The
GREAT DANE

Anna Katherine Nicholas

Title page photo: The Dinro trademark! Ch. Dinro Taboo Again and Ch. Dinro Talisman, two of the most famous of the Danes from Dinro Kennels, Mrs. Rosemarie Robert, Dinro Danes, Carmel, N.Y.

Distributed in the UNITED STATES by T.F.H. Publications, Inc., 211 West Sylvania Avenue, Neptune City, NJ 07753; in CANADA to the Pet Trade by H & L Pet Supplies Inc., 27 Kingston Crescent, Kitchener, Ontario N2B 2T6; Rolf C. Hagen Ltd., 3225 Sartelon Street, Montreal 382 Quebec; in CANADA to the Book Trade by Macmillan of Canada (A Division of Canada Publishing Corporation), 164 Commander Boulevard, Agincourt, Ontario M1S 3C7; in ENGLAND by T.F.H. Publications Limited, 4 Kier Park, Ascot, Berkshire SL5 7DS; in AUSTRALIA AND THE SOUTH PACIFIC by T.F.H. (Australia) Pty. Ltd., Box 149, Brookvale 2100 N.S.W., Australia; in NEW ZEALAND by Ross Haines & Son, Ltd., 18 Monmouth Street, Grey Lynn, Auckland 2, New Zealand; in SINGAPORE AND MALAYSIA by MPH Distributors (S) Pte., Ltd., 601 Sims Drive, #03/07/21, Singapore 1438; in the PHILIPPINES by Bio-Research, 5 Lippay Street, San Lorenzo Village, Makati Rizal; in SOUTH AFRICA by Multipet Pty. Ltd., 30 Turners Avenue, Durban 4001. Published by T.F.H. Publications, Inc. Manufactured in the United States of America by T.F.H. Publications, Inc.

Contents

About the Author

Since early childhood, Anna Katherine Nicholas has been involved with dogs. Her first pets were a Boston Terrier, an Airedale, and a German Shepherd Dog. Then, in 1925, came the first of the Pekingese, a gift from a friend who raised them. Now her home is shared with two Miniature Poodles and numerous Beagles.

Miss Nicholas is best known throughout the Dog Fancy as a writer and as a judge. Her first magazine article, published in *Dog News* magazine around 1930, was about Pekingese, and this was followed by a widely acclaimed breed column, "Peeking at the Pekingese," which appeared for at least two decades, originally in *Dogdom* then, following the demise of that publication, in *Popular Dogs*. During the 1940's she was a Boxer columnist for *Pure-Bred Dogs/American Kennel Gazette* and for *Boxer Briefs*. More recently many of her articles, geared to interest fanciers of every breed, have appeared in *Popular Dogs, Pure-Bred Dogs/American Kennel Gazette, Show Dogs, Dog Fancy,* and *The World of the Working Dog*, and for both the Canadian publications, *The Dog Fancier* and *Dogs in Canada*. Her *Dog World* column, "Here, There and Everywhere" was the Dog Writers' Association of America winner of the Best Series in a Dog Magazine Award for 1979. Also a feature article of hers, "Faster Is Not Better," published in *Canine Chronicle*, received Honorable Mention on another occasion.

In 1970 Miss Nicholas won the Dog Writers' Association Award for the Best Technical Book of the Year with her *Nicholas Guide to Dog Judging*. In 1979 the revision of this book again won this award, the first time ever that a revision has been so honored by this organization. Other important dog writer awards which Miss Nicholas has gained over the years have been the Gaines "Fido" on two occasions and the *Kennel Review* "Winkies" also on two occasions, these both in the Dog Writer of the Year category.

It was during the 1930's that Miss Nicholas's first book, *The Pekingese*, appeared in print, published by the Judy Publishing Company. This book, and its second edition, sold out quickly and is now a collector's item, as is her *The Skye Terrier Book* which was published during the 1960's by the Skye Terrier Club of America.

During recent years, Miss Nicholas has been writing books consistently for T.F.H. These include *Successful Dog Show Exhibiting, The Book of the Rottweiler, The Book of the Poodle, The Book of the Labrador Retriever, The Book of the English Springer Spaniel, The Book of the Golden Retriever, The Book of the German Shepherd Dog, The Book of the Shetland Sheepdog, The Book of the Miniature Schnauzer, The World of the Doberman Pinscher* and *The World of the Rottweiler*. Plus, in the newest T.F.H. series, *The Maltese, The Keeshond, The Chow Chow, The Poodle, The Boxer, The Beagle, The Basset Hound, The Dachshund* (the latter three co-authored with Marcia A. Foy), *The German Pointer, The Collie, The Weimaraner*, and numerous other titles. In the KW series she has done *Rottweilers, Weimaraners* and *Norwegian Elkhounds*. And she has written American chapters for two popular English books purchased and published in the United States by T.F.H., *The Staffordshire Bull Terrier*, and *The Jack Russell Terrier*.

Miss Nicholas's association with T.F.H. began in the early 1970's when she co-authored for them five books with Joan Brearley. These are *The Wonderful World of Beagles and Beagling* (also honored by the Dog Writers Association), *This is the Bichon Frise, The Book of the Pekingese, The Book of the Boxer*, and *This is the Skye Terrier*.

Since 1934 Miss Nicholas has been a popular dog show judge, officiating at prestigious events throughout the United States and Canada. She is presently approved for all Hounds, all Terriers, all Toys and all Non-Sporting; plus all Pointers, English and Gordon Setters, Vizslas, Weimaraners, and Wirehaired Pointing Griffons in the Sporting Group and Boxers and Dobermans in Working. In 1970 she became only the third woman ever to have judged Best in Show at the famous Westminster Kennel Club event at Madison Square Garden in New York City, where she has officiated as well on some sixteen other occasions over the years. She has also officiated at such events as Santa Barbara, Chicago International, Morris and Essex, Trenton, Westchester, etc., in the United States; the Sportsman's and the Metropolitan among numerous others in Canada; and Specialty shows in several dozen breeds in both countries. She has judged in almost every one of the United States and in four of the Canadian Provinces. Her dislike of air travel has caused her to refrain from acceptance of the constant invitations to officiate in other parts of the world.

Ch. Mountdania's Ashley was bred by Mountdania Kennels and owned by Don and Mary Lou Carmody. This outstanding Great Dane is the sire of 31 champions to date, was #1 Great Dane in 1979, and boasts a show record of four all-breed Bests in Show, 48 Group placements including 18 Group 1sts, and 112 times Best of Breed including 11 Specialty Shows. Photo courtesy of Mr. and Mrs. Lowell K. Davis.

Ch. Heidere's Kolyer Kimbayh bred by Heidere's Kennels, Erna Heidere and Kitty Kolyer, winning Best of Breed at the K.C. of Philadelphia in 1970. Bob Forsyth handling. Owned by Dr. James and Elizabeth W. Gribbin. This very famous dog of tremendous quality and influence on the breed was born in 1968, sired by Champion Big Kim of Bella Dane ex Champion Kolyer's Heidere Heidee.

Chapter 1

Origin and Early Development of the Great Dane

The Great Dane very definitely is a product of Germany, and quite likely was developed through a combination of Mastiff and Irish Wolfhound. There is a difference of opinion among historians as to whether the Mastiff or the Wolfhound is the more dominant ancestor, but it seems quite generally accepted that it is these two breeds which have been used in the creation of the modern Great Dane.

The antiquity of these dogs is not difficult to trace. It has been claimed that on Egyptian monuments dating back as far as several thousand years B.C. there are drawings of dogs closely resembling our Great Danes. Written descriptions of such dogs have been reported as having been found in Chinese literature of 1121 B.C. Since Mastiffs originated in Asia, this seems quite logical as does the presence of early Irish Wolfhound types, which ties in with the role of the ancestors of the present day Great Dane—that of a boar hound. What could have been more appropriate in hunting boar than a dog combining the strength, power and tenacity of the Mastiff with the speed, agility, and power of the Irish Wolfhound? The feeling is strong that in this combination, the Germans truly did create a superdog!

No one whose work I have read yet has come up with a valid reason for these dogs being called Great Danes, for while indeed they *are* Great Dogs, they have never, so far as has been discov-

9

ered, had anything whatsoever to do with Denmark! Strange how things come about! The literal translation of the French designation given by that country to these dogs, is "big Danish." Why the English, among numerous others, should have picked up and used that identification for the breed shall remain forever a mystery! Of course the other choices already in use then were not too definitive either! For example to call it a "Dogue Allemand" also was misleading since it translates to "German Mastiff." While there would be more point to including Mastiff in the identification of the breed than there is to implying that it is Danish, it still is not an accurate description of the dog, although it is a canine giant possessing more elegance and refinement in its head than does the Mastiff, a more massive head type dog. The head of the Great Dane actually adheres more closely to the head type of the Irish Wolfhound than that of the Mastiff; thus strictly speaking classifying him a Mastiff would have been another misnomer.

By whatever name he is known, the Great Dane is a very special and unique dog, dating back probably close to 500 years. He is a type of dog unto himself; a distinguished member of our canine world who combines to perfection strength with elegance.

It was during the year 1880 that Dr. Bodinus, a leading fancier of these dogs, brought together a group of people interested in the future of Great Danes in Germany. The purpose of the meeting was the establishment of a club to further the best interests of the breed there, and the preparation of a modern standard for the breed.

As might have been anticipated (and probably was) strong opposition was raised to permitting the dogs to continue to be known as Great Danes; the group undoubtly felt that since the breed was actually a German-made product, they were being robbed of rightful credit in this regard. Thus it was decided that in the future Germany would refer to them as the Deutsche Dogge, with all other designations being abandoned. This was fine as far as it went, but that territory was limited as they were unsuccessful in persuading the English-speaking world to do likewise. So in most of Europe they are "Deutsche Dogges"; but in many other countries of the world they remain Great Danes.

The Deutsche Doggen Club (German Great Dane Club) drew up and adopted an excellent standard for the breed in 1891. So

Ch. Fabian of Warrendane, the great "star" from Canyon Crest Kennels, with his handler Russell Zimmerman. Noted multiple Best in Show winner and sire of champions.

Ch. Eaglevalley Killamanjaro and son, Champion Eaglevalley Orbit. Two outstanding brindle Danes owned by Dorothy Montgomery, Eaglevalley Kennels, New Milford, Conn.

The famous winning Ch. Dinro Brandy was owned by Mrs. Frank Neuwirth of New York City. Note all the quality and elegance for which Dinro Danes are famous.

Dorothy (Mrs. Sewall) Montgomery poses informally on her lawn at New Milford, Conn. in the 1950's with several of her Danes. Ch. Eaglevalley's Crescendo, Sonata and Moonlight. Photo courtesy of Ed Lyons.

Ch. Estid Zeus was one of the splendid Great Danes owned by Ernest E. Ferguson in California in the late 1930's to early 1940's. All of the Estid Great Danes had names starting with a "Z" in tribute to Ch. Zelia v Loheland, the magnificent importation whom Ernie considered to be the soundest Dane he ever had known. Photo courtesy of Ed Lyons.

well thought out and satisfactory is this standard that it has been recognized around the world, and almost every other country has based its own standard of the breed on this one, using practically verbatim translations from the German—whether describing the Deutsche Dogge or the Great Dane.

It was from Germany that the early foundation stock for many kennels around the world was acquired. To the United States have come many great dogs which have helped in the development of type and quality here, as has been the case elsewhere, too. England, other continental countries, Canada, Australia, and the Americas all have had a share in the leading German bloodlines which have reflected on our homebreds. We view the results with pride as we note the judicious use that has been made of these fine dogs and bitches who have come to the United States over the years. Many, I am sure, will agree with my statement that I feel the United States has now become the leading producer anywhere of Great Dane quality. But let us never forget the great dogs of Germany who helped make this possible.

Int'l. Nordic Ch. Hotpoint's Be My Joy, by Int'l. Ch. Gerjos Shilo of Airways ex Int. Nordic Ch. Airways Nebula, fawn, by Allyndanes Alfie v Archduke with some Murlo breeding on her dam's side. Bred and owned by Borghild E. Sorensen, Kennel Hotpoint, Oslo, Norway. Top winning Dane in Norway, 1981.

Int'l. and Nordic Ch. Hotpoint's New Treasure as of mid-1985 is the top winner in Norway. One of the first Harlequin puppies born at Kennel Hotpoint, Oslo. Borghild E. Sorensen, breeder and Mrs. W. Enger, owner.

Chapter 2

Great Danes in Great Britain and on the Continent

England was quick to gain appreciation for the Great Dane, and the breed has enjoyed popularity there for numerous decades. British breeders have sent out excellent foundation stock to other countries, as you will note in reading this book. Dogs from there have gone to Australia with splendid results and proved highly successful in breeding programs "down under." They have also gone to various European countries where the dogs have made impact in a spectacular manner.

You will find photos of many English-bred dogs in this book, as well as some from France which I have tremendously admired, and the progeny of the imported bloodlines.

Thanks to Borghild Sorensen, of Oslo, we know that Great Danes are a popular breed in Norway and Sweden, and that breeders there have relied on English stock with which to augment their own. Hotpoint is Borghild Sorensen's well-known kennel, from which an impressive number of important dogs have come.

Borghild's first Great Dane was a family owned pet, a fawn bitch acquired in 1964, who shared their household (as do all Hotpoint Danes) as family members. Borghild's own first Dane followed in 1970, a fawn who lived to be only two years old. She was followed, in 1972, by the first import from England, a fawn dog called Simba Boy of Helmlake, who became a Norwegian and Swedish Champion and who sired several champions including the first two born at Hotpoint: International and Nordic Champions Sir Brutus Sebastian and Sheik Barbarian, the two who also became Best in Show winners.

The Hotpoint prefix was first used in 1976 with the arrival of the second litter from the fawn bitch, English International Nordic Champion Helmlake Curieuse. This bitch was from one of the premier British kennels, with partial American breeding.

The Swedish import, International Nordic Champion Airways Nebula, again a fawn, by Allyndanes Alfie of Archduke from a bitch with some Murlo breeding, produced very well at Hotpoint. Mated to International Champion Gerjos Shilo of Airways she produced, in her first litter, two International Champions of which the Sorensens kept Be My Joy; a Nordic Champion, a Norwegian Champion, and two Challenge Certificate winners. A repeat of this breeding produced a brindle bitch, Hotpoint's Fortuna of Walkmyll who was sent to England where she gained her championship. There was another Norwegian Champion in that litter, as well as two International Nordic Champions. The brindle dog, Hotpoint's Fortune Maker, has won several Bests in Show in addition to being Top Winning Dane in Norway for 1982, 1983, and 1984, and Top Winning Dane in Sweden for 1983.

It is a source of pride to Borghild that the Top Winning Dane in Norway since the award was started in 1977 was bred at Hotpoint Kennels or sired by their stud dogs.

In 1982 the first Harlequin puppies were born at Hotpoint. From this litter by another English import, International Champion French Fashion of Helmlake (by a dog with German bloodlines) came the bitch International Nordic Champion Hotpoint's New Treasure, who at present is the top winner there.

International Champion Hotpoint's Be My Joy, Norway's Top Winning Dane for 1981, has produced four champions of which Borghild has kept Norwegian and Swedish Champion Hotpoint's Kopi Me, who has also won Best in Show.

There are never more than five Great Danes kept at Hotpoint at any one time, and only one or two litters a year are bred there.

16

Great Dane puppies bred at Hotpoint Kennels in Oslo, Norway, who grew up to become important winners. Borghild E. Sorensen, owner and breeder.

Int'l. and Nordic Ch. Hotpoint's Fashion Maker was the Top Winning Great Dane in Norway for 1982, 1983 and 1984; also Top Winning Great Dane in Sweden for 1983. A representative of the Kennel Hotpoint bred by Borghild E. Sorensen in Oslo, Norway. Owned by Mr. C. Hilstan, Norway.

An important winner coast to coast, Champion Muldoon, owned by Canyon Crest Kennels in California, brought home the Best of Breed rosette from Westminster to his proud owners, Mr. and Mrs. William O. Bagshaw. Handled, as always, by Russell Zimmerman.

Italy is a busy center of Great Dane breeding activity, too, and it is interesting to note that they have their own separate name for the breed, never having adopted either the Great Dane or the Deutsche Dogge. In Italy it is called Alano, which translates "Mastiff." The Alano is accepted amicably by the Germans, however, and there is tremendous co-operation between fanciers in these two countries, Italian breeding programs being based almost entirely on German-imported or German-bred stock.

Chapter 3

Great Danes in the United States

The Great Dane Club of America was founded, in Chicago, in 1889 as the "German Mastiff or Great Dane" Club of America which title became The Great Dane Club of America two years later under re-organization by a membership majority of Eastern fanciers. A note of interest is that the famed artist, G. Muss-Arnolt, was a primary figure in the original organization of the Club and its first delegate. There are few of us who are collectors of art involving dogs who are not proud owners of at least one of Muss-Arnolt's fabulous paintings! And as one considers the classic beauty of a Great Dane, his admiration of the breed is clearly understandable as such a dog could not fail to please so appreciative an eye.

The author's personal memories of Great Danes reach back into the 1930's, when breed development in the United States was taking place from coast to coast. One of my early memories centers around the Warrendanes, owned by Florence and Harry Warren, who in 1937 had no fewer than ten of the breed at Westminster. Quite an impressive sight!

Warrendane was a major and important kennel which provided foundation stock for numerous other kennels. The three specials they had listed for Westminster 1937 were Champion James V. Loheland, by Elch Edler v. d. Saalburg ex Hilde v Falkenhurst, born November 1930, bred by Mrs. H. von Rohden; Champion Puma v. d. Saalburg, same pedigree, born in May 1932; and Champion Wirbelwind v Loheland, also bred by Mrs. von Rohden, by Orel v Loheland ex Else v. d. Linde. The latter became the dam of the famous Champion Gretchen of Warrendane (sired by Rungnir v Loheland of Warrendane). She in her turn produced the outstanding dog Champion Fabian of Warrendane who blazed a trail of glory for Mr. and Mrs. William O. Bagshaw at Canyon Crest Kennels.

Margaret ("Mig") and Bill Bagshaw and Canyon Crest are among my fondest memories, as we became good friends and the many hours I spent with them and their Great Dane breeder friends whenever they came to New York did much to generate my admiration for the breed. The Bagshaws were "into" several breeds, including Miniature Pinschers, Manchester Terriers and Greyhounds, always owning dogs of superb quality. But I think that no one could question the fact that the Danes were at the top of the list in their affections.

I first recall their fabulous dog Champion Muldoon, who Russell Zimmerman handled successfully to a lot of spectacular winning.

Fabian of Warrendane went out to the Bagshaws from the Warrens after a short, successful career as a puppy in the East, and promptly started on his way as a great show dog there. In addition, he became a superb stud dog, siring youngsters who did him proud as they reached show age.

Vincent J. Garrity was an exciting success story in Great Danes with his owner-handled Champion Hansi of Garricrest who at 27 months old had been shown 19 times, became a champion at 13 months, and won his first Best in Show on his first birthday! This record soon stood at six times Best in Show, 15 times Best of Breed, and 15 Group placements, including first nine times, and second six times! Surely most gratifying to his breeder-owner-handler! Hansi was, as well, a sire of champions.

A widely known kennel of the same period in California was Planetree, owned by Mrs. S. Daniel Wall and Miss Ruth Martin at Canoga Park. This was the home of that famed bitch Champion

20

The great Ch. Brenda of Brae Tarn with her owners just after winning one of her Bests in Show, at Beverly Hills K.C. Miss Ruth Martin handling; Mrs. S. Daniel Wall holding the trophy. A most outstanding bitch of her day.

Ch. Prinz Erik of Willow Run and Ch. Ozelot v Birkenhof, famous Danes from Estid Kennels, Ernest E. Ferguson, during the 1930's-1940's.

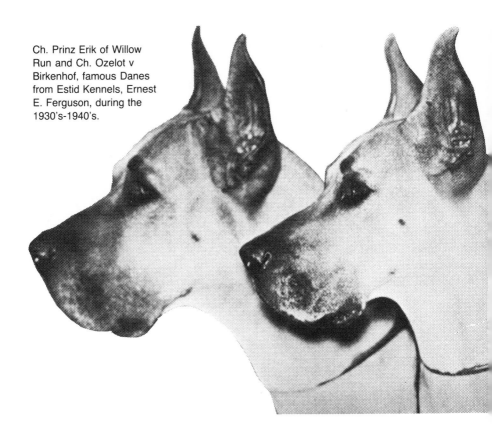

The great German bitch, German and American Ch. Etfa v d Saalburg with Josef Eigenbauer who brought her to the United States, where she was purchased by Mrs. Donald Hostetter. A tremendously admired bitch of truly outstanding merit.

Ch. Oerlang v Loheland, famous importation of the 1930's owned by Estid Kennels, Ernest E. Ferguson in California.

Ch. Eaglevalley Crescendo and Ch. Eaglevalley Moonlight making a "clean sweep" of things for owner, Mrs. Dorothy Montgomery, Eaglevalley Kennels, New Milford, Conn., at the Westchester Kennel Club Dog Show in 1954. Photo courtesy of Ed Lyons.

Brenda of Brae Tarn, winner of some prestigious Bests in Show among other honors. She was a daughter of Champion Czardas von Eppeleinsprung-Noris ex Champion Quia of Brae Tarn. Champion Planetree Cyrus, a handsome dog, was, like Brenda, a Best in Show winner at some of the leading West Coast events.

There were Warrendane dogs at Planetree, too. Champion Jaga of Warrendane and Champion Kuno of Warrendane, C.D., both from top quality imported stock and both with definite obedience talents.

One of the most memorable fanciers of all was the late Colonel Ernest E. Ferguson, owner of the Estid Kennels. Often thought of primarily as a Poodle fancier, Ernie Ferguson actually had a deep love and admiration of Danes as well, and many famous dogs of both breeds have represented him over the years in dog show competition.

The first of the Ferguson Great Danes was a dog named Baron Content, who took runner-up to Best in Show his first time in the ring, and then embarked on a career in the movies. We are told that he was the first Great Dane ever to appear in a talking picture, which he did in the film "Big Boy" starring Al Jolson.

International Champion Prinz Eril of Willowrun, who was to become an American and Canadian Champion, came to Estid Kennels having been purchased as a puppy, and lived to become 14 years old. He was the product of the Danes raised by Francis X. Bushman, a famous matinee idol movie star of the period, and was a handsome fawn dog bred by Mr. and Mrs. Albert Gardiner.

Colonel Ferguson was extremely admiring of a bitch in Germany, Champion Etfa von der Saalburg, whom he has been quoted as considering the finest, at that time, ever bred. As his plans for breeding Danes seriously shaped up, he sought dogs descended from her for his own kennel, and brought over her granddaughter, Champion Ozelot v Birkenhof, who became the granddam of some very lovely Danes in California. The next Estid importation was Champion Oerlang v Loheland, a son of Ozelot (thus great-grandson of Etfa)—a stunning dog who proved to be a fine stud, siring four champions in one litter and quality youngsters in them all. He was to be found in the pedigree of several of the Eastern Dane winners of the 1940's.

This is the famous Ch. Hycrest Prince owned by Lester Sawyer winning at the Morris and Essex Kennel Club in June 1955. This son of Foray's Bismarck ex Ch. Heidere's Alexi was a homebred and born on October 16, 1951. Mr. and Mrs. Sawyer owned many noted Dane winners at their kennel in Leominster, Mass. Photo courtesy of Ed Lyons.

Famous Great Danes of the Past. "Pop" Gilbert handling Ch. Dinro Aslan and Ch. Dinro Aelric to Best Brace in Working Group several decades ago for owner, Rosemarie Robert, Dinro Danes, Carmel, N.Y. Photo courtesy of Ed Lyons.

Then came the great Champion Zelia v Loheland, a great-granddaughter of Ozelot, thus great-great-granddaughter of Etfa. Ernie Ferguson is said to have stated that she was the soundest Dane he had imported. Her success here was instantaneous and spectacular! She made her championship in three straight shows, going Best in Show each time. To honor Zelia, all names of the Estid Danes started with a "Z" once she joined the kennel.

It is interesting to note that Mrs. Donald Hostetter imported the immortal International Champion Etfa v d Saalburg from Germany, who was brought to her here by Josef Eigenbauer. Mrs. Hostetter had been a Dane owner since 1928, having acquired her first of the breed at about the time she moved from New York to Flintridge, California. We understand that Etfa became her constant companion, and that she was really something to see as a picture of elegant magnificence. Etfa usually was handled by Mrs. Hostetter personally, standing in a gorgeous natural pose as Mrs. Hostetter held a tidbit before her in a gloved hand!

The Hostetter Kennel was known as Ridge Rest, and the Danes were noted for their perfect temperament. It was customary for Mrs. Hostetter to travel with her dogs and family, during which she attended many shows in Germany. During a trip there in 1931, a daughter of Etfa's, Little Sister of Ridge Rest, was sold to Josef Eigenbauer who had originaly brought Etfa to the United States, returned to Germany, and at that period was associated with Birkenhof Kennels. Later Little Sister was sent to England, sold to von Send Kennels, where we assume the bloodlines became beneficial. Eventually her offspring returned to the east coast of the United States.

Mrs. Hostetter and her young son, Donald, were both deeply involved with a love of Great Danes. They both became popular judges and during 1931 Mrs. Hostetter was instrumental in the organization of the Great Dane Club of California which she served as its first President. Later she also participated in organizing the Great Dane Club in Northern California.

Ch. Paradise's Desiree, bred, owned, and handled by Joan and Vince Mulligan, was #5 Great Dane and #2 Dane bitch in 1978, having won 40 Bests of Breed and nine Group placements including three 1sts. By Tallbrook's Akamai of Alii ex Tallbrook's Vicki of Paradise.

Chapter 4

Great Dane Kennels in the United States

A kennel name is important to a breeder, and should be selected and used from the time of one's first homebred litter. Kennel names are chosen in many different ways. Some people select for them the name of the street on which they live, or did live at the time the kennel started. Others will use a form of their own name, such as the Johnstons did with "Marydane," or a coined combination of the names of family members. Some will name the kennel for a child or children who may be especially enthusiastic over the dogs. Many use the name of the foundation dogs behind a breeding program, either the proper names or the call names of these dogs. Anything that strikes your fancy and isn't burdensome or an infringement of someone else's rights is fine, provided that it's appropriate and will identify you and your Great Danes down through the generations—especially important in those that you yourself have bred. And keep in mind that the American Kennel Club permits only 25 letters in the registered name of a dog, including the kennel name.

A kennel name can be registered with the American Kennel Club, which gives the registrant the exclusive right to that name in registering dogs, and no breeder or owner other than the one to whom it is registered is permitted to include it in the registered name of a dog unless the application is accompanied by written consent of the person to whom the kennel name is registered during the period in which this registration is effective. Detailed information on this subject is available through the American Kennel Club, 51 Madison Avenue, New York, N.Y. 10010. There are specific requirements in making application, and a fee is to be paid if one chooses this course.

To be of greatest value, kennel names should be applied to all dogs bred by your kennel, as then it immediately identifies your dog and its background. A good way is to work out a system by which your homebreds will bear names *beginning* with the kennel name, while dogs purchased from others and already bearing their breeder's kennel name will have your kennel name added to the end. Adopt whatever type of system appeals to you as a way to indicate whether the dog was actually bred by you or was purchased.

We take very special pride in our kennel stories for this book, for their wide range and for the many prominent and successful breeders who are represented. We feel that they bring you the history of Great Danes as it has unfolded in America in a complete, interesting, and authoritative manner. We hope that you will agree and find these chapters and their many illustrations as enlightening and representative as they seem to us.

GREAT DANE KENNELS
IN THE CONTINENTAL U.S.

ADDIDAS

Addidas Great Danes are owned by Marci Iler and situated at Boonsboro, Maryland. Marci and her husband, Jim Iler, have been raising and showing Danes since the 1970's, their foundation stock having been headed by Monsey Abiding Affection, C.D. and Addidas Chamonile, C.D., both of whom are the dams of champions and pointed progeny. Addidas Orange Pekoe was also part of the early Addidas background.

Among the early winners at this kennel were Addidas Jovan, Chamonile's son by Champion Von Raseac Westwind, C.D., born in April 1977. Jovan, a handsome dog, was pointed and figures in a number of current pedigrees.

28

Champion Addidas Andiamo, brindle son of Abiding Affection, was sired by Champion Von Raseac Westwind, who was the dominant sire in the Ilers' early litters. Andiamo did extremely well at the shows, having gained his championship with ease, going on to Group placements from the classes, and with Specialty wins. Bred at Addidas, he was later owned by Carol Lamberto and Nancy Welsh. He is the sire of the handsome Addidas Piscataway who is out of Addidas Autumn Acorn. This combination also produced Champion Addidas Amtrack, bred by Marci and owned by Jim Iler. Amtrack, despite a knee injury, fully recovered to gain his title during 1984.

Other current winners from this kennel are Champion Addidas Up N Coming Star, born in November 1984, who at his first show, when only nine months old, went clear through to Best of Breed over specials competition, and finished quickly owner-handled.

Another current campaigner is the striking black dog, Addidas Friday, bred, owned, and handled by Marci.

BMW

BMW Harlequin Great Danes have earned a position of admiration and respect in the Great Dane world, owing to the talents and breeding ability of their owner, Laura Kiaulenas of Farmingville, New York. It is now about 28 years since Laura started her breeding program of Great Danes. This was the culmination of her early childhood love of animals, and her longing to have one (or more). Laura finally, at the age of 12 years, received as a Christmas present from her mother a German Shepherd whom she turned into an incredibly well trained dog. Laura soon had him working like a machine; obeying hand signals, whispered commands, and even several commands given in a row.

But even before Laura had been permitted the German Shepherd, she had lost her heart to another breed, the Great Dane, an event which took place when she was seven or eight years old and the noted Dane breeder, Fred Finkle, moved right around the corner from her family's home. Laura spent a lot of time at his house, becoming deeply attached to a fawn bitch of his called Kathy. Upon occasion she was permitted to walk Kathy, always with

BMW Michelle Ma
Belle, dam of Ch. BMW
Quincy, owned by
Laura Kiaulenas,
Farmingville, N.Y., who
is also the
photographer.

Addidas Piscataway,
by Ch. Addidas
Andiamo ex Addidas
Autumn Acorn at age
16 months. Owned by
Marci Iler, Addidas
Great Danes,
Boonsboro, Md.

the sworn promise that she would hold tightly to the leash no matter what. Thus it was that during one of these walks, Kathy looked up ahead and saw her owners getting out of their car, leading her to drag Laura, flat on her stomach, holding on valiantly every inch of the way, the entire block to meet them as they were alighting from the car.

It was Mr. Finkle who invited Laura to accompany him to Westminster, a red letter day for her. Mr. Finkle's newly imported bitch at that time, Champion Heide von Meistersinger, whom she thought to be the most beautiful dog she ever had seen, took Best of Opposite Sex at that prestigious event. Her dream right then became to own a dog who looked like Heide!

At that time Laura was about ten years old. Half a dozen years later she finally got her first Dane, a granddaughter of Heide. Laura's two favorite dogs at that time were Heide and her half brother, Champion Amor von Meistersinger, also owned by Fred Finkle. They were bred and produced a son called Bill Miller's Village Squire, whose first litter was born right in Greenwich Village in New York. Laura wanted just *one* thing for Christmas—a puppy from that litter. And she got it!

That puppy was Biche, a Harlequin bitch to whom the entire BMW breeding program goes back many times over. Laura's Mom's love and support for the dogs has made BMW possible.

Harlequins held a fascination for Laura, even as they do now, with their spectacular coloring.

Her kennel identification, BMW, was selected because she wanted a name that would immediately make clear the fact that the dog was a Harlequin; these letters refer to Black, Merle and White, the Harlequins. On some of her early dogs, which were only black and white, she identified them with B & W. Her show dogs all carried the initials; thus they just sort of naturally evolved into her kennel name.

Laura has by now produced what I would guess to be somewhere in the area of 25 to 30 champions (probably more by the time you are reading this book). This is a notable accomplishment when one considers that she breeds about one litter annually and the majority of her bitches are bred only once or twice during their lifetime, then retired.

Laura keeps five Great Danes at her house. Her good friend, Holly Sayvetz, who has a lovely farm in Virginia, keeps several adults and a few puppies. Both have fenced areas for their dogs, but basically they are raised as *house* dogs. They are housebroken, well mannered, and go through obedience school as a matter of course. It is important to them that their dogs be good pets as well as show dogs, since, if all goes well, they have many years after the close of their show and breeding years in which to enjoy being family pets. They are socialized from their whelping box days onward and, since they are selected for temperament, both Laura and Holly feel that they have been quite successful in this regard.

Laura is a successful full-time architect who lives part time in New York City. It is difficult with the dogs, but a system has been developed. There are numerous people involved with the BMW breeding program, folks whom Laura started but of whom she says, "I do not want it thought that it was I alone." It really is teamwork. They refuse to put up kennel runs, but with the co-ownership method they can work with numerous dogs—quite a different method from that of the big kennels of earlier times, but successful all the same.

Lorraine Gatti, co-owner with Laura of Champion ZL's BMW Quincy, has been another key person in the program. She attends shows whether or not Laura will be showing Quincy, and is involved in assisting with the training and conditioning of the dogs, in housebreaking puppies, and in everything else that goes along with it.

Both Laura and Holly put a great deal of themselves into their co-ownerships, which is probably why they work so well. One of the principal aims in co-owning the Danes is that the co-owners are people who want Great Danes as pets, which has enabled Laura to use quite a few individuals in her breeding program who might not otherwise have been available.

She has worked a number of her Great Danes in obedience, with good results. Her first obedience winner was BMW Zero, who got his C.D. degree in three shows with his lowest score 196½.

Laura was a professional handler back in the days before the license system was terminated. She still handles Danes of all colors as well as some of the other Working breeds.

32

BMW's foundation bitch was inbred to a Harlequin dog named Champion I.W. Harper, and the first couple of dogs to whom she was bred also were inbred on I.W., who was by Champion Rux-Conny out of Champion Wodka v.d. Stadt-Hamburg, and Laura comments, "It is these two dogs who show up over and over in the newer generations." The champion brothers, Hanibal and Herold v St. Magn-Obertraubling are by Conny-Rux out of Ramona who was a sister to the latter. There is also Jagla v.d. Stadt Hamburg and Marko v.d. Kreuzschanze whose sire is by Rux-Conny, the latter also the sire of I. W. Harper. Thus the BMW pedigrees go back to just a few dogs who are of almost identical breeding. The abovementioned dogs all were Harlequins and all from the 1950's. They were bred in Germany, but at least several of them journeyed subsequently to the United States. To quote Laura, "They are very definitely the basis for Harlequin breeding in the United States, and the total in this regard for BMW."

In further pedigree research, Laura calls attention to the "key" names in the half dozen or so generations behind her foundation dogs. Especially she notes the numerous repetitions of two key names, Jagla Moguntia and Dolf v St. Magn-Obertraubling. Jagla Moguntia was a Harlequin son of the famed Dolf v. d. Saalburg. Rux-Conny and Ramona have eight crosses apiece to Jagla; Conny-Rux has eleven.

DAVIS

Davis Great Danes are famous around the world, each bearing the family name of their breeders-owners, Arlene and Lowell K. Davis of Covina, California.

Mr. and Mrs. Davis started in Great Danes in the early 1960's. Ironically, it was not their original intention to become exhibitors, for Lowell had shown Dachshunds as a child, and was not really anxious to return to that hobby. So they asked for the *smallest* Dane in the litter of 13 bred by Caroline and Jerry Mobley, Jecamo Kennels, when they went to make their selection. Since Lowell had been involved with purebred dogs and thus had an appreciation of quality, this had to be a *good* member of its breed, and this was the third repeat of a highly successful breeding which had produced champions.

Ch. Jessica Davis, by Ch. Sunridge's Chief Justice ex Ch. Abigail Davis of Tallbrook, winning Best in Show at the Santa Maria K.C. in September 1976. The dam of five champions, Jessica is a multiple Group and Specialty Best in Show winner, and was among the Top Ten Great Danes in the U.S. for 1976. For two years consecutively won the Top Winning Dane Award, Club Member Owned from the Great Dane Club of California. Mr. and Mrs. Lowell K. Davis, owners, Covina, Calif.

The rest is history. Each week when the Davises returned to Jecamo for ear rolling on their puppy, they were told that they had ended up with the pick-of-the-litter. So they allowed themselves to be persuaded to enter her at a match show, got rave reviews, and at the same time were bitten by the show bug.

This first of the Davis Great Danes became Champion Jecamo's Lucy Ann, C.D. She was a Specialty winner and the dam of two champions, with whom the Davises really "hit the jackpot" as these dogs were Champion Abner Lowell Davis and Champion Archibald Lowell Davis, both of whom have contributed importantly to the breed.

Arlene and Lowell adhere to the policy of breeding only when they wish to keep a puppy for themselves, thus their breeding program has been limited in size. Arlene comments that she "just could not raise a litter and have to sell them all"; and with the exception of their good friend Peggy McQuillen, they did not want to enter into any co-ownerships. Despite this limited breeding program, the Davises have made some tremendous contributions to the Great Dane breed, their outstanding homebreds including three Best in Show winners and many Specialty and Group winning dogs. They are proud of the many Davis Danes who have become top producers, whom they have bred, and that a goodly number of leading Danes from the present era go back to Davis bloodlines—not only in the United States, but in Canada, Europe, Japan and Taiwan.

Champion Abner Lowell Davis, from Lucy Ann's and their first litter, was the most famous of the Davis dogs, with fabulous records both in the ring and as a producer. His show career was culminated with the winning of his sixth all-breed Best in Show at the San Mateo Kennel Club in December 1971, and it is especially noteworthy that this splendid dog's Bests in Show all were gained in entries averaging over 2500 dogs! He was winner of 33 Group 1sts at the West Coast's most important shows, including Beverly Hills (twice), Santa Barbara, Orange Empire and Pasadena. He also acquired 75 additional Group placements and 113 Bests of Breed, 13 of the latter having been at Specialties. When the final records were tabulated, Abner was #1 Great Dane, #4 Working Dog, and #5 all-breeds under all systems for 1971.

As an influential sire, Abner was equally successful. His ability to stamp his get with his own soundness, movement and elegance earned for him the respect of outstanding breeders.

Abner's litter brother, Archie, also made his mark as a sire.

Champion Jessica Davis was another very famous Dane from this kennel, as was Champion Don Lu's Maggie Davis. Abner, Jessica and Maggie all were all-breed Best in Show winners.

DAVISDANE

Davisdane Kennels are owned by Susan Davis of Hanover, Massachusetts, where the "head man" among her dogs is the handsome Harlequin, Champion Davisdane's Double Exposure, C.D., by Champion Shalako's Repeat of Maitau, C.D. ex Double D. von Maitau, C.D.

"Kodak," as Double Exposure is known, is a third generation Specialty winning Champion and a fourth generation obedience title holder, making him perhaps the only Great Dane in the country with this distinction.

Kodak earned two points as a young dog. Moving up to Open he earned his remaining minors in three consecutive weekends. His majors include a Great Dane Club of Maryland Specialty win and a finish during the New England Specialty weekend.

Linebred to Champion Dinro Longsock of Charm, Kodak is the first homebred champion and third obedience titleholder at Davisdane. May there be many to follow him for Susan Davis!

DR. AND MRS. ANTHONY DINARDO

When Tony and Sheila DiNardo became interested, and then participants, in the showing of a working breed, the first with which they were involved was the Great Dane. Their original purchase was Champion Kim's Sabu of Lyndane who was campaigned for them by Jane Forsyth in 1972 and 1973.

Then came Champion Castile's Carousel who was handled for the DiNardos by Jeffrey Brucker to become a Best in Show winner.

They loved the Danes, but finally it was a Doberman which captured the hearts of the DiNardo family, and the latter breed is the one with which they have stuck since, taking two dogs, a father and son, to outstanding records. More will follow we are certain, as the DiNardos are breeding Dobes of exceptional quality.

Seven-week-old Harlequin puppies by Ch. Davisdane's Double Exposure, C.D. ex Hasheba Del Royal Black. Owned by Susan Davis, Hanover, Mass.

Ch. Abigail Davis of Tallbrook, by Ch. Abner Lowell Davis ex Ch. Brenda Von Overcup, 1971-1979. During her short lifetime, she produced four champions. Finishing her title at 18 months, Abigail gained her championship with three majors including Best of Winners at the Great Dane Club of San Diego Specialty and Best of Opposite Sex from the classes. Owned by Mr. and Mrs. Lowell K. Davis, Covina, Calif.

Ch. Castile's Carousel, Best in Show winning Great Dane during 1974, was handled by Jeffrey Brucker for Dr. Anthony and Mrs. Sheila DiNardo, West Hartford, Conn.

DINRO

Dinro Danes are a legend in their own time in the Great Dane world. They have reached many enviable heights through the years during the lifetime of their owner, Mrs. Rosemarie Robert, which came to so abrupt an end with her murder on March 31, 1978, just three days past her 66th birthday at her home in Carmel, New York. The entire Dane Fancy and all of the dog show world mourned her loss and continues to do so, for Rose Robert was a devoted breeder and exhibitor of Danes for more than 40 years. The quality of her dogs speaks for itself when one examines pedigrees and realizes the number of winners they are behind. They were famous individually and collectively, noted for outstanding type and highest quality.

Looking back through show catalogues of the 1950's, one finds that Mrs. Rose Tong (who was later to become Mrs. Robert) was exhibiting Champion Gilbert's Braemar Blossomtime, bred by the William P. Gilberts, born in 1949, by Champion Gilbert's Dolf Crusader ex the famous and admired bitch of the 1940's, Champion Senta. Mrs. Robert's own homebred Champion Dinro Aslan was born a year earlier, in March 1948, by Champion Ajax Telemon of Brae Tarn (the latter kennel one of the truly *great* early ones whose dogs are to be found behind much quality) ex Cathy of Danecroft.

Champion Dinro Yorge was another homebred born in 1949, by the popular sire Champion Dinro Don ex Dinro Cam. Champion Dinro Aelric was a littermate of Aslan. Champion Dinro Brandy was sold to Mrs. Neuwirth in New York City who did good winning with him. He was born in August 1947 by Dinro Herke ex Dinro Greer.

Champion Dinro Taboo is another dog from this kennel well remembered for his own quality and for what he produced, especially his son Champion Dinro Taboo Again, as well as the aptly named Champion Dinro Legend; American and Canadian Champion Dinro Ovation; Champion Dinro Diplomat; Champion Dinro Talisman; Champion Dinro Kimberly, and so very many more.

We are deeply indebted to Ed Lyons for having loaned us numerous of his Dinro photographs so that we may share them with the readers of this book. Study them well, as they are definitely worth your attention.

Although Mrs. Robert is no longer here to personally continue the Dinro breeding program, the line is being continued under the joint kennel identification "Dinro-Sounda" owned by Dr. Louis Grant Bond and Robert E. Layne of Millbury, Massachusetts. From the success of their own Sounda homebreds, it is obvious that these gentlemen also possess "the talent." Already the good results of Dinro being in their hands is becoming apparent.

DORRIDANE

Dorridane Kennels are owned by Dr. and Mrs. (Patricia) Robert J. Crawley and are located in Merrywood Estates, at Folsom, Louisiana, in the heart of Louisiana's numerous thoroughbred horse farms and ranches.

Their first Great Dane joined the Crawleys in 1960. The foundation bitch was representative of such noted bloodlines as Marydane, Roxdane, Heidere, and Dinro. She became Champion Kensinomens Countess, known to her friends as "Brandy," and she was Pat's 1960 Christmas gift.

Brandy made her championship in good order, winning both of her majors at Specialty Shows. Bred to American and Canadian Champion Daneridge Cliban, she whelped a litter of four on March 31, 1963, all of which grew up to become champions. They were Champion Anzacs Marcher of Dorridane who became the winner of two Group 1sts, one of them from the classes at 13 months and amateur handled. The others were Champion Hamlet of Dorridane, Champion Dorridanes Cinda, and Champion Diablo of Dorridane. All were breed winners from the classes, and all those shown in Group competition placed. Unfortunately, a hormone shot ruined Brandy for breeding after this great litter.

Wanting to keep their kennel small (all Dorridane Great Danes live as house dogs with their owners), the Crawleys have bred their bitches sparingly, thus have produced only 12 litters plus one other of which Pat was co-breeder, making their record of 12 homebred champions (plus two others they have owned) all the more outstanding.

Of the homebred champions, four of them have been Group winners with three of them *multiple* Group winners.

40

The foundation bitch at Dorridane Kennels, Ch. Kensinomens Contess. Dam of an all champion litter of four. Dr. Robert and Mrs. Patricia Crawley, owners, Folsom, La.

Ch. Dinro Taboo Again, outstanding representative of Rosemarie Robert's Dinro Danes, Carmel, N.Y.

Champion Dorridanes Sweet Molly is a bitch of tremendous importance to the Dorridane breeding program, having produced seven champions, six of whom are American Champions and one a Mexican Champion. Her progeny includes three Group winners: Champion Tomike's Ringer of Dorridane who was #2 Great Dane for 1977, and a daughter, Champion Ding's Impulse of Dorridane, who was Best of Opposite Sex at the First Regional National in 1977; plus Dorridane's Aphrodite, pointed but retired after bloating on a show circuit.

Dorridane has bred, also, two Specialty winners, not counting Impulse's Winners Bitch victory in an entry of 140 of her sex at a Regional National.

FAHMIE'S

Fahmie's Great Danes are owned by Mr. and Mrs. John Fahmie, Miami, Florida.

This is the home of Champion Fahmie's Golden Vulcan v Fury who completed his title in April 1976.

Vulcan's career as a special included winning a Group 1st his first time out as a special under judge Helen Miller Fisher (breed) and Louis Murr (Group), followed by other Group successes and three Specialty Bests of Breed. Vulcan also retired the Great Dane Club of Southern Florida challenge trophy by winning Best in that Club's Specialties three times consecutively, 1976, 1977, and 1978.

Vulcan has proven himself an outstanding stud dog. Two of his well-known progeny are a son and daughter, Champion Thor Dane's Pat Hand Poker and Champion Thor Dane's Page v Brass Rail. Pat Hand Poker went Winners Dog and Page was Best in Sweepstakes and Winners Bitch at the Southern Florida Specialty, going on to win Best Stud Dog for their sire there.

FALCONROC

Falconroc Great Danes are owned by Janet Purdy at Schodack Landing, New York. Janet's first Great Dane was Champion Buck's Ruler of the Gods, who was whelped in 1966, and it was due to him that she has become so involved in and devoted to the breed.

A few years after acquiring him, she decided that she would like to breed Great Danes; thus she purchased a bitch and the first of

Ch. Harmony Hill Riff Song, by Ch. Harmony Hill Fortissimo ex Peanut Candy of Marydane. Owned by Mr. and Mrs. Robert C. Thomas, Harmony Hill Kennels, Marlboro, Mass. Winning Best of Breed at Windam County in 1967.

Six-week-old puppies sired by Barban's Falconroc Alexander ex Ch. Barban's Peach Parfait. Bred by Anthony and Barbara Tolintino.

Ch. Ju-Wil's Danes Charisma, by Joker ex Roc A Ril Rhapsody, bred and owned by Paul Szabo. A Best in Show winner.

Am., Can., and Bda. Ch. Harmony Hill Sherwood Joker winning Veterans and Stud Dog Class at G.D.C.N.E. Specialty in 1973. Owner-handled by Mrs. Carolyn A. Thomas, Marlboro, Mass.

the Falconroc litters was born in 1969. After recurrent problems which she was unable to tolerate, she decided to start over, this time with another line.

A visit to the Lovetts in 1978 to see a brindle bitch puppy led to Janet's return home not with a puppy but instead with a three-year-old bitch with whom she was very taken. Shortly thereafter this bitch came into season and was bred, producing Champion Tyler Lovett of Falconroc and his beautiful sisters. This inbred litter provided the solid foundation that Janet had been needing and which she put to good use. Tyler, at the time of writing, has produced ten champions. These bloodlines are strong producers of bitches, and can also be counted on for handsome heads and bites, fronts and feet, movement (particularly reach and drive), angulation, bone and substance, and tails.

HARMONY HILL

Harmony Hill Great Danes at Marlboro, Massachusetts, got under way in 1956 with the purchase by Mr. and Mrs. Robert C. Thomas of Lane's Turn Kirschwasser (of Marydane-Dinro background). Carolyn and Robert Thomas began breeding very selectively, a total of 27 litters that would span a period of 25 years. During these years, despite keeping only nine dams and five sires for their limited breeding program, there were 141 Champions directly bred from Harmony Hill sires. Many of their most promising Danes were sold to others sincerely interested in the breed.

Marydane, Kolyer, Tivoli, and Gilbert bloodlines proved to be the most successful when combined with the Harmony Hill stock.

From their first litter, Harmony Hill All By Myself was the winner of the 1959 Great Dane Club of America Futurity. When bred to the Johnson's great sire, Champion Heidere's Devil D of Marydane, she produced Champion Harmony Hill Dream Girl, Best of Opposite Sex at the 1959 Futurity. Later purchased by the Kents as the foundation bitch for their Northcliff Danes, Dream Girl became the dam of three champions. One of her sons, Champion Kent's Brandt of Northcliff, by Champion Dinro Taboo, won the Futurity in 1963 and started the Booxbaums in Danes. A repeat of the Missy-Devil D breeding accounted for the first stud kept by Harmony Hill, American and Canadian Champion Harmony Hill Fortissimo, who was Best of Opposite Sex at the 1961 Futurity.

45

Although never bred to a champion bitch, Fortissimo was the sire of twelve champions. The breeding of Fortissimo to Peanut Candy of Marydane (purchased from the Johnsons by Harmony Hill) accounted for five champions. A daughter from this breeding, Champion Harmony Hill Lady Be Good, was the foundation bitch for the Lovetts. Another son from the breeding, American and Canadian Champion Harmony Hill Riff Song, when bred to Harmony Hill Xmas Eve, produced two Danes who were to have great impact on the International scene after being sold to Mrs. Magnusson's Airways Kennel in Sweden. International and Nordic Champion Harmony Hill Linda of Airways was the 1969 Dog of the Year, All Breeds; was the dam of six champions; and still holds the record for most Bests in Show in one year. International and Nordic Champion Harmony Hill Lied of Airways was the top stud dog, all breeds, for several years, and sired 39 champions, among them Champion Airways Wrangler of Impton who gained 24 Challenge Certificates for Margaret Everton in England.

Harmony Hill Xmas Eve was sired by Champion Kolyer's Kissin Kurt from a Fortissimo daughter. Her brother, Champion Harmony Hill Xmas Lyons Pride, was sold to Ed Lyons. Although used sparingly at stud, he was the sire of 14 champions. One of his daughters, Leo Duffer's Champion Timberlakes Rejoice of O'Kala, was later linebred to the Thomas's American, Canadian, Bermudian Champion Harmony Hill Sherwood Joker to produce a number of champions. Among them Champion Pinehollow's Smoki Jarva, the sire of Champion Edeldane's Wildfire who was a top rated Great Dane Club of America Regional Specialty winner, and grandsire of Champion Temple Dell's Odin v Branstock (Davis lines).

Fortissimo, when bred to Gilbert's Gallant Lady, produced the kennel's leading sire, American, Canadian and Bermudian Champion Harmony Hill Sherwood Joker. Bred by Gwen McAlmond. The Thomases were fortunate in selecting him as a stud puppy as Joker became the sire of 46 champions, 23 of which were American. A daughter, American and Canadian Champion Davos Baroness Zareba, bred by the Drs. Fletch and owned by June Cowie, was Canada's Top Dog All Breeds in 1972.

Roxanne Mahan's breeding of Joker to Tivoli's Dilema produced a number of champions, among them the Presley's Champion Tivoli Newt v Harmony Hill who was owner-handled to Best in Show. The Bob Vances' Champion Rochar's Bittersweet (Joker bred to their Champion Tivoli Democrat) often topped the Working Group and was a Specialty Best of Breed winner.

Another Best in Show Joker daughter was Champion Charisma of Ju-Wil's Dane, one of four champions of this breeding by the Szabos out of Roc n Rils Rhapsody (Marydane background). Another sister, Champion Corina of Ju-Wil's Dane was purchased by the Thomases and when bred to their Canadian Champion Harmony Hill Witch Doctor produced the Dermotts' Harmony Hill Monday Monday, winner of the 1976 Futurity, as well as the Stows' Champion Harmony Hill Sugar On Sunday. Bred to the Koopmanns' Champion Harmony Hill Midas of Delphi, Corina produced their Champion Harmony Hill Indian Summer.

HONEY HOLLOW

Honey Hollow Kennels are almost legendary in their greatness and in their owner, Lina Basquette, who is a former premier danseuse and movie star, and describes herself as "breeder/exhibitor/professional handler, and, as of September 12, 1985, prospective judge." To which she adds, "is not only alive and well but going strong at an unbelievable age of 78½ years." The latter is a fact difficult to make people believe since her appearance, energy, and animation combine to make her seem about half that number of years.

Lina's kennels at Chalfont, Bucks County, Pennsylvania are world-famous for the dogs they have housed and produced. The kennel was sold in the mid-1970's when Lina retired from breeding Danes and moved to Wheeling, West Virginia. From there she has operated on a very small scale as a professional handler, taking on a show ring career only one Great Dane at a time provided she considered it to be of exceptional quality. Now she is retiring from handling and soon to become a judge. What knowledge she will bring to the rings in that capacity!

Lina started "in Danes" back at the close of the 1940's. Her first champion was Champion Gilbert-Duysters Linda Mae back in 1950. Her first male champion and stud dog was Champion Duyster's Lord Jim. His impact on the breed was tremendous; among others, he sired Gregory of Kent, the dog Lina so enormously admired. His story is part of Lina's chapter elsewhere in this book.

The great Ch. Honey Hollow Stormi Rudio with his daughter, Sunny. Bred and handled by Lina Basquette, Honey Hollow Kennels, Chalfont, Pa. Owned by Kay and Bill Clarke, Medford Lakes, New Jersey, "Stormi" was the winner of eight Best in Show awards.

Ch. Shalott's Sir Allistair, Ch. Dion of Kent (fawn) ex Ch. Honey Hollow Ebony Maid (black), was the sire of the great Ch. Honey Hollow Stormi Rudio. Photographed at 18 months.

Probably Champion Honey Hollow Stormi Rudio was Lina's greatest and most famed homebred, winner of eight Bests in Show at a time in the late 1950's when Great Danes were seldom honored with winning *Groups* much less the top award! Stormi Rudio was by Champion Shalott's Sir Allistair ex Honey Hollow Ruda Kazoota. Lina dubbed Stormi the "Cinderella Dog." As she puts it (reverently) "a glorious gift from heaven." For you see, Stormi was the result of an accidental mating (*not* clever insight!) between a golden fawn sire and a solid *black* female, which subsequently set off a veritable revolution in the Great Dane Club of America that exists even until the present day. Yet Lina still stands by her opinion and maintains "until I am six feet under" that such a breeding *"when carefully and intelligently done"* produces the finest in blacks and often the most desirable golden fawns. Although Stormi Rudio was the product of a kennel man's mistake, "somebody upstairs must have tried to tell us lowly humans *something,*" again using Lina's words.

Stormi was sold as a pet at two months of age for $150.00---because Lina liked the people involved. Again quoting her, "Kay and Bill Clarke of Medford Lakes, New Jersey, were such *nice* folks—didn't have much money, but the love they showered on that puppy was something to behold."

Lina did not see Stormi again until he was about two years old, and then he stood before her "the epitome of what a Great Dane should be." Lina demanded, begged, and implored that he *must* be shown. She succeeded in persuading the owners, and at his first show, Philadelphia, Stormi went Best of Breed from the Open Dog Class, defeated several famous Dane specials, then placed fourth in the Group under Henry Stoecker. The Clarkes were not in a position to campaign the dog, so Lina took him on gratis, so great was her pride and faith in him. Seldom shown more than two hundred miles from home, Stormi Rudio wound up his career with eight Bests in Show, sired about six litters, then was summarily retired from shows and stud. But not until after Stormi had scored one of the most prestigious of all his exciting wins, that of first in the Working Group at Westminster under judge John W. Cross, Jr., in 1959—one of only four Great Danes to date who have gained Group 1st at this most respected of all dog shows, two of which were handled by Lina herself.

Stormi Rudio lived to be past ten years of age, and to his dying day, "remained sound as a gold-backed dollar."

Another of Lina's own Honey Hollow prefixes was that on the solid black Champion Honey Hollow Great Donner, like Stormi from a mixed color breeding, who remains the top winning Black Great Dane of all time, despite a relatively limited career. He was owned by Dr. and Mrs. James Childress of Wexford, Pennsylvania, and his show successes included 45 Group 1sts and four Bests in Show.

Another black, Champion Honey Hollow Rameses, belonged to J. Council Parker.

Champion Honey Hollow Great Dion, a golden fawn, although owned by Virginia and Garnett Matthews of Missouri remained at home at Honey Hollow. He thoroughly disliked dog shows and the show ring, for which reason he was not campaigned as a special.

In her own separate chapter of this book, Lina makes many comments and tells you of the numerous dogs she has handled and/or admired over the years. She will be missed in the ring as a handler; but at the same time she will be a marvelous addition to the ranks of truly knowledgeable judges. We wish her many, many years of success in this, to her, new phase of the Fancy.

HORIZON'S

Champion Tara's Wonder Woman V Horizon's whirlwind success in the show ring began at the very early age of six months and four days with a four-point major reserve winners under Mr. Hugo Gamboa. One month later she gained her first points, going on to Best of Breed.

Wonder Woman's career continued to blossom. "Ginger", as she is called, made her championship while still in the puppy class at only 11 months of age. She then became a multiple breed and Group winner who in a very short time had accumulated 41 Bests of Breed, 15 Group placements, and three Specialty wins. This has placed her in the Top Ten both in breed and Group, and has made her the #1 Great Dane bitch in the South.

Wonder Woman now has six lovely puppies, all fawns, sired by Champion Tara's The Gold Card v Norella. She is therefore shown less frequently than formerly, but still, when she has the opportunity, continues her winning ways.

Charles and Debbie Kirksey, at Houston, Texas, co-own Wonder Woman with her breeders, Marilyn K. Riggins and Cindy Fisher, owners of her dam, Champion Tara's On To Glory; and with Sharon G. Fulford, who is her excellent (and devoted) handler.

In looking to the future, Debbie Kirksey comments that Wonder Woman, who is sired by the American and Canadian Best in Show winning Champion Tara's Sir Fredric Freeloader has followed in her sire's footsteps in a very satisfactory manner. Thus all concerned are hoping that these puppies, in their turn, will follow in Wonder Woman's footsteps with success equal to her own. Sir Fredric Freeloader, incidentally, was the number 1 Great Dane, All Systems, for 1977 and 1978.

KEETRA

Keetra Great Danes are owned by Bernard and Francine Schwartz at Lake Forest, Illinois, who are primarily interested in the breeding of Harlequins.

Francine Schwartz started out as an exhibitor with her dogs back in the early 1960's, at which period it was rough going for black color Great Danes even to achieve championship honors. The first of Mrs. Schwartz's was a black bitch out of a Boston and Harlequin breeding who had been Reserve Winners on 27 occasions. So what did the Schwartzes do but go from the frying pan into the fire by purchasing a Harlequin, Lancer V. Meistersinger at age four months from Mrs. Toni Pratt who finished his title and then was specialed briefly, acquiring a few Best of Breed wins in the process.

Next, also at age four months, Timbaleca V. Meistersinger was purchased and finished quite quickly by Mrs. Schwartz. To her credit, Timbaleca defeated some Best in Show Danes during her show career.

Then came Champion Keetra's Bruno V. Dog, "Jaws" to his friends. He is a Specialty and Group winner, and lives with a ten-year-old Dobe bitch. He has sired champions, but, to quote Mrs. Schwartz, "His claim to fame is his temperament. He has *charisma.*"

Future Ch. Tara's Wonder Woman V Horizon's at her first dog show, age six months and four days, taking reserve winners at a four-point major— very nice going for so young a puppy. One month later she earned her first points going through to Best of Breed. Owned by Charles and Debbie Kirksey, Marilyn K. Riggins, and Sharon G. Fulford (her devoted handler) of Houston, Texas.

This handsome Harlequin puppy is Keetra's Valentine, by Ch. Carrosel's The Showboat ex Keetra's Ariana. Bred by Bernard and Francine Schwartz. A lovely show prospect Harlequin puppy.

Regarding her much-loved Harlequins, Mrs. Schwartz writes the following: "Today we are seeing some with very few blotches, and this is not proper. White fronts and necks are what we aim for, but it should not be at the cost of losing black. I feel it is necessary to use blacks out of Harlequins every few generations to keep color. I stress *black out of Harlequin* because many so-called blacks have blue or fawn in their background, and we do not want that in the breeding of our Harlies."

LONGO'S

Longo's Great Danes are owned by Joseph and Tootie Longo at Mentor-on-the-Lake, Ohio, where black Great Danes are featured.

The "star" of the kennel is the magnificent Best in Show winner, Champion Longo's Chief Joseph who was born on September 1, 1980. This splendid dog completed his championship at 18 months of age, not having taken his first points until he was more than a year old as he was like a fine wine, a slow maturing dog becoming excellent with maturity.

On the other hand, Chief Joseph's sister, Champion Longo's Double De Luxe, breezed through her championship taking a 4 point major first time in the ring from the 6-9 months puppy class. She is the first black Great Dane bitch ever to have finished from the Bred-by-Exhibitor Class.

Champion Longo's Chief Joseph is the seventh champion in an unbroken seven generation line of champion sires. He is also the first black Dane ever to have won 13 Specialty Shows; the first black to go Best of Breed at Westchester Kennel Club Dog Show. And the first black in 22 years to win an all-breed Best in Show, making him only the second black in history to have gained this honor in the breed. He was retired with two Bests in Show, all-breeds, and was handled during his career by Carol Whitney.

Chief Joseph has been used sparingly at stud, yet has produced four champions to date with numerous others pointed. He was the Top Producing Sire for the first half of 1985, Canine Chronicle System, #1 male Great Dane and #2 Great Dane for 1983 and 1984.

Chief Joseph won Best of Breed at Westchester Kennel Club in 1984, and the following year his daughter, Champion Vera's Annastacia v Brislyn, was Winners Bitch there, the first time at this show for a black Dane bitch. She went on to finish with four majors.

Champion Longo's Chief Joseph and Champion Longo's Double De Luxe are sired by the black Champion Shadowbrooks Pask (Champion Charlemagne Du Lac-Rebelro's Satanic Lady) ex Longo's Foxxy Lady (black) by Champion Charlemagne Du Lac ex Honey Hollow Dark Grumbles. Thus they are the result of half brother to half sister breeding.

LYNDANE

Lyndane Great Danes, at Salem, Connecticut, are owned by Joel and Lynn Rosenblatt who are successful as Great Dane breeders as well as Joel being a highly regarded and extremely popular professional handler.

The Rosenblatts have raised a goodly number of Dane champions, and in addition, they have finished many others for their clients. Pride of place among their own dogs, we feel certain, goes to the magnificent Champion Lyndane's J.J., who, while being campaigned back in 1978, became one of the Top Great Danes in both breed and Group competition for that period. J.J. is representative of the finest in Marydane breeding combined with that of Champion Big Kim of Bella Dane.

Champion Lyndane's Special Edition is another fine example of the Danes bred at Lyndane. Owned by Henry Thunhorst, handled by Joel, "Eddy" was a multi-Group and Specialty winner and one of the Top Great Danes for 1981-1982—another handsome, successful Lyndane homebred.

Champion Darrdane's Opening Bid is by Champion Windane's Zephyr ex Champion Lyndane's La-Di-Da. Now a Specialty and multi-Group winner, Opening Bid was #3 Great Dane in the United States for 1983. As a youngster, his success was obviously already assured as he completed his championship at the age of nine months! Dr. and Mrs. Robert A. Rothenberg, Avon, Connecticut, are the owners and breeders, Joel Rosenblatt the handler and co-breeder.

Owned by Laurie and Michael Maulucci, the lovely bitch Champion MJM's Class Act of Lyndane has been a leading special during 1985 and is a Group and Specialty winner. Bred by Joyce Vukic, "Katie" is a daughter of Champion Darrdane's Opening

Front view of Ch. Longo's Chief Joseph, famous Best in Show winner owned by Joe and Tootie Longo, Mentor-on-the-Lake, Ohio.

Ch. Lyndane's J.J., owned and bred by Joel and Lynn Rosenblatt, is one of the Top Great Danes under both breed and Group system. A grandson of Ch. Big Kim of Bella Dane combined with Marydane breeding.

Ch. Calhoun of Tamerlane, owned by Mrs. J. Bruce Morey, was bred by owner and Lucy A. Lyons', sired by Ch. Mr. Pacific of Marydane ex Ch. Lyons' Pride Heidi.

Am. and Can. Ch. Lyons' Pride Heidi was the Top Great Dane Bitch for 1969, and is the only Dane bitch to have produced a Best in Futurity brother and sister. Owned by Lucy Lyons, Somers, Conn., and the Illinois fancier, Mrs. J. Bruce Morey.

Bid ex Champion Murlo Scarlett O'Harris. She is handled by Joel Rosenblatt.

Joel has had a very striking black bitch at the shows and doing nicely. She is Wildwind Blaze of Glory owned by Susan Carlin and bred by Jill Ferrera, well on the way towards her championship as we write.

Another of the Rosenblatt-handled Danes, Champion Zeno's Jedi Master is among the photos in this book. Owned and bred by Barbra Oliva and David Zeno, this dog is a handsome representative of the Harlequin coloring.

LYONS' PRIDE

Since 1959 Ed Lyons and his wife, Lucy, have been "Great Great Dane people," involved as breeders in the earlier days, although at present Mr. Lyons is a very successful and popular professional handler which is the reason he concentrates on his clients and their dogs rather than on many dogs of their own.

Their first Dane was a rescue case, an unwanted Dane whom they took on for the purpose of giving it a home. The second one came to join the family to be company for the first, which indeed she was, as in due course there came the day when the Lyons arrived home to find no less than 12 tiny puppies along with sire and dam waiting to greet them.

We bring you herewith some of the Lyons' Pride dogs among our illustrations. Ed probably takes most pleasure in the fact that he and his wife bred littermates who won Best Dog and Best Bitch at the National Futurity—certainly a tremendous satisfaction to any breeder so fortunate as to have something so exciting happen!

It must be equally gratifying for Ed to have piloted dozens of noted Danes to outstanding ring success. His proficiency as a handler makes him extremely popular with Dane exhibitors; he must regard the roster of his big winners with great pleasure!

MARYDANE

Marydane Great Danes, at Wilton, Connecticut, carried the banner high over at least several decades for those dedicated breeders Jerry and Mary Johnston, or as they were more formally known, Mr. and Mrs. Gerard C. Johnston. Right up to the time of her death, Mary Johnston was involved with Danes, even after

Jerry's death some half dozen years ago. These people made a tremendous contribution to Danes in the United States, and although the kennel is now closed, I am including their story with the currently active ones as they were until so very successful.

Mary Johnston acquired her first Great Dane from the Roxdane Kennels in New Jersey during 1942, having previously owned Scottish Terriers. Ironically, she brought the Dane home on the very day that food rationing went into effect during World War II, which did not faze her in the least.

This was the lovely bitch Champion Molle of Roxdane, for whom Mary selected as a stud Champion Neil of Brae Tarn. Call it beginner's luck or call it prophetic, whichever pleases you most. But from this very first litter came the Johnstons' first champion, Gerhardt of Marydane. Molle proved herself to be an excellent producer, which carried through two breedings, the second to Champion Fergus of Daynemouth. Each of these litters produced several champions. It was by Fergus that she gave her owners Marshmallow of Marydane, a bitch who quickly became a champion and then went on to become the foundtion bitch at Marydane Kennels.

At the time of their first Great Dane, the Johnstons were residents of Detroit. Whey they moved to Wilton it was necessary for them to build the kennel on the New York side of their property owing to rigid rulings prohibiting kennels in that exclusive Connecticut community.

Mary Johnston had owned dogs all her life when she bought the Danes; Jerry had not ever had one previous to their marriage. His love of them, however, was proven quite clearly when one evening, prior to the Danes, Mary came home to find a Scottie in the living room, brought there by Jerry! One thing for sure, Jerry's interest in dogs surfaced in short order along with ownership of them. It was he who owner-handled many of the Danes (although some went out with professionals, too)—never Mary when she could avoid it—and his Sherlock Holmes type cap became a trademark at the shows and in the rings. It speaks well of his handling abilities when we point out that Jerry Johnston personally handled five of the Marydane Great Danes to Best in Show!

We do not have a total count of the Marydane champions, so on that subject can only say that there were very, very many of them. From the first of the homebred champions, Gerhardt, on to the 1980's, Marydane was in competition with dogs of striking quality and excellence.

Undoubtedly the "star" of the Marydane campaigners was the famous Champion Reggan's Maddas L of Marydane, known as "Maddo." Born in May 1964, by Champion Heidere Devil D of Marydane ex Regendane's Fame, she was bred by R. and G. Parks and handled to her stunning show career by Stuart S. Sliney. Maddo was the daughter of a most dominant and successful stud dog, Champion Heidere's Devil D of Marydane having been the sire of a total of 34 champions. On all of them, to quote Mary, "he put his stamp regardless of the bitch to whom he was bred. You couldn't miss one—they all looked alike and acted like him." Devil D was bred by Heidere, by Champion Lucky Adolph of Marydane ex Champion Heidere Turka of Carlsdane, and was born in 1957.

But returning to Maddo: by seven months' age she already had 14 points. Mary took her out on a circuit with another dog purely as company for him, Maddo being just a puppy, and by nine months of age she was a champion, winning her first Working Group when she was still less than a year old. When her show career ended, she had amassed a total of 25 times Best in Show, 149 Group placements, 18 Specialty Shows, and 230 times Best of Breed. She was in the Top Ten, all breeds, in 1966 and 1967, and among the Top Ten Working Dogs over a consecutive period of four years. Maddo also had a litter brother who was an extremely handsome Dane and who did some good winning although he was overshadowed by his sister. This was Champion Reggen's Marcus of Marydane.

Other illustrious Danes who helped to make Marydane so widely renowned a kennel include Autopilot of Kanedane whom Jerry Johnston himself handled to Best of Breed at Westminster in 1952 when Marydane dogs were just becoming really established. Champion Mr. Pacific of Marydane, who was sired by Laird of Tallbrook Farm ex Reggen's Mona of Marydane (a bitch who had been sold to the West Coast) is a dog whom one recalls with admiration, as is the triple Best in Show winner, Champion Honey Bun of Marydane, who had the distinction of winning a Working Group 1st at Westminster. Champion Amobi of Marydane during

Ch. Akobi of Marydane, littermate to Ch. Ayo of Marydane, by Ch. Abner Lowell Davis ex Ayo of Marydane, taking points towards his title, handled by Jack Houser for the late Mr. and Mrs. Gerard Johnston, Marydane Kennels, Wilton, Conn., some years back.

Ch. Waterwood's Brew Meister, January 1980-January 1985, by Ch. Tilpadane Barnaby Neustadt ex Hearth Hill's Golden Kinde, C.D., was handled and finished by Linda Springthorpe. Owned by Sally and Paul Harris, Peach Danes, Covington, Ga.

the 1970's was also going along nicely at the shows.

Mary Johnston, in addition to her enthusiasm for Danes, enjoyed club work, thus involved herself with some of the local all-breed show giving clubs, doing so most effectively. She was closely involved with the Newtown Kennel Club and the running of its shows over at least several years. After that she became Show Chairman for Longshore Southport, again handling the job well. Her most recent club affiliation was with the Greenwich Kennel Club which organization she headed as President for numerous years, up to the time of her death.

As one who thoroughly enjoyed the task, bringing knowledge and integrity with her into the ring, Mary Johnston was a respected and popular dog show judge.

The closing of Marydane and the loss of the Johnstons certainly takes away considerably from the Great Dane world. As one well-known member of the Fancy commented when we all heard the sad news, "It is the end of an era." Which I am sure many of us agree is all too true.

PEACH

Peach Great Danes are owned by Sally and Paul Harris at Covington, Georgia. Top dog here has been the very handsome late Champion Waterwood's Brew Meister, who died in January of 1985 at the age of five years.

Brew was a son of Champion Tilpadane Barnaby Neustadt ex Hearth Hill's Golden Kinde, C.D. He was handled by Linda Springthorpe who finished him at 19 months with a Best of Breed and Group 3rd.

As a special, Brew had multiple Group placements and multiple Bests in Specialty Shows. He was #5 Great Dane in 1984, *Great Dane Reporter System*. His breeders were Herb and Margaret Shappard.

RIKA

Rika Great Danes are owned by Richard and Kathy Varian of Reseda, California. Although Richard has owned Danes for more than 27 years, it was not until 1973 that he and Kathy started showing; thus the kennel name did not come into being until that time.

Ch. Rika's Tattletale of Kino, by Best in Specialty Show winning Ch. Rika's Rendition of Kingswood ex MTC Madame, was bred by Floyd and Nicole McGinnis and is owned by Pam Robles and Kathy Varian. Sylvia Rodwell handling.

The Varians exhibited many dogs, mostly owner-handled, for years and did little breeding due to their conviction that when they began breeding they wanted to breed only the best. During this time Kathy also handled other breeds on a non-professional basis, including an American/Mexican champion St. Bernard who had several breed wins, Group placements, and other impressive accomplishments.

The Varians' first litter was co-bred with Kathy Jacobs and whelped by her. This litter was born in 1977 and produced Canadian Champion Merry Meadows Carmine and several other point-winning puppies. In 1980 things began to fall into place for Rika Danes, and they bred and whelped their first litter "at home" that year out of Champion Regal Aires Amy of Amstar and sired by Champion Von Raseac Tybo O'Lorcain. This litter produced three champions.

The total number of litters whelped in their home and bred by the Varians, at the time of writing, is five. Co-bred litters number four. Kathy and Richard take great pride in these litters due to the fact that each has produced champion or major pointed puppies before the age of one year. They feel that the quality and breed type represented in these puppies is exceptional, and plan to continue their breeding program as they are doing now, on a limited basis with thought and consideration going into each.

Most of the Varians' champions are co-owned as they feel that the individual attention necessary to bring a dog to its fullest potential is better achieved in a home environment.

Currently the Varians have four champions who live in the house with them. They are the famed Best in Show winning Champion Brierdane's Indian Amber, Best in Specialty Show winning Champion Rika's Rendition of Kingswood, Champion Kingswood Phoebe Snow, and Champion Rika's Putn On The Ritz M'Mdws. One other bitch is currently kept in their kennel, Rika's Patent Pending.

Richard and Kathy Varian have owned and/or bred 14 champions to date as follows:

Can. Ch. Alexis McDavis of Rika
Ch. Regal Aires Amy of Amstar
Ch. Winfall's Papillon v Mako
Can. Ch. Merry Meadows Carmine

Ch. Kingswood Phoebe Snow
Ch. Brierdane's Indian Amber
Ch. Sierra's Let's Rip v Rika
Ch. Rika's Tattletale at Kino
Ch. Rika-Warwick LeRoi v Equidane
Ch. Warwick's Tybo Diyanu v Rika
Ch. Rika Rumor Has It Merry Meadows
Ch. Rika's Plain Jane v Hauer
Ch. Rika's Putn On The Ritz M'Mdws
Ch. Rika's Rendition of Kingswood

The greatest thrill of all for the Varians to date as Dane owners has been, of course, the sensational success they have achieved owning and campaigning the famous bitch Champion Brierdane's Indian Amber, who is a multi-Best in Show winner. To quote Kathy Varian, "She has that special charisma required in a top show dog, and made 'specialing' fun. We have also taken great pride in our puppies, almost all of whom have been pointed from the puppy classes."

The foundations of the Rika breeding program rest upon Champion Rika's Rendition of Kingswood, Champion Kingswood Phoebe Snow (who are littermates) and the incorporation of a prepotent stud dog, Champion Hauerdane's War Bonnet, a famous Best in Show winner who is the sire of Amber.

Champion Brierdane's Indian Amber has to her credit as a show bitch four all-breed Bests in Show; 52 Group placements including 20 Group 1sts; and 80 Bests of Breed including eight Bests in Specialty Shows. She was #1 Great Dane, Best of Breed System, at the year end 1984; #2 Great Dane, Group System, as of the aforementioned date, and ranked among the Top Ten Great Danes, both breed and Group, in 1983, 1984 and 1985. She was the youngest California-owned Dane bitch to complete a championship, finishing at 12 months with four majors. At seven months' age she took Winners Bitch at the Great Dane Club of America Regional Specialty Show. And she was the Top Club Owned Dog in 1984 by a member of the Great Dane Club of California and of the Great Dane Club of San Diego.

Another very important Dane in this kennel is the dog, Champion Rika's Rendition of Kingswood, a Best in Show winner sired by American and Mexican Champion Jecamo's Aalborg v Dibo ex

Champion Kingswood Lily Langtry. The Varians co-own this dog with Richard N. Gebhart. The breeders are Evelyn Porter and Gary Catron, and he is handled by Doug Toomey. Rendition is a multiple Best of Breed winner with a Group 1st and a Specialty Best of Breed to his credit, who has ranked in the Top Ten, both breed and Group, in 1982 and 1984. He is the youngest California-owned Great Dane to complete a championship, which he did at 13 months with four majors, including two Specialty Best of Winners awards and four consecutive Best Puppy at Specialty awards.

Bred 11 times, Rendition has sired 11 litters to date. He is the sire of Champion Rika's Tattletale of Kino, Champion Riko Rumor Has It Merry Meadows, Canadian Champion CJ's Brittania Jeans v Baydane, Champion M and M's Wind Drift v Hauer, and some half dozen others who are pointed at time of writing.

ROCHFORD

Rochford Great Danes of Kansas City, Missouri, are owned by Gary and Janet Quick who are tremendous Dane enthusiasts.

The foundation bitch here is the lovely Champion Edeldane's Celebration, by Lazycroft Murlo Harris ex Edeldane's Lothario (whose four grandparents are American and Canadian Champion Harmony Hill Sherwood Joker, Champion Timberlake Rejoice O'Kala, Champion Reisenhof's The Boss, and Champion Earl-Mar's Sandpiper). Celebration was bred by Nancy Thompson and Betty Harris.

A handsome brindle bitch, Celebration completed her title at two years old owner-handled, then went on to multiple breed wins and Group placements. Her first litter, sired by Champion Templedell's Odin v Brandstock (Champion Edeldane's Wildfire-Champion Sarah Davis of Templedell) has, to quote Janet Quick, been "like a dream come true." Two of the puppies are already finished, Champion Rochford's Essex and Champion Rochford's Cumbria, while two littermates were pointed at that time, Rochford's Devon (13 points) and Rochford's Cambridge (6 points).

Champion Rochford's Essex now belongs to Valerie and Jerry Parsons in DeSoto, Kansas. A big fawn male, he has had an impressive career from the puppy classes finishing his title at 11 months old. Owner-handled all the way, this 37" male has been a consistent breed winner.

Champion Rochford's Cumbria is an exceptionally tall bitch with plenty of substance who took multiple breeds from the classes and completed title at less than two years of age.

Rochford's Devon is owned by Lourdes Carvajal in Kansas City, to whom she has been a source of much pleasure. Needing just a major to finish as this was written, we are sure that she now is sporting the title of Champion.

Janet Quick has some strong convictions about Great Danes which guide her in her breeding program. She feels that the Great Dane is still truly a working dog, and that even though not required to work, these dogs should be able to do so. Thus substance is to her of tremendous importance, and her goal is to produce Danes who combine this necessity with the elegance and outstanding heads necessary in the show ring. The photos she has sent us of the Rochford puppies and dogs speak for themselves!

SHADAM

Great Danes of Shadam, owned by M. Arthur and June Shafer at Fort Wayne, Indiana, had their beginnings with the purchase of Champion Ardlyn's Adam of Marydane, a large brindle dog who breezed through to his title and became a Top Ten Great Dane with multiple Bests in Specialty Shows to his credit. His sire was Champion Han Dan's Alfie, a nice fawn dog owned and shown by the late Mary and Jerry Johnston of Marydane Kennels.

Adam was killed in a tragic accident at a very early age. Fortunately he had been used a few times at stud, and had sired several champions. He was bred to a fawn bitch from the Marydane line, and this is the combination which produced that very special bitch, Champion Shadam's A Girl Called Charlie. Although only specialed five months, Charlie became #5 Dane in that limited time. Better yet is her record as a producer! She was bred to Champion Windane's Zephyr (a Champion Von Riesenhof The Boss grandson) and from this event five puppies entered the show ring, going through to complete their titles. They are Champion Shadam's Aliage, Champion Shadam's A. Lucas, Champion Shadam's Aboard the Merrimac, Champion Shadam's Aaron, and Champion Shadam's A. Haley, C.D. Having been so successful with this litter, the Shafers one year later repeated the breeding.

A future show bitch at age seven weeks. Owned by Rochford Great Danes, Janet Quick, Kansas City, Mo.

Ch. Edeldane's Celebration in 1983 relaxing on the lawn. Owned by Rochford Great Danes, Gary and Janet Quick, Kansas City, Mo.

67

Ch. Shadam's Chessa proudly carrying her dumbbell. Photo courtesy of Nancy Gilbert, Everett, Wash.

Ch. Shadam's A Girl Called Charlie winning the Brood Bitch Class at the Great Dane Club of Western Pennsylvania Specialty with her seven-month-old offspring, Ch. Shadam's Aaron and Ch. Shadam's A. Lucas and Ch. Shadam's Aliage. Arthur and June Shafer, owners, Ft. Wayne, Ind.

Again five puppies entered the ring, this time four of them finishing and the fifth needing just a major to complete her title. They are Champion Shadam's Benson, Champion Shadam's Brooke, Champion Shadam's Booker T., and Champion Shadam's Bernadette.

Champion Shadam's A Girl Called Charlie was #1 producer for several years and won the Brood Bitch Class at the National Specialty. She is the dam of nine living, healthy champions. Most of them are multi-Specialty Best in Show winners; many are Group winners; and all have produced a litter and many champion offspring.

In mid-1985 the Shafers are campaigning three youngsters. They are Sargon Chadsworth V. Shadam, a Charlie great-grandson who at age 15 months has earned 14 points; Shadam's Gideon, a Charlie grandson, major-pointed although still in the puppy classes; Shadam's Hillary, a six-month-old Charlie granddaughter who, in her thus far short career, has several Bests in Sweepstakes and three reserve wins in major entries. The Shafers are greatly excited over all three of them. They are all out of Charlie children bred to a Champion Dagon's Pixie son, Champion Dagon's In A Flash. All of the Shadam litters are based on linebreeding, which the Shafers have found is definitely "the way to go" for them. These last three litters are all linebred on Champion Von Riesenhof The Boss and the Shafers' original Marydane lines.

Breeding and exhibiting Great Danes is a hobby which the Shafers thoroughly enjoy. Breeding takes place only when they specifically need something new for themselves. The dogs are companions to their owners and temperament shares equally the importance of conformation. Although they have had many handlers, including their dear friend Lina Basquette, the Shafers also have had the fun and pride of personally finishing their most recent six or seven Danes themselves—as breeder-owner-handlers.

SHEENWATER

Sally Chandler and her husband, Ed, who, sad to say, passed away in 1980, purchased their first Great Dane shortly after their marriage in 1949. They showed a bit, and even bred a litter, but it was not until 1961 when they met Mary and Jerry Johnston, that they really "got into" Danes.

It was at a show in Rochester, New York, and the Johnstons were showing Caliban at the time. It turned out they had a litter at home, just a few days old, by Champion Daneridge Caliban ex Champion Squirerun Meadowview's Ada (both sired by Devil-D). And so a few weeks later the Chandlers drove to Connecticut to see the litter. When they returned home, it was with a lovely fawn bitch called Cheerio Cathy of Marydane, who eventually was bred to Champion Reggen's Marcus of Marydane (also by Champion Devil-D of Marydane), and it was from this breeding that the Chandlers got Champion Sheenwater Capital Gains.

About the time that "Profit" (Capital Gains) finished in Canada, the Chandlers moved from Western New York to the Chicago area. Apparently "Profit" was too "Eastern" in type to do well against the mid-West dogs, and they never did finish him.

Their next purchase was a bitch, regarding which they of course consulted the Johnstons. In 1968 a lovely brindle bitch, Singing Sue of Marydane, arrived at the Chandlers'. She also was sired by Marcus, and when bred to her half brother Capital Gains, Singing Sue produced Sheenwater Grassfire who became the dam of eight champions from three litters.

From the first of Grassfire's litters, sired by Champion Mr. Pacific of Marydane, the Chandlers found themselves with a very beautiful and typey fawn bitch who became Champion Sheenwater Heat Wave. The second and third of her litters were sired by Champion Ashbun Acres Avant-Garde, resulting in seven champions! They were Jokers Wild, Joie de Vivre, Jubilee, Jackpot, Knock Out, Kiss and Tell, and Koenig. Joker won the National Specialty at Westchester in 1977, and is to be found close up in the pedigrees of some of the leading producers on the West Coast. Knock Out sired a Westchester winner, and is influential in many Eastern bloodlines.

Champion Sheenwater Heat Wave was bred to both Joker and Knock Out. From the Joker breeding came Champion Sheenwater Phoenix, grandsire of the brindle Champion Sheenwater Ace In The Hole. From Knock Out came Sheenwater Open Sesame, sire of the gorgeous Champion Stone River's Delta Dawn, whose dam, Rockbridge's Texas Lady, goes back to both Champion Sunridge's Chief Justice and Champion Sunridge's Lil Liza Jane, thus this breeding doubles up on both sides on Champion Mount-dania's Timber, sire of Avant-Garde as well as Chief Justice and Liza.

Coming to more recent events at Sheenwater Kennels, which are now located at Loganville, Georgia and their current Danes: Champion Stone River's Delta Dawn is owned by Sally Chandler with Chris O'Connell. Bred to the Top Producing Avant-Garde son, Champion Reann's French Aristocrat, she has produced Champion Sheenwater Gamble On Me (currently Top Winning Great Dane in the United States), Champion Sheenwater Georgia Pacific, Champion Sheenwater Jump for Joy, Sheenwater Juris-prudence (10 points) and three others who are pointed—this from a total of nine puppies.

As can be seen from the foregoing, Sheenwater has relied heav-ily on close linebreeding, including several half brothers to half sisters. Basically, everything goes back to the two stud dogs, Champion Dinro Taboo and Champion Heidere Devil-D of Mary-dane, who themselves are half brothers. Sally Chandler's feeling is that linebreeding plus rigid selection within the bloodline is the only way to "set" the qualities which are important at Sheenwater, including temperament, balance, beauty of outline, good strong hindquarters and smooth, precise movement, to which Mrs. Chandler also adds dark eyes, and good clean color. That, truly, is a dog that says "I am a GREAT DANE."

SHERIDANE

Sheridane Kennels are owned by Mike and Eileen Sherman at Hebron, Connecticut, who finished their first homebred cham-pion, Sheridane Iroquois Hope, during the late 1970's with a Spe-cialty win over 71 bitches.

Star of the kennel, and a most widely admired dog, is the four-year-old (as of mid-October 1985) fawn male, Champion Sheri-dane Prince Valiant. Bred by Eileen Sherman and Diane Dodson, "Val" is a son of Champion Bodane Tourister (by the Champion Mountdania's Timber son, Champion Ashbun Acres Avant-Garde ex Bodane Sophisticated Lady) from Champion Sheridane Joyful Jade (Champion Devrok's Zartanian v Sheboane, he by Avant-Garde, thus a Timber grandson, ex Sheridane Camoflage Cameo). "Val" was chosen by the Great Dane Club of America Committee

Ch. Sheridane Aarlo v Danebridge, owned by Dale and Karen Dasjardin. Bred and handled by Mike Sherman, Sheridane Kennels, Hebron, Ct.

Ch. Dinro Latoya at Westchester K.C. in 1981. Owned by Dr. Louis Grant Bond and Robert E. Layne, Dinro-Sounda Danes, Millbury, Mass.

in charge of the judge's teaching slide presentation by the American Kennel Club to be one of the dogs represented as an example of overall balance and movement.

Champion Sheridane Viking Prince, litter brother to Prince Valiant, was finished for his owners by Mike Sherman and, shown since by his owners as a special, has already a Specialty Best in Show win to his credit.

Champion Sheridane Iroquois Shenandoah is one of the very few blue Dane champion males alive in the United States. He is by Rissone's Super Blu v Iroquois, (grandson of four blue champions, Zoro Aus Dem Schwartzwald, Mako's Fancy Blue Lace, Jecopa's Blue Nearli Ned, and Sloanes Renata of Iroquois) ex Sheridane Iroquois Heather (granddaughter of one black, Champion Charlemagne Du Lac and three blue champions, Bantry Hazel D Sangrai Azul, Jecopa's Blu Nearli Ned, and Sloanes Renata of Iroquois).

Champion Sheridane Aarlo v Danebridge was finished owner-handled and is a multiple group placing and winning dog.

Champion Sheridane Quidny, a big, very typey dog, finished under all breeder judges including a Specialty win. He was not specialed as the Shermans were showing Val.

Now Val's daughter from his first litter, Champion Sheridane Easy Money, is a brand new champion as we write. Her litter sister has 14 points, and there are three others pointed from another litter by this dog. Val's contributions to the breed as a sire are now just starting to come into focus.

SOUNDA (DINRO-SOUNDA)

Now known as Dinro-Sounda since taking over a large portion of the Danes and the breeding program of the late Rosemarie Robert following that lady's sad death in the late 1970's, Sounda Kennels has been synonymous with quality Danes on its own over a lengthy period of time.

Owned by two very enthusiastic Great Dane fanciers, Dr. Louis Grant Bond and Robert E. Layne, the kennel is located at Millbury, Massachusetts.

Among the Danes who have brought fame to Sounda one thinks of American and Canadian Champion Sounda's Marathon Man, the stunning Harlequin dog who made history in the breed when

73

Stone Valley's Dream Hustler owned by Stone Valley Great Danes, Chuck and Darcy Quinlan, Kennesaw, Ga.

Stone Valley's Carina, born Sept. 1983 by Ch. Rojon's Oh Boy V Meccadane ex Ch. Stone Valley's Midnight Dream. Bred and owned by Chuck and Darcy Quinlan, Kennesaw, Ga., taking Winners at Queensboro K.C. in 1985.

four of his get completed their titles within the same year. This dog, interestingly, was used to illustrate gait in the American Kennel Club's first Dane slide show, depicting what one looks for in evaluating a correct Great Dane.

Champion Dinro Sounda Nijinsky (by Champion BMW Ruffian ex Sounda Curtain Call) is another handsome Harlequin champion from this kennel, who completed title during 1985.

There are famed Sounda Great Danes in brindle, fawn and black in addition to the Harlequins. Among the winners from this kennel so far in the 1980's are Champion Reann's Dark Side of Sounda, a black dog; Champion Sounda's Illiad Bracis, a very stunning brindle; Champion Sounda Flash Gordon; Champion Sounda's Duke of Earl, to name just a few.

Probably one of the most outstanding dogs at Dinro-Sounda is the magnificent Champion Dinro Legend. He is another from this kennel to have been selected for presentation in the A.K.C. slide show on Great Danes. An honor which is well deserved!

STONE VALLEY

Stone Valley Great Danes are owned by Chuck and Darcy Quinlan at Kennesaw, Georgia.

Foundation of this kennel is the homebred Stone Valley Dream Weaver, by Champion Wallach's Gordia Howe, C.D.X. ex Fanta's Echo of Stone Valley. She has been an invaluable bitch in Stone Valley's breeding program—one who has repeatedly produced fine progeny.

Champion Stone Valley's Midnight Dream is from Dream Weaver sired by Bray's Waldorf V Lesliedane. Known as Cleo, she started her show career by going Best Puppy at the 1981 Great Dane Club of America Regional Specialty, finishing her championship at two years of age. She is also the dam of two litters with puppies from the first of these nearing completion of their championships.

Stone Valley's Dream Hustler is also from Dream Weaver and sired by the Best in Show winning American and Canadian Champion Windanes Zephyr, the latter a top producer for several years. Hustler is a handsome brindle dog who has been shown sparingly on a very limited basis and presently is working towards his C.D.

Stone Valley's Carina, by Champion Rojons Oh Boy V Mecca-dane ex Champion Stone Valley's Midnight Dream has enjoyed a highly successful puppy career winning at many Specialties and Sweepstakes and taking a Best in Match, all breeds. She was Best Junior at the 1984 Great Dane Club of America Futurity in West-chester. Nearing her title, she has taken a maternity leave from the show ring for a short while, but shortly will be back in there for those additional needed points.

Champion Windanes Breeze of Stone Valley, by Best in Show winning American and Canadian Champion Windanes Zephyr ex Champion Jebas Jennifer of Windane, was bred by Phyllis Ryan and is owned by Darcy Quinlan and June Herbst. This gorgeous young bitch finished title with two 5-point majors taking Best of Breed from the classes. It is felt that she will prove a tremendous asset to the Stone Valley breeding program.

STOCKDALE

Stockdale Great Danes, at Bakersfield, California, are owned by Larry and Carleen Radanovich, who comment on their very good fortune in that the puppy they purchased more or less blindly, with none of the recommended methods of study, researching and learning which are the more accepted ways to start out, led them into good hands nonetheless. This first Dane was, Larry tells us, actually a compromise between himself and his wife; one of them wanted a family pet, the other a horse. The compromise, a dog of a huge breed, turned out to be a very happy choice which has led to great pleasure for this couple.

The puppy was located through a newspaper advertisement placed by a very reliable breeder who sold them the pet type puppy they requested. When the pedigree arrived, the new own-ers were impressed to find that it contained the names of very many champions. The sire and dam turned out to be both champi-ons Barnetts Bravo and Polldane's Merry Merrily. So enthusiastic did they become over their new pet that Larry and Carleen began to think of match shows (which by then they had learned about), and asked the breeder for help. The breeder reminded them, gently, that they had bought the puppy as a *pet* and to expect not too much from it in the ring. The next six months were spent in showing their dog here and there while at the same time going through the study process—all available books on the breed, studying the Danes they saw at the shows, learning to talk with and make friends of the other exhibitors. By the time their puppy had reached a year's age, it had been decided that this was, indeed, a delightful and lovable *pet,* not show quality, and that they wanted to really show dogs and, hopefully, to contribute to the breed.

Then it was that a brindle bitch was purchased, sired by American and Mexican Champion Treseders Brother Jeptha out of a Dinro-Lovett bred dam. This was Gypsy, who in due time was bred to Champion Von Raseac's Caesar's Quote, a fawn dog, which produced an all-brindle litter, thus starting these breeders on the road to success.

With the birth of the litter, a kennel name was chosen—Stockdale, originating from the area of Bakersfield where the family lived. Included in the litter were Champion Stockdale Rudolph v Raseac, American and Canadian Champion Stockdale King's Ransom, and Champion Stockdale's Twilight Twinkle. All, at one time or another, were Specialty winners.

Prior to the arrival of this litter, another bitch was purchased for Stockdale, this one a fawn, Polldane's Sparkle Plenty, sired by Champion Jeffry McDavis. This was "Gladys," who became Carleen's constant companion and favorite Dane.

With two good bitches to start them off, the Radanoviches felt they had a nice foundation for their future breeding program. This takes time, however, and so Larry and Carleen, to keep them busy meanwhile, purchased a German Wirehaired Pointer, whom they finished, then used for hunting. This dog, called David, was Champion The King of Wireland, who also became the king of the house and the sire of champions, including a son who is also now siring champions. As Larry puts it, "This kept our thinking straight as we were struggling with our Danes in a handler-oriented breed."

Since even one extra Dane is not really needed in a new breeding program, the Radanoviches were delighted to learn, from Lillian McEdwards (owner of the renowned Dane Edens) and Jackie White (owner of the Tallbrooks) that a friend of the McEdwards, Stan Meyers, had recently lost his Great Dane and was looking for an older well-trained dog. The ideal home for the first Dane the

Radanoviches had purchased as a pet! Mr. Meyers thought so, too, and "Mac," as the Dane was known, soon was encsonced in a beautiful home (actually we understand that it was Betty Grable's former estate) at Encino where he lived happily for years. Interestingly, years after Mac had gone there to Mr. Meyers, a fire broke out in the main house, and Mac was the hero of the occasion, awakening the family to the danger, thus permitting everyone to safely escape. The house burned to the ground, however, and Mac just never got over its loss, spending hours lying in front of the debris, obviously mourning. A few months later this lovely dog died of what the veterinarian termed "a broken heart," just in case one does not appreciate the loyalty of this breed!

In due course, Larry and Carleen bred their Sparkle Plenty bitch to Champion Rudolph, thus starting the consolidation of their own line. Champion Stockdales Rory O'More, brindle, was in this litter and stayed with his breeders; also Champion Stockdales Union Jack, who went to Carla Curts in Oklahoma, finishing and becoming a Group winner from the classes.

It is unfortunate that Rudolph, a dog with much to recommend him, broke his tail and never would give it a chance to mend properly despite all the best efforts of everyone concerned with him. His own show career was, therefore, a brief one prior to the tail finally having to be amputated. He is leaving his mark as a sire, however, in both the United States and Brazil.

Under co-ownership with Maggie White in Texas, the Radanoviches bred Champion Stockdales Twilight Twinkle to Champion Ajax v Ashgrove, which produced several champions.

Other noted winners carrying the Stockdale kennel prefix include Champion Stockdales Maria De Gruccia, who finished at age 13 months and is expected to make a valuable addition to the breeding program; Champion Viking Danes Valient V Stockdale (who now has pointed progeny), owned by Tom and Connie Stimmell; Champion Viking Vaquiro V Stockdale; Champion Stockdales Corporate Dividend, co-owned with Chuck and Pam Richtor, who finished with five majors and is now being specialed with marked succes; and the bitch who is currently #1 Great Dane bitch in the nation after ten months of showing as a special, Champion Stockdales Savannah, owned by the Radanoviches and handled for them by Eric Ringle. During the past nine months (as of November 1985) she has won the Great Dane Club of America Regional Specialty, 29 Bests of Breed, 24 Bests of Opposite Sex, six Group 1sts, and ten additional Group placements. After a few additional months in the show ring, Susannah, although now only age two and a half years, will be retired and it is hoped reproduce her quality.

TALLBROOK FARMS

Tallbrook Farms, at Los Angeles, California, started its climb to fame in the Great Dane world during the 1960's with some show and producing members of the breed. Among them were the marvelous bitch Champion Brenda von Overcup, a Producer of Merit, who is the dam of five or more champions. Also during this same period, Tallbrook was represented by American and Mexican Champion Amber of Tallbrook Farms, and Champion Sun-E-Bane's Heavenly Halo.

Herb and Kathleen Twaits and Frank and Jacqueline White are the owners of this kennel and these dogs. Their enthusiasm for their breed seems to escalate with each passing year and the 1970's found a lot of important Tallbrook Great Danes in the picture, headed by three who are on the Producer of Merit Honor Roll, these being Champion Tallbrook's Dapper Dan, Champion Tallbrook's Bit O'Honey, and Champion Grenadilla's Bit O'Tallbrook.

Additionally, for the decade of the 1970's, one finds Champion Tallbrook Farms Taly Overcup, Champion Abigail Davis of Tallbrook, Champion Tallbrook's Happy Holiday, Champion Tallbrook's Salute, Champion Walker's Luv of Tallbrook, Champion Tallbrook's Akami of Alii, Champion Tallbrook's Ginger of Alii, Champion Tallbrook's Bit O'Darby Davy, Champion Tallbrook's Happy As A Lark, Champion Tallbrook's Vicki of Paradise, Champion Bit O'Tallbrook's Brenda, and Champion Bit O'Tallbrook's Honey Chile. It seems appropriate to mention here that in order to become recognized on the Producer of Merit Honor Roll in Great Danes, a bitch must be the dam of five or more champions; a dog, the sire of ten or more.

Champion Tallbrook's Wild Chile is co-owned with Cathy Schaefer and handled by Dick Schaefer, and has carried over into the 1980's, keeping the Tallbrook banner high. Others doing so in

Ch. Walker's Luv of Tallbrook, by Ch. Abner Lowell Davis ex Laric of Tallbrook Farms, dam of four champions, was bred by Tallbrook Kennels and owned by Louise Van Alystyne. An important winner of the 1970's.

Am. and Mex. Ch. Amber of Tallbrook Farms, a champion of the 1960's owned by Tallbrook Great Danes, sired by Ch. Sham's Sacerdotes ex Ch. Thendara Henriette Kerpen.

this decade are Champion Tallbrook's My Honey, Champion Tallbrook's Natalie Borelli, and Champion Tallbrook's Folly v Romano, the latter co-owned with Penny Eversole.

As for the future, there are as usual some exceptionally outstanding youngsters at Tallbrook Farms who undoubtedly will be making their presence in the show ring felt by the time you are reading this book.

THOR DANE

Thor Dane Kennels, owned by Ed and Linda Springthorpe, Ball Ground, Georgia, are noted for excellence in this breed.

As a professional handler as well as a breeder, Linda Springthorpe has piloted numerous Danes to outstanding show records, among them Champion Waterwood's Brew Meister, who completed title at 19 months old with a Group 3rd from the classes. Brew earned multiple Group placements and multiple Bests in Specialty Shows during his career. He was #5 Great Dane in the United States during 1984. His sire, Champion Tilpadane Barnaby Neustadt, was the #1 Great Dane in 1979, *Great Dane Reporter* system. This splendid dog was bred by Herb and Margaret Shappard and owned by Sally and Paul Harris of Covington, Georgia.

Another dog piloted by Linda was Champion Fahmie's Golden Vulcan v Fury owned by Mr. and Mrs. John Fahmie of Miami, Florida. He finished his championship in April of '76 with a 4-point major under Hugo Gamboa.

The next time out as a Special he took Best of Breed and a Group One under Louis Murr. He was only specialed for a limited time but had many Best of Breeds, two Group one's and three Best in Specialty wins at the Great Dane Club of South Florida to retire the challenge Trophy by winning Best of in three consecutive years 1976-1977-1978.

Vulcan was the sire of two exciting progeny, a dog and a bitch, both of whom bear the Springthorpes' Thor Dane kennel prefix, who were making their championships during the same period that their sire was out as a special. These are Champion Thordane's Page v Brass Rail and Champion Thor Dane's Pat Hand. Pat Hand had a Specialty major among this points towards the title, Page the same, in addition to a Best in Sweepstakes to her credit.

Champion Thor Dane's Churchill Downs is a very excellent dog who has done well for the Springthorpes. He is owned by Pam Hebreickson, bred by Ed and Linda Springthorpe, and handled by Linda. His show record includes a number of fine victories.

Champion Thor Dane's Butterfly, owned by Sally Chandler, is another successful winner bred by the Springthorpes and handled by Linda.

A very lovely bitch of the early 1980's, Champion Thor Dane's Class Action, is another Springthorpe homebred who has attracted much approval for quality and elegance from the judges. She, too, is handled by Linda and holds her own well in keenest competition.

A famous and highly admired bitch belonging to the Springthorpes is Champion Guevric's Dawns Early Light whose prestigious ring successes include Winners Bitch at the Great Dane Club of America South East Regional Specialty in May 1981. Additionally, she has already contributed well as a producer, her progeny including Champion Thor Dane's Churchill Downs, Champion Thor Dane's Class Action, Thor Dane's Alias Vegas (needing just three points to finish as we write), and Thor Dane's Alias Crystal who also has championship points.

TYDWIND

The De Gruccios, Dennis and Joy of Orange, California, are owners of two exceedingly famous and outstanding Great Danes. The first of these is Champion Von Raseac's Tybo O'Lorcain, who was born on June 3, 1974, bred by Brucie Mitchell and Harriet Larkin. This black masked fawn stands 35" tall at the withers. His sire, Champion Sunridges Chief Justice, was a son of Champion Mountdania's Timber ex Champion Troy's Wendy of Hearth Hill. His dam, American, Mexican, and Canadian Champion Von Raseac's Quintessence, a granddaughter of Champion Dana's Zeus of Quindane, Champion Caesar's Lorelei v Overcup, and Champion Overcup's Jason Sacerdotes.

Tybo sired 21 champions from a total of 16 litters. He was a multiple breed and Group winner who in 1977 earned *Working Dog Magazine's* #3 Top Producing Sire and #7 Great Dane in Group and Best in Show points. Then in 1980 he was the *Kennel Review* #1 Great Dane Sire and #7 Sire among the Working breeds.

Thor Dane's Debutant at age four and a half months. Bred and owned by Ed and Linda Springthorpe, Thor Dane Kennels, Ball Ground, Ga.

Sheenwater Herman v Thor Dane at eight weeks is already receiving lessons on being "stacked" for the show ring. Bred by Sally Chandler, he is owned by Ed and Linda Springthorpe, Thor Dane Kennels, Ball Ground, Georgia.

Ch. Von Raseac's West Wind, bred by Brucie Mitchell and Clare Lincoln, owned by John and Donna Bolte, Pikesville, Md. A National Specialty winner and sire of 11 champions, West Wind was by Ch. Von Raseac's Tybo O'Lorcain ex Am. and Can. Ch. Von Raseac's Quite A Gal.

Am. and Can. Ch. Lincoln's Our Rina Von Raseac, by Jecamo's King Ranson V Lincoln ex Ch. Laurado's Czarina. Bred by Raymond and Clare Lincoln; owned by Brucie Mitchell and Clare Lincoln. A multi-breed, Specialty, and Group winner.

The present big winner for the De Gruccios is American and Mexican Champion Tydwind's Sail Maker, brindle dog born on May 13, 1982, bred by Dennis and Joy De Gruccio and E. Mitchell, owned by the De Gruccios. Sail Maker is a grandson of Tybo (and a very worthy one!), being by Champion Temple Dell's Odin V Branstock (Champion Edeldane's Wildfire-Champion Sarah Davis of Temple Dell) from Champion Von Raseac's Whirlwind v Tybo (Tybo-Champion Von Raseac's Quite A Gal).

Sail Maker finished his championship at 12 months of age and is already a multiple breed and Group winner, finishing in the Top Ten for 1984. His progeny are now starting out in the show ring, with two having become champions so far in 1985.

VON RASEAC

Von Raseac Great Danes are named in honor of the first of their many famous show winners of this breed owned by Gene and Brucie Mitchell at San Luis Rey, California. This was American, Canadian, and Mexican Champion Jecamo's Caesar of A.A.A. ("Raseac" is "Caesar" spelled backwards).

The Mitchells purchased their first Great Dane as a companion to the family in 1961, then a few years later bought a fawn male with the intention of showing a dog. This was Caesar, and, unknowingly at the time, the Mitchells were entering into a new life style, being introduced to an all-consuming hobby!

Caesar went on to become a show dog of note. A Group winner and a Canadian Best in Show winner, but his true prowess was as a great sire, and the legacy he left the Fancy were the many splendid sons and daughters he left behind to carry on.

It was not until after retiring Caesar from the show ring that the Mitchells decided to try their hand at some serious breeding—and Von Raseac was born. Since that time they have bred 25 champions, owned five others, and their personally owned stud dogs account for 25 champions.

The Mitchells have always bred their Danes from a home situation, with no kennel dogs. They have never had more than four Great Danes at one time, although they have co-owned some lovely animals with their friends who had helped keep their breeding program afloat. Von Raseac started with bloodlines provided by Caesar, who was basically a dog of Eastern lines. Through his

85

dam he carried bloodlines from the famous Gilbert and Mount-dania Kennels and from his sire picked up Duyster/Brae Tarn and Heidere/Dinro bloodlines. The Mitchells' first attempts at breeding met with only moderate success, but they finally reached the genetic-pool to breed from when they bred a double grandson of Caesar's, Great Caesar's Ghost V Raseac, owned by Dick and Cathy Schaefer, to a bitch they had bought who was linebred to the Denios' great Champion Deacon's Golden Fury V Geordan. In that litter they also doubled on the pedigree of Champion Thend-ara Henriette Keppen, who is tied for Top Producing Dam with 17 champions.

Three of the four champions whelped in that litter went on to make a real contribution, both in the show ring and in the prog-eny they produced. Those three are Champion Von Raseac's Great Caesar's Quote, Champion Von Raseac's Quite A Gal, and Cham-pion Von Raseac's Quintessence, whom the Mitchells co-owned with Kenyon and Harriet Larkin. Quote was the sire of nine champions; Quite A Gal the dam of seven champions. And Quin-tessence the dam of four champions, one of which became the famed sire Champion Von Raseac's Tybo O'Lorcain, owned by Dennis and Joy De Gruccio, who has sired 21 champions as of Oc-tober 1985.

From the breeding of Tybo and Quite A Gal came Champion Von Raseac's West Wind, who became a fine showman and a sire as prepotent as his own sire before him. Also from that litter came Champion Von Raseac's Windsong, a lovely bitch whose cham-pion progeny is being used to continue the line. West Wind was owned by the John Boltes of Maryland, while the Mitchells co-own Windsong with Linda Epperson Welsh in Missouri.

With pride we note that West Wind is the sire of Champion C. and K.'s Special-K Gribbin who recently became the Top Win-ning Great Dane of all time; and that his littermate, Lincoln's Winstead Von Raseac, who resides now in England, has among his numerous champion offspring Champion Daneton's Amelia whom the Mitchells understand now to be the Top Winning Bitch in the United Kingdom.

In recent years, the Mitchells have bred very sparingly but plan to continue their limited breeding program. In the past they have had some very successful litters, and some not so successful,

A lovely informal photo of Gene and Brucie Mitchell with "Ch. Corky" on the back lawn. "Corky" is by Ch. Von Raseac's Valor of Tybo ex Ch. Von Raseac's Windsong. His formal name is Ch. Von Raseac's County Cork.

Ch. Woodcliffe's Bold Bracken winning a Group 3rd at Providence County in 1985, agent Fred Olson handling for owner, Richard E. Nelson, Woodcliff Lake, N.J.

87

which is sort of par for the course. All have been planned with a great deal of thought and preparation.

The Mitchells are very widely admired in the Dane Fancy both for their good sportsmanship and for the quality of their dogs. These are extremely knowledgeable people who truly deeply love Great Danes. Brucie says, very modestly at the close of her note to me, "We sincerely hope we have made a contribution to this wonderful breed of dog, and that we will have fulfilled our aim, that of keeping the Great Dane the regal and gentle companion he should always be." All one needs to do is to see some of these magnificent Danes, or study their pictures, to realize that the Mitchells have, indeed, made a very great contribution to their breed.

WOODCLIFF

Woodcliff Great Danes, owned by Elizabeth and Richard Nelson (Peg and Dick to their friends) at Woodcliff Lake, New Jersey, came into being because of a yellow Labrador named Maggie. Peg Nelson, as her husband was training and running a black male Lab in field trials, decided that she would like to get herself a pretty yellow Lab. That was Maggie, who turned out to be an even better field trial dog than the black male. By 1973, Peg decided that her husband should take over Maggie, and that she would go out and find for herself a breed not used in field trials.

This is what led to the purchase of Champion Kolyer's Dame Daphne, C.D., from Kittie Kolyer in 1973. She was the foundation bitch for Woodcliff Great Danes, giving her then-novice owners a great thrill when she finished her championship and her C.D.

Including Daphne, the Nelsons have shown six Great Danes as of October 1985, all of whom have completed their titles. These are, of course, Daphne herself, who is by Kolyer's Mr. Beau of Glenwood ex Kolyer's Sweet Cinnamon; Daphne's daughter, Champion Woodcliff Gentle Greaves, who is by Champion Kolyer's Big Ben Be Mine; Gentle's daughter, Champion Woodcliff's Sister Carrie, who is by Champion Castile's Gent of Mountdania; Carrie's daughter, Champion Woodcliff's Sweet Rebecca and her son Champion Woodcliff's Bold Bracken, these by Champion Reann's French Aristocrat; and Champion Brandelyn Derek of

Woodcliff, by Champion Ashbun Acres Avant Garde ex Champion Brandelyn's Encore.

Daphne's sire, Kolyer's Mr. Beau of Glenwood, was a son of the great Kimbayh, one of the top Great Danes of all time. So the Nelsons bred her therefore to Big Ben as he was a litter brother to Champion Heidere's Kolyer Kimbayh. Peg Nelson describes Daphne as a cobby fawn bitch with a magnificent front and head. Big Ben was also a fawn. Their daughter, Gentle, was "a sweet faced fawn lady."

Gentle was outcrossed to Gent of Mountdania "to get size." The result was Sister Carrie, "a tall and elegant" brindle who finished her championship in great style by going Winners Bitch over 140 others at the Westchester National Specialty in 1981.

Sister Carrie was bred to "the top stud dog in the East, Canadian and American Champion Reann's French Aristocrat," producing a litter of 13! The Nelsons kept the showy brindle bitch Sweet Rebecca, who completed championship at only 13 months. They also kept the handsome fawn male, Bracken, who matured more slowly than Rebecca, but finished his championship at two years, then went on to Bests of Breed and Group placements.

GREAT DANES IN HAWAII

PAT VALDEZ ADAMECK

Pat Valdez Adameck of Kailua, Hawaii, has owned Great Danes since 1942, but did not start exhibiting until 1969 in Hawaii. She took her dogs to California in 1977 through 1981, then returned to the islands where she is still very active in the dog fancy.

Over the years Mrs. Adameck has had many lovely Danes, but without a doubt the one in which she has taken very particular pride is the Best in Show winning Champion Temple Dell's Fleetwood v Alii whom she co-owns with Paula Schmidt.

Fleetwood, during an exciting show career, has accounted for two all-breed Bests in Show, multiple Group wins, and has been a consistent Specialty winner to the point where he became one of only two Great Danes to qualify for the *Kennel Review* 1984 Tournament of Champions, doing so as well again the next year which he had to miss due to the four-month Hawaiian quarantine for dogs. He was Hawaii's #1 Great Dane since 1981; Hawaii's #1 Dog, All-Breeds, 1983; and #2 All-Breeds in 1984.

Born in July 1979, Fleetwood was sired by Champion Edeldane's Wildfire ex Champion Sarah Davis of Temple Dell. His breeders were Stephen and Elizabeth Temple.

Mrs. Adameck was a tremendous admirer of the lovely bitch Champion Honeygold Von Overcup, an important winner from the 1960's. Honeycup belonged to Edna and James Hatch and was, in Mrs. Adameck's opinion, one of the all time "great" Great Danes. Honeycup was bred twice; the first time to the Mitchells' Champion Jecamo's Caesar of A.A.A.; the second time to Champion Abner Lowell Davis.

The two puppies from the Abner litter were owned by Pat Adameck, but the bitch died in quarantine and the dog broke his shoulder, also in quarantine, so neither ever made it to the show ring. The male, however, did produce some nice puppies.

Among the Caesar-Honey Cup litter there was a truly handsome American and Canadian Champion, Honey Cup's Juno of St. James. She belonged to Dick Fitzsimmons but was leased to Mrs. Adameck who bred her to Champion Tallbrook's Dapper Dan by whom she produced just one puppy, Alii's Fascination, who belongs to Mrs. Adameck.

Two other Danes whom Mrs. Adameck considers among her finest are Champion Tallbrook's Akamai of Alii and sister Champion Tallbrook's Ginger of Alii. These were born in 1972, bred by Kathleen Twaits and Jackie White. Both finished with ease in California competition, on several occasions winning Best of Breed and Best of Opposite Sex from the classes.

The opportunities for Great Dane competition are quite limited in Hawaii, with only four all-breed events and two Great Dane Specialties annually, which, coupled with the four-month quarantine period if one leaves the state with dogs to be shown on the mainland, certainly limits the opportunity for campaigning.

Opposite page: Ch. Tallbrooks Ginger of Alii, litter sister to Ch. Tallbrook's Akami of Alii, both owned by Pat Adameck, Kailua, Hawaii. Like her brother, finished title promptly in California competition. They were born in 1972.

An early highly successful Great Dane breeder in Canada, Mrs. Betty Hyslop of Brockville, Ontario, with two of her brightest "stars" from the Dane branch of her Cairndania Kennels, these from the 1940's.

The great bitch, Am. and Can. Ch. Gilbert's Nancy of Brae Tarn was Best in Show at the Canadian Winter Fair in 1946; and Best in the Working Group at Westchester Kennel Club, Rye, N.Y., after winning the Great Dane Club of America National Specialty that same day. A Westminster Best of Breed winner of the mid-1940's, owned by Mrs. Betty Hyslop, Cairndania Kennels.

Chapter 5

Great Danes in Canada

Cairndania Kennels, owned by Mrs. Betty Hyslop, is one of the most famous in the world; and is the first in Canada that owned Great Danes with which the author was personally acquainted. Exceptionally handsome, sound and typical ones, as Betty Hyslop is a perfectionist and nothing but the best could ever have satisfied her in Great Danes anymore than in her Cairns.

The first Dane champion here was American and Canadian Champion Pax von Birkenhof who came to Mrs. Hyslop in the early 1930's. She was a daughter of the widely admired Champion Etfa v d Saalburg, of whom you have read earlier in this book, so great a favorite with Colonel Ferguson and owned by Mrs. Donald Hostetter who had imported her from Germany. Pax was a lovely brindle bitch who became an American Champion in 1933 (Mrs. Hyslop has always been a consistent and successful exhibitor in both the States and Canada); then for three years she was campaigned in Canada, remaining practically undefeated in her breed. During this time she annexed five all breed Bests in Show. She led the Montreal Show in both 1934 and 1935, was Best in Show at Aurora in 1934, and carried off the highest honors at Ottawa and at Toronto in 1935.

The next Great Dane champion for Betty Hyslop was the brindle bitch American and Canadian Champion Quagga von Lohe-land, finishing in 1935. She started her show career principally in the United States, faring very well indeed. Then came Canada for her, where she went Best in Show at Brantford on her first ring appearance there.

The next Dane to become a champion for Betty was American and Canadian Champion Max of Cairndania, by Champion Cyrus v.d. Pissa ex Champion Irongood Queen Sheba, a homebred. This beautiful fawn dog gained his American Championship in 1935. In the States he had six Best of Breed awards, one Group 1st, and three seconds in Group.

In 1937 Champion Senta Hexengold, a stunning two-year-old fawn bitch, hit the show ring, taking Winners Bitch at the Morris and Essex Kennel Club Dog Show in keenest competition. Senta was a German importation and had been the German Siegerin for 1936. Her purchase by Mrs. Hyslop was a marvelous addition to her young kennel.

Canadian and American Champion Aslan von Loheland was another worthy addition to the kennel during the 1930's—another Best in Show winner.

Canadian Champion Inge Hassia, a notable daughter of Zorn v Birkenhof, was imported in the late 1930's, as was Venus Hexengold.

Betty Hyslop dearly loved her Great Danes, and enjoyed them over the years. Eventually, however, she decided to concentrate all her efforts on the Cairns, and so since then her major activity in Great Danes has been as a judge of them upon occasion.

HANNADALE

Hannadale Great Danes are owned by Bill and Aila Treloar of Mississauga, Ontario, whose kennel is headed by the great Canadian Best in Show Champion Davos Deacon, C.D., TT, who was whelped on August 28, 1980, bred by Drs. Andy and Sheilah Fletch.

Deacon is a son of American and Canadian Champion Daneadair's T.J. of Harmony Hill (Champion Harmony Hill Witch Doctor-Daneadair's Rebecca Galloway) from Canadian Champion Davos Rinky Twink (American Champion Rojan's The Hustler-Canadian Champion Davos Zarina's Star Noelle).

Best in Show Ch. Davos Deacon, C.D., TT, was Canada's # 1 Great Dane in 1983. Photographed in October 1983 at age three and a half years. Bred by Drs. Andy and Sheilah Fletch. Owned by Bill and Aila Treloar, Hannadale Great Danes, Mississaugua, Ontario.

Can. Ch. Hannadale's Deacon's Fury at six weeks old sired by Ch. Davos Deacon, C.D., T.T. out of Ch. Davos Isis Hannadale. Owned by Bill and Aila Treloar, Hannadale Great Danes, Mississaugua, Ontario.

Am. and Can. Ch. Devrok's Zartanian v Sheboane, by Ch. Ashbun Acres Avant Garde ex Devrok's Quite A Doll, owned by Bonne and Gayle Klompstra, Sombra, Ontario. Sire of Great Dane Club of America winner and of several additional American and Canadian Champions.

At age eight years, Am. and Can. Ch. Devrock's Zartanian v Sheboane was the first champion at Sheboane Kennels and also Best in Show winner. Owned by Bonne and Gayle Klompstra. Sire of Great Dane Club of America winner and of several additional American and Canadian Champions.

Deacon's wins include an all-breed Best in Show; numerous Group placements; 40 times Best of Breed; Specialty Best Canadian Bred and Best of Opposite Sex; and undefeated in the classes.

The first Great Dane in Canada to be successfully temperament tested by the American Temperament Test Society (1982), Deacon is, as well, the sire of champions whose wins include several Bests of Breed and Specialty Bests in Sweepstakes.

There are at present a number of highly promising puppies sired by Deacon "standing in the wings" as they await the start of their show careers.

SHEBOANE

Sheboane Great Danes are owned by Bonne and Gayle Klompstra, situated at Sombra, Ontario, Canada, the home of some of Canada's most distinguished Great Danes.

The Klompstras are enthusiasts of the Harlequins, which immediately is taking on a challenge as this is far and away the most difficult color to breed in its most correct form. The challenge did not prove to be insurmountable to these dedicated fanciers, however, and they point with pride to some very successful and noted dogs who represent their breeding program.

Head man among these Danes is Canadian and American Champion Queststar Valdez of Sheboane, who came to the Klompstras as a stud fee puppy for a breeding to their homebred Canadian and American Champion Harlequin dog, Sheboane's Johnnie B. Goode. Gayle Klompstra describes Valdez as truly a "once in a lifetime puppy," one of two Harlequin males in the litter, possessing perfect markings and correct structure. Of course Valdez' sire was a dog to be reckoned with too, for he, Johnnie B. Goode, was the first Canadian-bred Harlequin Dane in 25 years to complete the American championship title. So Valdez obviously had things going for him!

Valdez came to Westchester, to the Great Dane Club of America National Specialty and Futurity, for his first visit to the States. There he took Best in Futurity and Reserve Winners Dog from the Junior Puppy Class. His second U.S. appearance was at the Great Dane Club of Michigan Specialty where again he was Reserve Winners. The following day, at his third show here, he took his first U.S.A. major, thus was on his way.

Entered at three Canadian shows, Valdez was awarded three 5-point majors going on to Best of Breed one day (under Ed Dixon) and Best of Opposite Sex the other two (judges Joyce MacKenzie and Edna Joel), followed by Best Puppy in Group. All three of these judges, who admired Valdez as a puppy, have gone on to later award him Bests in Show.

As a beginning Valdez came out as a special in the autumn of 1983, at Michigan Great Dane Specialty. He came home the winner; then two weeks later, on his first appearance as a special at an all-breed event, he went Best in Show at London, Ontario and also won the Great Dane Specialty on that same day—all this while still less than two years old.

Valdez was seriously specialed during 1984, competing in 59 all-breed shows and two Specialties. His wins included 57 times Best of Breed, one Best of Opposite Sex, and one Specialty Best of Breed, plus 37 Group placements and ten all-breed Bests in Show including one at the prestigious Barrie event and at Credit Valley.

Despite his comparative youth, Valdez has already distinguished himself as a sire. Among his offspring are American and Canadian Champion Amherst Mylan who was Best of Winners at the 1984 Great Dane Club of Canada Specialty; Canadian and American Champion Amherst Gingerbread Girl, who was Winners Bitch at Great Dane Club of Canada and Winners Bitch and Best of Opposite Sex at Great Dane Fanciers of Ontario the same year, and Canadian Champion Lynnmars Teddybear, who was Best Puppy in Show at Seaway in 1985.

The first champion, and a Best in Show winner, owned by the Klompstras, was American and Canadian Champion Devrok's Zartanian v Sheboane, who was by American Champion Ashbun Acres Avant Garde ex Devrok's Quite A Doll.

The sire of Valdez, Champion Sheboane's Johnnie B. Goode, finished very quickly in both Canada and the United States. A Specialty Show winner, he is also the first Canadian-bred Harlequin to complete an American championship. He is a son of Bonne's Adonis Von Sheboane ex Devrok's Windsong Von Sheboane.

Early in 1985 Bonne Klompstra went to England to see the Crufts Dog Show, and also to look at some Danes in Europe. As

Am. and Can. Ch. Davos Baroness Zareba, by Am., Can., and Bda. Champion Harmony Hill Sherwood's Joker ex Am. and Can. Ch. Davos Zarina of Dukay, bred by Drs. Fletch and owned by June Cowie. This was the Top Dog, All Breeds in Canada in 1972.

a result, Barbel von Harlekin was acquired for the Sheboane Kennels, a new bloodline for the breeding program and a dog with many assets.

Also, future "stars" being watched with anticipation are Vi-Dayne's Desire v Sheboane and Vi-Dayne's Pride of Sheboane, the latter co-owned with Mrs. Sandi Brown-Todd.

Vi-Dayne's Pride of Sheboane was BOW at the 1985 Westchester show over 122 dogs and 160 bitches, from the Puppy Class.

The Klompstras take pride in Valdez having been one of Canada's Top Ten Dogs during 1984. Sheboane is very much a family project with the children, Mark, Jackie and Matthew, all joining their parents in the pleasure of these magnificent dogs.

Ch. Daymondane
Forever, by Hildydane
El Cid ex Urdos
Jodella, here winning
Best Opposite at the
Sydney Royal, which is
Australia's leading dog
show. Owned and bred
by Ted and Viv Helliar,
Pennant Hills, N.S.W.,
Australia.

Aust. Ch. Impton
Kestrel, one of U.K.
import littermates
brought to Australia for
the breeding program
of Mr. and Mrs.
Arrowsmith at Cooroy,
Queensland.

Chapter 6

Great Danes in Australia

In the United States, we are becoming steadily and increasingly aware of the successful activities of our dog show friends "Down Under"; of the enthusiasm existing among Australian dog breeders; and of their sincere desire not only to *own* dogs of highest quality but also to breed them. So well are they succeeding that in numerous breeds, dogs from there are being exported from New Zealand and Australian breeders to the United States, Canada, the United Kingdom, Europe, and Japan.

As for importing top bloodlines into their own country, the Australians have never hesitated to do so when it seemed the logical move. Even the stringent quarantine regulations have not proved discouraging to them; thus finest dogs of outstanding bloodlines have gone there from Europe, from the United Kingdom, and from the Americas.

Many American authorities have judged there during the past dozen years, and they return home with glowing accounts of the really good Australian dogs as well as the enthusiasm and energy displayed by their owners. This country is becoming a strong force in the world of purebred dogs. Their shows are not only huge in numbers (the Royals run around 5,000 entries, we understand) but are also filled with superb quality. Competition is no cinch here. In order to win in Australia, one must present dogs of *excellence,* and from all reports this is exactly what is taking place. I am sure that you Dane enthusiasts who may not have seen the dogs personally will agree with this opinion as you study the photos of some of the important Danes on these pages representing what is taking place for the breed there.

AMASA

Amasa Great Dane Kennels, located at Schofields, N.S.W., are co-owned by Sue and Alan Whyte with Denise and Fred Bennett. This kennel is regarded with tremendous esteem, with a show record between the mid-1970's and mid-1980's which includes having won eight out of ten Royals attended, with the same ratio at Specialty Shows. Additionally these splendid dogs have won more than 50 in Show awards in all breed competition, during only the past five years.

Among the dogs who have so well represented this kennel in keenest competition are Australian Champion Amasa Extraordinaire, who, standing 36 inches tall alongside his handler's seven foot height makes a very impressive picture in the ring. He has been one of the kennel's leading winners, and was Great Dane of the Year for 1979-1980.

First place among the bitches at Amasa is Champion Amasa The Enchantress, Top Winning Great Dane Bitch in Australia, who at only three years of age has amassed more than twenty All-Breed "in Shows." She is Great Dane of the Year 1983-1984 and 1984-1985, honors earned by enormous margins.

Then there is Australian Champion Sherain Scharach, an importation from U.K., who is a popular sire with outstanding puppies in all parts of Australia.

The youngsters, Amasa Cygnus and Amasa Chardonnay, go back to United States bloodlines on their sire's side, being descended from the Jacamos line. Both youngsters are showing splendid promise.

MR. AND MRS. ARROWSMITH

Mr. S. and Mrs. L. Arrowsmith of Cooroy in Queensland, Australia, are breeders of some very beautiful and successful winning dogs. They have used mainly imported bloodlines on which to base their breeding program, and they are well pleased with the results.

This magnificent dog is Aust. Ch. Airways Adrian, Best in Show at Australia's National Great Dane Specialty Show in 1984. One of Australia's All Time Top Winning Great Danes. Owned by Mr. S. and Mrs. L. Arrowsmith, Cooroy, Queensland.

Aust. Ch. Amasa Extraordinaire, by Astatines Kabaka ex Ch. Raatu Astrid. One of the leading winners from Amasa Great Dane Kennels, Sue and Alan Wyler and Denise and Fred Bennett, owners, Schofields, N.S.W.

103

Aust. Ch. Impton Eagle (1977-1981) in his limited show career won many breed and Group awards. Owned by Mr. S. and Mrs. L. Arrowsmith, Cooroy, Queensland.

Aust. Ch. Oby Des Terres De La Rairie (French import), is a multiple Best in Show winner and was Best of Breed at the Sydney Royal in 1984 and sire of the winner at the Melbourne Royal the same year. Bred by Mme. Pincenin Merat, France; owned by Mr. L.R. and Mrs. V.E. Hogan, Banachek Kennels, Kurmond, N.S.W.

The Arrowsmiths' first import was Impton Eagle, who arrived in Australia in 1977 from Margaret Everton's Impton Kennels in England. He was by Freda Lewis's imported dog Danelagh's Eurus of Walkmyll ex Impton Tibble. Eagle was highly successful in the Australian show ring, quickly gaining his title there.

In an effort to build up on these bloodlines, the Arrowsmiths then imported Impton Kestrel and Impton Peregrine, two litter sisters from Margaret Everton's Swedish import, Airways Optimist of Impton and Impton Harmony. These two also excelled in the Australian show ring, achieving the Australian Champion status with numerous Specialty and all-breed wins.

More recently the Arrowsmiths have acquired, from Ulla and Curt Magnussen of Sweden, Airways Adrian and Celebers Kilroy, both dogs being from their highly successful American import, Gerjos Shiloh of Airways. Both Adrian and Kilroy were shown in England during the compulsory 12 months stay there, Margaret Everton having taken them to some of the British shows. Kilroy delighted his new owners by winning the South Wales Great Dane Show. Then following an additional three months' quarantine in Australia before they could be released to the Arrowsmiths, they were received in their new home on Christmas Day in 1982. These Danes have both had exciting careers in the show ring, with Airways Adrian winning Australia's first National Specialty Show under esteemed U.S. specialist judge Nancy Carroll Draper.

The puppies whom the Arrowsmiths so far have bred are having very satisfactory success in the show ring, in all states of Australia and in New Zealand. Some have had Best in Show in all-breed competition; many are "in Group" winners. They all represent splendid European and American stock judiciously used by the Arrowsmiths.

BANACHEK

Banachek Great Danes are owned by Mr. L.R. and Mrs. V.E. Hogan at Kurmond, in New South Wales.

This is the home of the magnificent French import, the black Australian Champion Oby Des Terres De La Rairie, the only Great Dane in Australia to have come from France. Just to look at this handsome dog's photo is to admire his excellence! He was born on November 30, 1978, a son of French Champion Luigi Du

Mont Simon ex International Champion Taila Von Haus Fresena (German importation), and he was bred by Mme. Pincenin Merat. A multiple Best in Show winner, Oby was Best of Breed at the Sydney Royal in 1984 and sire of the Best of Breed at the Melbourne Royal that same year, two of Australia's most important and prestigious events!

A very outstanding young son of Oby, Banachek Morgan, also black, was born on July 16, 1984, and is just starting out on what should prove to be an exciting show career. His dam is Banachek China Blue, and he is a homebred belonging to Mr. and Mrs. Hogan.

Banachek Petra is another promising youngster at this kennel, sired by Australian Champion Wilksdane Bandit ex Australian Champion Amasa Atouch O'Class.

CHELSHAR

Chelshar Great Danes are owned by Mrs. Sharyn Wright, at Schofields in the New South Wales section of Australia.

The foundation bitch of Mrs. Wright's Chelshar kennel prefix was Cazdane Chelsea, her first Great Dane who was her very best friend and so spoiled that Mrs. Wright did not show her very often. However, she was awarded Reserve Challenge on most of her outings.

Chelsea's first litter produced Australian Champion Chelshar Ursula, who gained her title at two years of age in five shows over four weekends. She went on to win Reserve Challenge at the Sydney Royal in an entry of 59 bitches at 18 months, and also the Sydney Spring Fair (46 bitches) at age four and a half years. She also became a multi class, in Group, and in Show winner plus constant Best or Best Opposite class winner at the Australian Specialty Shows.

In her first litter, Ursula produced Australian Champion Chelshar Saffron. Cabaret continued in her mother's paw prints, also winning Reserve Challenge at the Sydney Royal (42 bitches) and Best of Best Opposite at the Specialty Shows, plus many Group and in Show awards again with numerous Bests of Breed.

Saffron was shown only sparingly, and with her first litter by Ursula's litter brother, Chelshar Brook, produced Australian Champion Chelshar Vashti who won Best Puppy of the Day at the

Aust. Ch. Chelshar Wild Honey by Dharug Edric ex Aust. Ch. Chelshar Cabaret, photographed in January 1984 at one year of age. Bred by Mrs. S. Wright, owned by Miss J. Kawka, Australia.

Cazdane Chelsea at age three and a half. the dam of Aust. Ch. Chelshar Ursula, she is a daughter of Aust. Ch. Raatu Riley ex Aust. Marydane Jacquline. Bred by Miss C. Stuart, owned by Mrs. S. Wright, Schofields, Sydney, N.S.W.

107

Aust. Ch. Daymondane Apollo, by Ch. Raatu Atlas (fawn) ex Urdos Jodella (brindle), owned and bred by Ted and Viv Helliar, Pennant Hills, N.S.W. This was Great Dane of the Year for 1981-1982 and this same photo appears on all T-shirts representing the breed sold throughout Australia.

Sydney Royal. She was awarded her first Challenge at age seven months and gained her title at age two years with many prestigious awards. Vashti is to be mated in late 1985.

Cabaret, with her first litter, produced Australian Champion Chelshar Wild Honey who gained her title at only 12 months of age, with many enviable wins including Reserve Challenge at 13 months at the Canberra Royal. Honey's slower-to-develop litter sister, Chelshar Claim To Fame, was awarded her first Challenge and class in Group at 12 months old, and as we write in mid-1985 is well on her way to Australian championship.

DAYMONDANE

Daymondane Great Danes are owned by Ted and Viv Helliar at Pennant Hills in New South Wales. These folks are the breeders-owners of the very handsome Australian Champion Daymondane Apollo, who was born in March 1978.

Apollo is a son of Australian Champion Raatu Atlas, owned by Graeme Haerse, who was also a "Great Dane of the Year" during his show career and was sired by Champion Airlie of Auchnacraig ex Raatu Honey. Apollo's dam, Urdos Jodella, owned by his breeders, is a daughter of Champion Daneswalk Chance ex Norse-dane Astrid.

He has been highly successful as a show dog, taking honors at Royals and other prestigious events. Additionally, he is a famous celebrity as the dog whose likeness is depicted on all T-shirts in Australia which feature his breed.

There is also a very lovely bitch at this kennel, she, too, a homebred, Australian Champion Daymondane Forever. She is of English breeding on her sire's side, being by Hildydane El Cid, whose parents are imports from the United Kingdom and whose grandparents include English Champion Simba of Helmlake (a Crufts and Dane of the Year winner in England), English Champion Helmlake Praslin, and English Champion Halindi of Helmlake. Forever is half sister to Apollo, both being from Urdos Jodella who has among her grandparents Champion Danestadt, Champion Dantipaws Diana, and Champion Daneswalk Amber Honi.

Apollo, upon his retirement, had amassed over 2,000 Challenge Certificate points; 10 all-breed Bests in Show; and for two years running (1981 and 1982), was chosen to compete in the "Contest of Champions" which is for the Top Twenty Dogs in Australia, All-Breeds. Also, as already mentioned, he was Great Dane of the Year for 1981 and 1982.

Champion Daymondane Forever, nicknamed Matilda, retired in 1984, by which time she had amassed 1,300 C.C. points, four Bests in Show (all breeds), and in 1983 was chosen to compete in the "Contest of Champions" as one of the Top Twenty Dogs, all breeds, in Australia.

HILDYDANE

The Hildydane Great Danes are owned by Hildegarde Mooney at Box Hills in New South Wales, where their enthusiastic owner is breeding some truly outstanding Harlequin representatives of the breed.

Australian Champion Hildydane Lord Thor is a dog of very special merit, and takes "pride of place" with his owner. At eight years old, he hardly ever misses a weekend of showing, and was Top Working Dog for 1984-1985 in the point score of the Great Dane Club of New South Wales. He was Reserve Challenge Dog at the Melbourne Royal in 1985 and also at the Sydney Royal in 1984, beating some splendid dogs only a quarter his age. At the Canberra Royal in 1985, he was Runner Up to Best in Show All Breeds, just to list a few of his current achievements.

As a puppy, Lord Thor won 18 Puppy in Show awards. Most of his major wins were at the prestige events under judges of international fame from Europe, Japan, and the Americas. Every so often Thor has to be retired temporarily so that another Hildydane youngster can make up his title. Thor does not like these retirement periods!

Lord Thor's parents are Australian Champion Helmlake Dazzling Igor, C.D. and Australian Champion Helmlake Darling Fashion, C.D.X. (both imported from U.K.). These two really put the Harlequin on the map in Australia. They were by the German import into the U.K., Helmlake Ben Eik vom Forellenparadies. Igor and Fashion both were Top Winning Danes, Igor having been Dane of the Year 1975 and 1976 and Best of Breed three years consecutively at the prestigious Spring Fair Show. He was a constant in Group and in Show winner. At seven years he came

110

Aust. Ch. Hildydane Carisma New York, by BMW Sydney ex Hildydane Baronessa, bred and owned by Hildydane Kennels, Hildegarde Mooney, Box Hill, N.S.W.

Aust. Ch. Hildydane Lord Thor winning R.U. Best in Show, Canberra Royal. Owned by Hildydane Kennels, Hildegarde Mooney, Box Hill, N.S.W.

Ranadane The Performer, by Amasa Sir Midas ex Jaysdane Rebecca, another lovely Dane from the Amasa Kennels in Australia, owned by Sue and Alan Whyte and Denise and Fred Bennett, Schofields, N.S.W.

Aust. Ch. Kochak Biba is a homebred by Aust. Ch. Airways Adrian ex Aust. Ch. Impton Peregrine. A product of the first full imported breeding at this kennel has won Best of Breed at only 11 months age; Puppy of the Day at the Brisbane Royal National, and has many in-Group and Best of Breed awards. Owned by Mr. and Mrs. L. Arrowsmith, Cooroy, Queensland.

out of one of his semi-retirements for the big Spring Fair under an American judge, winning the C.D.; and his daughter, Australian Champion Hildydane Janushka, gained the C.C. for bitches, then beat her sire to the Best of Breed, the Dane entry numbering 180! A couple of years later, they went down to Melbourne for the Great Dane Specialty under another American judge, the Dane breeder Mr. Davis. He awarded Thor the Reserve C.C. and Janushka the C.C. This same bitch won the Best of Breed at the Tasmanian Fiesta under the German judge Dr. H. Wirtz, and went on to win Best of Opposite Sex in Group. Janushka and Lord Thor were a beautiful winning team, taking over from their parents.

Janushka is now retired to a beautiful home from where, to quote Hildegarde, "she writes letters to me regularly in dog talk."

An Igor son, New Zealand Champion Hildydane Count Amour, was exported by Hildydane Kennels to New Zealand, where he became Great Dane of the Year three years running.

Hildegarde Mooney states, "Every good Harlequin in this country goes back to Igor and Fashion and Kempson's Venus, the latter imported from U.K."

Another importation at Hildydane is a daughter of the Crufts Best of Breed English Champion Leesthorphill Sultan of Escheatsland; Igor and Fashion's grandsire is the famous Harlequin, German Champion Eik Imperial who for three years was the Bundessieger and was an International Champion. Thus Hildydane is well supplied with leading British and German bloodlines.

Hildegarde Mooney is proud of having bred the only Danes in New South Wales, Victoria, or Western Australia to have earned dual titles. Also she notes that Great Danes from Hildydane have been exported to Singapore, Fiji, and New Guinea as well as to New Zealand.

Almost without question, the most exciting day for Hildydane at a dog show was in Melbourne at the Australia Day International Show, where they made history under the American judge Mr. John Patterson when every bitch in the lineup for the selection of the C.C. consisted entirely of Harlequins carrying the Hildydane kennel prefix.

Australian Champion Hildydane Titan King is a product of the kennel's original lines and a French imported dog who also goes

Aust. Ch. Celebers Kilroy has won Best in Show all breeds, and Best in Group, at many major Australian dog shows. Owned by Mr. S. and Mrs. L. Arrowsmith, Cooroy, Queensland.

back to the German dogs. This dog, at age two years, was Best of Breed at the 1985 Melbourne Royal.

To her original successful and beautiful lines, Ms. Mooney has recently added another outstanding element by the importation of her new American boy, BMW Sydney, son of American Champion BMW Quincy. He had to fly first to England, where he spent a year in quarantine, followed by another two-month quarantine period in Australia. He now is settled in his new home and has become the sire of Australian Champion Hildydane Carisma New York, who has been a consistent Puppy Sweepstakes winner and has in Group and in Show honors as well. At only 12 months she took out the Reserve C.C. at the Melbourne Royal in 1985, a remarkable achievement for so young a bitch. At 16 months she was a champion.

Sydney's first son, Hildydane's The Yank Tank, still a "lanky teenager," will soon be ready for some serious showing, and hopes are high for his success.

114

Chapter 7

The Standard of the Breed

The standard of the breed, to which one sees and hears such frequent reference wherever purebred dogs are written of or discussed, is the word picture of what is to be considered the ideal specimen of that breed. It outlines, in minute detail, each and every feature of these dogs, both in physical characteristics and in temperament, accurately describing the dog from whisker to tail, creating a clear impression of what is to be considered correct (or incorrect); the features comprising "breed type" (i.e., those which set it apart from other breeds, making it distinctive and unique); and the probable temperament and behavior pattern to expect in typical members of that breed.

The standard is the guide for breeders endeavoring to produce quality dogs, and for fanciers wishing to learn what is considered beautiful and typical within this individual breed. It is the tool with which judges evaluate and reach their decisions in the ring. The dog it describes as correct is the one in our mind's eye as we compare dogs and make evaluations. It is the result of endless hours spent in consideration and study of the breed, its history, its reasons for being; and of its description and previous standards in our own country and the countries of the breed's origin and development from earliest days up until modern times. All such factors have been studied and examined by your breed's parent specialty club (in this case the Great Dane Club of America), usually by a special committee selected for the task; then by the board of directors, and later the general membership. When all are in agreement to that point, the results are turned in to the American Kennel Club for their study and possible comments or suggestions, followed by publication, with an invitation to interested parties to comment, in the official Pure Bred Dogs/American Kennel Gazette. Following the satisfactory completion of all these steps, the Standard, or any changes in it which may have been under consideration, are approved and become official.

A similar routine is followed in other countries, too, in the writing of breed standards.

In Great Danes, the first standard of the breed was adopted in 1891 by the Great Dane Club of America, and this is the standard basically behind all for the breed since that time. Germany's authority in the matter has stood unchallenged in this matter around the world. Great Dane Clubs in England, France, Holland, India and Italy as well as in the United States, Canada, Australia, and South Africa, all adhere closely to the literal translation from the German as adopted by the Deutsche Doggen Club.

OFFICIAL STANDARD FOR GREAT DANES
1. GENERAL CONFORMATION

(a) GENERAL APPEARANCE: The Great Dane combines in its distinguished appearance, dignity, strength, and elegance with great size and a powerful, well-formed, smoothly muscled body. He is one of the giant breeds, but is unique in that his general conformation must be so well balanced that he never appears clumsy and is always a unit—the Apollo of dogs. He must be spirited and courageous—never timid. He is friendly and dependable. His physical and mental combination is the characteristic which gives the Great Dane the majesty possessed by no other breed. It is particularly true of this breed that there is an impression of great masculinity in dogs as compared to an impression of femininity in bitches. The male should appear more massive throughout than the bitch, with larger frame and heavier bone. In the ratio between length and height, the Great Dane should appear as square as possible. In bitches, a somewhat longer body is permissible. *Faults:* Lack of unity; timidity; bitchy dogs; poor musculation; poor bone development; out of condition; rickets; doggy bitches.

116

An owner-handled Best in Show winning Champion, Tivoli's Newt v Harmony Hill, was bred by Roxanne Mahan and owned by Pat Presley.

Two noted Danes from the Dinro Kennels, Mrs. Rosemarie Robert, Carmel, N.Y. The fawn *(left)*, Ch. Dinro Aslan; the brindle *(right)*, Ch. Dinro Yorge. Photo courtesy of Ed Lyons.

Ch. Shalott's Lady
Alicia in 1949, winning
the Cleveland Great
Dane Club Specialty
handled by Jane Kamp
Forsyth for Mr. and
Mrs. Gilbert Freeman.

Ch. Eaglevalley
Moonlight, one of
Dorothy Montgomery's
splendid Great Danes
from the 1960's era.

(b) COLOR AND MARKINGS

(I) BRINDLE DANES: Base color ranging from light golden yellow to deep golden yellow always brindled with strong black across stripes; deep-black mask preferred. Black may or may not appear on the eyes, ears, and tail tip. The more intensive the base color and the more distinct the brindling, the more attractive will be the color. Small white marks at the chest and toes are not desirable. *Faults:* Brindle with too dark a base color; silver-blue and grayish-blue base color; dull (faded) brindlings; white tail tip. Black fronted, dirty colored brindles are not desirable.

(II) FAWN DANES: Light golden yellow to deep golden yellow color with a deep black mask. Black may or may not appear on the eyes, ears, and tail tip. The deep golden yellow color must always be given the preference. Small white spots at the chest and toes are not desirable. *Faults:* Yellowish-gray, bluish-yellow, grayish-blue, dirty yellow color (drab color), lack of black mask. Black fronted, dirty colored fawns are not desirable.

(III) BLUE DANES: The color must be a pure steel blue, as far as possible without any tinge of yellow, black or mouse gray. Small white marks at the chest and toes are not desirable. *Faults:* Any deviation from a pure steel-blue coloration.

(IV) BLACK DANES: Glossy black. *Faults:* Yellow-black, brown-black, or blue-black. White markings, such as stripes on the chest, speckled chest and markings on the paws are permitted but not desirable.

(V) HARLEQUIN DANES: Base color: pure white with black torn patches irregularly and well distributed over the entire body; pure white neck preferred. The black patches should never be large enough to give the appearance of a blanket nor so small as to give a stippled or dappled effect. (Eligible, but less desirable, are a few small gray spots; also pointings where instead of a pure white base with black spots, there is a white base with single black hairs showing through which tend to give a salt and pepper or dirty effect.) *Faults:* White base color with a few large spots; bluish-gray pointed background.

(c) SIZE: The male should not be less than 30 inches at the shoulders, but it is preferable that he be 32 inches or more, providing he is well proportioned to his height. The female should not be less than 28 inches at the shoulders, but it is preferable that she be 30 inches or more, providing she is well proportioned to her height.

(d) CONDITION OF COAT: The coat should be very short and thick, smooth, and glossy. *Faults:* Excessively long hair (stand-off coat); dull hair (indicating malnutrition, worms, and negligent care).

(e) SUBSTANCE: Substance is that sufficiency of bone and muscle which rounds out a balance with the frame. Faults: Lightweight, whippety Danes; course, ungainly proportioned Danes— always there should be balance.

2. MOVEMENT

(a) GAIT: Long, easy, springy stride with no tossing or rolling of body. The back line should move smoothly, parallel to the ground, with minimum rise and fall. The gait of the Great Dane should denote strength and power showing good driving action in the hindquarters and good reach in front. As speed increases, there is a natural tendency for the legs to converge towards the center line of balance beneath the body and there should be no twisting in or out at the joints. *Faults:* Interference or crossing, twisting joints; short steps; stilted steps; the rear quarters should not pitch; the forelegs should not have a hackney gait. When moving rapidly, the Great Dane should not pace for the reason that it causes excessive side-to-side rolling of the body and thus reduces endurance.

(b) REAR END (Croup, Legs, Paws): The croup must be full, slightly drooping, and must continue imperceptibly to the tail root. *Faults:* A croup which is too straight; a croup which slopes downward too steeply; and too narrow a croup.

Hind legs: The first thighs (from hip joint to knee) are broad and muscular. the second thighs (from knee to hock joint) are strong and long. Seen from the side, the angulation of the first thigh with the body, of the second thigh with the first thigh, and the pastern root with the second thigh should be very moderate, neither too straight nor too exaggerated. Seen from the rear, the hock joints appear to be perfectly straight, turned neither towards the inside nor towards the outside. *Faults:* Hind legs, soft, flabby, poorly muscled thighs, cowhocks which are the result of the hock joint

Ch. Dinro Simon Templar, handled by Jane Kamp Forsyth for Dana Knowlton and Antonia Pratt. Important winner of the early 1970's, a son of Ch. Dinro's Yogi Bear ex Dinro's Irresistible Charm. Born November 1969.

Ch. Dinro Squire was one of the famous Great Danes from the late Mrs. Rosemarie Robert's Dinro Kennels at Carmel, N.Y. One of the most respected and important kennels in the history of this breed.

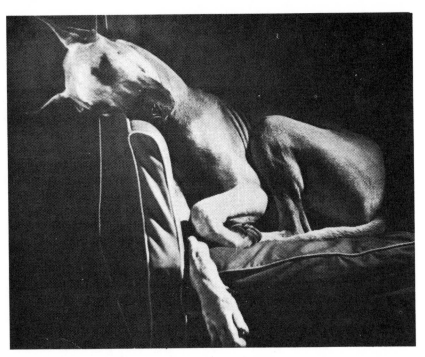

Ch. Gilbert-Duysters Linda Mia, Honey Hollow's first champion in 1950. Lina Basquette, owner, Chalfont, Pa.

Am. and Can. Ch. Dinro Goliath taking points towards his title during the 1960's for owner, the late Rosemarie Robert. Photo courtesy of Ed Lyons.

turning inward and the hock and rear paws turning outward; barrel legs, the result of the hock joints being too far apart; steep rear. As seen from the side, a steep rear is the result of the angles of the rear legs forming almost a straight line; overangulation is the result of exaggerated angles between the first and second thighs and the hocks and is very conducive to weakness. The rear legs should never be too long in proportion to the front legs.

PAWS: Round and turned neither toward the inside nor toward the outside. Toes short, highly arched and well closed. Nails short, strong, and as dark as possible. *Faults:* Spreading toes (splay foot); bent, long toes (rabbit paws); toes turned toward the outside or toward the inside. Furthermore, the fifth toe on the hind legs appearing at a higher position and with wolf's claw or spur; excessively long nails; light colored nails.

(c) FRONT END (Shoulders, Legs, Paws):

SHOULDERS: The shoulder blade must be strong and sloping and seen from the side must form as nearly as possible a right angle in its articulation with the humerus (upper arm) to give a long stride. A line from the upper tip of the shoulder to the back of the elbow joint should be as nearly perpendicular as possible. Since all dogs lack a clavicle (collar bone) the ligaments and muscles holding the shoulder blade to the rib cage must be well developed, firm, and secure to prevent loose shoulders. FAULTS: Steep shoulders, which occur if the shoulder blade does not slope sufficiently; overangulation; loose shoulders which occur if the Dane is flabby muscled, or if the elbow is turned toward the outside; loaded shoulders.

FORELEGS: The upper arm should be strong and muscular. Seen from the side or front, the strong lower arms run absolutely straight to the pastern joints. Seen from the front, the forelegs and the pastern roots should form perpendicular lines to the ground. Seen from the side, the pastern root should slope only very slightly forward. *Faults:* Elbows turned toward the inside or toward the outside, the former position caused mostly by too narrow or too shallow a chest, bringing the front legs too closely together and at the same time turning the entire lower part of the leg outward; the latter position causes the front legs to spread too far apart, with the pastern roots and paws usually turned inwards. Seen from the side, a considerable bend in the pastern toward the

123

front indicates weakness and is in most cases connected with stretched and spread toes (splay foot); seen from the side, a forward bow in the forearm (chair leg); an excessively knotty bulge in the front of the pastern joint.

PAWS: Round and turned neither toward the inside nor toward the outside. Toes short, highly arched, and well closed. Nails short, strong and as dark as possible. *Faults:* Spreading toes (splay foot); bent, long toes (rabbit paws); toes turned toward the outside or toward the inside; light colored nails.

3. HEAD

(a) HEAD CONFORMATION: Long, narrow, distinguished, expressive, finely chiseled, especially the part below the eyes (which means that the skull plane under and to the inner point of the eye must slope without any bony protuberance in a pleasing line to the full square jaw), with strongly pronounced stop. The masculinity of the male is very pronounced in the expression and structure of head (this subtle difference should be evident in the dog's head through massive skull and depth of muzzle); the bitch's head may be more delicately formed. Seen from the side, the forehead must be sharply set off from the bridge of the nose. The forehead and the bridge of the nose must be straight and parallel to one another. Seen from the front, the head should appear narrow, the bridge of the nose should be as broad as possible. The cheek muscles must show slightly, but under no circumstances should they be too pronounced (cheeky). The muzzle part must have full flews and must be as blunt vertically as possible in front; the angles of the lips must be quite pronounced. The front part of the head, from the tip of the nose up to the center of the stop, should be as long as the rear part of the head from the center of the stop to the only slightly developed occiput. The head should be angular from all sides and should have definite flat planes and its dimensions should be absolutely in proportion to the general appearance of the Dane. *Faults:* Any deviation from the parallel planes of skull and foreface; too small a stop; a poorly defined stop or none at all; too narrow a nose bridge; the rear of the head spreading laterally in a wedgelike manner (wedge head); an excessively round upper head (apple head); excessively pronounced cheek musculature; pointed muzzle; loose lips hanging over the

124

lower jaw (fluttering lips) which create an illusion of a full deep muzzle. The head should be rather shorter and distinguished than long and expressionless.

(b) TEETH: Strong, well developed and clean. The incisors of the lower jaw must touch very lightly the bottoms of the inner surface of the upper incisors (scissors bite). If the front teeth of both jaws bite on top of each other, they wear down too rapidly. *Faults:* Even bite, undershot and overshot; incisors out of line; black or brown teeth; missing teeth.

(c) EYES: Medium size, as dark as possible, with lively intelligent expression; almond-shaped eyelids, well developed eyebrows. *Faults:* Light colored, piercing, amber colored, light blue to a watery blue, red or bleary eyes; eyes of different colors; eyes too far apart; Mongolian eyes; eyes with pronounced haws; eyes with excessively drooping lower eyelids. In blue and black Danes, lighter eyes are permitted but are not desirable. In Harlequins, the eyes should be dark. Light-colored eyes, two eyes of different color and walleyes are permitted but not desirable.

(d) NOSE: The nose must be large and in the case of brindled and "single colored" Danes, it must always be black. In Harlequins, the nose should be black; a black spotted nose is permitted; a pink-colored nose is not desirable.

(e) EARS: Ears should be high, set not too far apart, medium in size, of moderate thickness, drooping forward close to the cheek. Top line of folded ear should be about level with the skull. *Faults:* Hanging on the side, as on a Foxhound.

CROPPED EARS: High set, not set too far apart, well pointed, but always in proportion to the shape of the head and carried uniformly erect.

4. TORSO

(a) NECK: The neck should be firm and clean, high set, well arched, long, muscular and sinewy. From the chest to the head, it should be slightly tapering, beautifully formed, with well-developed nape. *Faults:* Short, heavy neck, pendulous throat folds (dewlaps).

(b) LOIN AND BACK: The withers forms the highest part of the back which slopes downward slightly toward the loins which are imperceptibly arched and strong. The back should be short and tensely set. The belly should be well shaped and tightly muscled, and, with the rear part of the thorax, should swing in a pleasing curve (tuck-up). *Faults:* Receding back; sway back; camel or roach back; a back line which is too high at the rear; an excessively long back; poor tuck-up.

(c) CHEST: Chest deals with that part of the thorax (rib cage) in front of the shoulders and front legs. The chest should be quite broad, deep and well muscled. *Faults:* A narrow and poorly muscled chest; strong protruding sternum (pigeon breast).

(d) RIBS AND BRISKET: Deals with that part of the thorax back of the shoulders and front legs. Should be broad with the ribs well sprung out from the spine and flattened at the side to allow proper movement of the shoulders extending down to the elbow joint. *Faults:* Narrow (slab sided) rib cage; round (barrel) rib cage; shallow rib cage not reaching the elbow joint.

5. TAIL

Should start high and fairly broad, terminating slender and thin at the hock joint. At rest, the tail should fall straight. When excited or running, slghtly curved (saberlike). *Faults:* A too high, or too low set tail (the tail set is governed by the slope of the croup); too long or too short a tail; tail bent too far over the back (ring tail); a tail which is curled; a twisted tail (sideways); a tail carried too high over the back (gay tail); a brush tail (hair too long on lower side). Cropping tails to desired length is forbidden.

DISQUALIFICATIONS

Danes under minimum height.

White Danes without any black marks (albinos).

Merles, a solid mouse-gray color or a mouse-gray base with black or white or both color spots or white base with mouse-gray spots.

Harlequins and solid-colored Danes in which a large spot extends coatlike over the entire body so that only the legs, neck and the point of tail are white.

Brindle, fawn, blue and black Danes with white forehead line, white collars, high white stockings and white bellies.

Danes with predominantly blue, gray, yellow or also brindled spots.

126

Am., Can., and Mex. Ch. Jecamo's Caesar of AAA, by Trailblazer of Los Vientos ex Ch. Kelsey's Annie Laurie. Best in Show, multi-Group winner. Sire of 10 champions. Bred by Jerry and Caroline Mobley. Owned by Gene Mitchell, San Luis Rey, Calif.

Any color other than those described under "Color and Markings."

Docked tails.

Split noses.

Approved August 10, 1976

KENNEL CLUB (GREAT BRITAIN) VARIATION TO STANDARD

HEAD: entire length of head varies with height of dog. There should be a decided rise or brow over eyes but no abrupt stop between. NOSE: bridge of nose should be very wide, with slight ridge where cartilage joins bone. A butterfly or flesh-coloured nose is not objected to in Harlequins. MOUTH: teeth should be level and not project one way or other. FEET: light nails permissible in Harlequins. HINDQUARTERS: stifle and hocks well bent, hocks set low. COLOR: *Brindle:* eyes and nails preferred dark. *Blues:* Color varies from light grey to deepest slate. HEIGHT AND SIZE: (minimum) dogs 30 inches and 120 pounds, bitches 28 inches and 100 pounds.

We have been urged by a number of important Great Dane fanciers to include the following *Code of Ethics* in this book. While all Great Dane breeders are not in agreement with it, a goodly number feel that is is an important step in protecting the future of the breed, and are asking their members, or those wishing to join the club, to abide by its words. With numerous disqualifications within the breed coming under the heading of color or markings, greater emphasis than ever is now being placed on these features.

BREEDERS CODE OF ETHICS
as endorsed by
THE GREAT DANE CLUB OF AMERICA

There are only five recognized colors: all these basically fall into four color strains: 1. FAWN and BRINDLE, 2. HARLEQUIN and HARLEQUIN BRED BLACK, 3. BLUE and BLUE BRED BLACK, 4. BLACK. Color classifications being well founded, the Great Dane Club of America, Inc. considers it an inadvisable practice to mix color strains and it is the club's policy to adhere only to the following matings:

Color of Dane	Pedigree of Sire and Dam		Approved Breedings
1. FAWN	Pedigrees of FAWN or BRINDLE Danes should not carry BLACK, HARLEQUIN or BLUE upon them.	1.	FAWN bred to FAWN or BRINDLE only.
1. BRINDLE		1.	BRINDLE bred to BRINDLE or FAWN only.
2. HARLEQUIN	Pedigrees of HARLEQUIN or HARLEQUIN BRED BLACK Danes should not carry FAWN, BRINDLE or BLUE upon them.	2.	HARLEQUIN bred to HARLEQUIN. BLACK from HARLEQUIN BREEDING or BLACK from BLACK BREEDING only.
2. BLACK (HARLEQUIN BRED)		2.	BLACK from HARLEQUIN BREEDING bred to HARLEQUIN, BLACK from HARLEQUIN BREEDING or BLACK from BLACK BREEDING only.
3. BLUE	Pedigrees of BLUE or BLUE BRED BLACK Danes should not carry FAWN, BRINDLE or HARLEQUIN upon them.	3.	BLUE bred to BLUE, BLACK from BLUE BREEDING or BLACK from BLACK BREEDING only.
3. BLACK (BLUE BRED)		3.	BLACK from BLUE BREEDING bred to BLUE, BLACK from BLUE BREEDING or BLACK from BLACK BREEDING only.
4. BLACK (BLACK BRED)	Pedigrees of BLACK BRED Danes should not carry FAWN, BRINDLE, HARLEQUIN or BLUE upon them.	4.	BLACK from BLACK BREEDING bred to BLACK, BLUE or HARLEQUIN only. (See note below.)

Note: Black Bred Great Danes may be bred to Blacks, Blues or Harlequins only; Puppies resulting from these breedings will become Blacks or Harlequins from Harlequin breeding (category 2 above), Blacks or Blues from Blue breeding (category 3 above) or Blacks from Black Breeding (category 4 above).

It is our belief that color mixing other than that set forth above is injurious to our breed.
   ALL COLORS SHALL BE PURE COLOR BRED FOR FOUR (4) GENERATIONS
Breeders of Black, Blue or Harlequin Danes will be expected to clear their lines to provide pedigrees that are 4 generations pure color bred.

128

◀Overleaf:

This is the great Ch. BMW Ruffian, sire of many champions, owned and photographed by Laura Kiaulenas.

1. Three generations of Am. and Can. Champion Harlequins. *Left to right*, Am. and Can. Ch. Sheboane's Johnnie B. Goode; Am. and Can. Ch. Queststar Valdez of Sheboane; and Am. and Can. Ch. Amherst Mylan. The judge, Jean Lanning of England. Owned by Bonne and Gayle Klompstra, Sombra, Ontario, Canada.

2. *From left to right*, Ch. Keetra's Bruno V. Dof, by Dof Huben V. Meistersinger ex Frits's Devil May Care; Ch. Keetra's Geronimo, by Ch. Keetra's Bruno V. Dof ex Shana V. Keetra; and Ch. Keetra's Lance (six months old at the time) by Ch. Keetra's Bruno V. Dof ex Shana V. Keetra. All bred by Bernard and Francine Schwartz, Lake Forest, Ill.

3. Family portrait! Laura Kiaulenas surrounded by some of her noted winning Harlequins. *Left to rigt*, Ch. BMW Leprechaun, Ch. BMW Prima Donna, BMW Reggae, and Ch. BMW In Vogue. Taken informally at a recent dog show.

131

1▲   ▼2

3▼

1 ▲   ▼ 2

3 ▼

◄Overleaf:

1. Best in Show winning Ch. Longo's Chief Joseph winning 1st place in the Stud Dog Class, Heart of Ohio Great Dane Club Specialty Show, 1985. *Second from left*, Ch. Winhurst Joshua J. Justice owned by Nancy Welsh, handled by Rick Zahorchack. *Third from left*, Longo's Baby Face Brislyn owned by Joe and Tootie Longo, handled by Linda Kazam. *On right*, Ch. Vera's Annastacia v. Brislyn, owned by Tootie Longo and Vera Smith, handled by Tootie Longo.

2. A very impressive line-up, headed by Ed Lyons with his famed Ch. Harmony Hill Xmas Lyons Pride and some of the "younger generation," the latter all progeny of Xmas. Ed Lyons owner-handling Xmas.

3. Ch. Fahmie's Golden Vulcan v Fury, sire, with his offspring Ch. Thor Dane's Pat Hand Poker and Champion Thor Dane's Page v Brass Rail. Vulcan owned by Mr. and Mrs. John Fahmie, Miami, Fla. Pat Hand and Page bred by Mrs. Linda Springthorpe, Ball Ground, Ga.

1. Ch. O'Lorcain's Tullamore Dew, by Ch. Von Raseac's Great Caesar's Quote ex Ch. O'Lorcain's Triscuit von Raseac. Was bred by Harriet and Kenyon Larkin and is owned by Mr. Larkin with Judy Phillips.

2. Ch. Winfall's Papillon v Mako with Doug Toomey. By Ch. Castile's Gent of Mountdania ex Ch. Sunridge's Butterfly McQueen. Owned by Kathy Varian, Rika Danes, Reseda, Calif. Handled by Doug Toomey.

3. Ch. Jessica Davis, born in 1973, whose classic head is ideal for a Great Dane bitch. Note clean lines and correct planes. Best in Show and multiple Specialty winner, Jessica was among the Top Great Danes in the United States during 1976. Owned by Mr. and Mrs. Lowell K. Davis, Covina, Calif.

4. Rochford's Devon at the age of 11 months. Daughter of Ch. Temple Dell's Odin v Branstock ex Ch. Edelweis Celebration. Bred by Gary and Janet Quick. Owned by Lourdes Carvajal, Kansas City, Mo.

◀Overleaf:

1. Ch. BMW Leprechaun, owned by Laura Kiaulenas, illustrates good muscular strength, balance and coordination without which it would be difficult for a dog so large to achieve and hold this position with such nonchalance.

2. A very promising Harlequin puppy at eight weeks. Litter sister to Am. and Can. Ch. Queststar Valdez of Sheboane ex Vi-Dayne's Sabrina. Owned by Bonne and Gayle Klompstra, Sombra, Ontario, Canada.

3. Headstudy of Ch. Von Raseac's Quintessence, the dam of four Group winning champions. Bred by R. Harris and Brucie Mitchell; owned by Kenyon and Harriet Larkin, co-owned with Brucie Mitchell. Sired by Cameo's Lilabet of Jason ex Great Caesar's Ghost V Raseac.

4. The magnificent Best in Show winning Am. and Can. Ch. Dinro Diplomat from the kennels of the late Mrs. Rosemarie Robert, owned by Robert Heal. Note the exceptional head and front of this highly successful dog. Photo courtesy of Ed Lyons.

Overleaf:

1. Best in Show winning Ch. BMW Bull Lea, by Ch. BMW Ruffian ex Ch. BMW Fantasia, co-owned by Mary Anne Zanetos and Laura Kiaulenas. Photo by Barbara Dane.

2. The magnificent head of Ch. BMW Prima Donna, owned by Laura Kiaulenas, Farmingville, N.Y., who was also the photographer!

3. Ch. BMW Fantasia, by BMW Ouzo ex BMW Vanilla, finished title from the puppy class. Bred, owned, and handled by Laura Kiaulenas. Photo by owner.

4. Ch. Keetra's Lance, by Ch. Keetra's Bruno V. Dof ex Shana V. Keetra, pictured with present owner, Antonia Pratt. Bred by Bernard and Francine Schwartz, Lake Forest, Ill.

5. Ch. Rockbridge's BMW Rachel, by Ch. BMW Ruffian ex BMW Danskin, was bred by Leon Reimert and Laura Kiaulenas, owned by Mr. Reimert and David Houtz.

6. Am. and Can. Ch. Queststar Valdez of Sheboane, by Am. and Can. Ch. Sheboane's Johnnie B. Goode ex Can. Ch. Morrisons Miss Behaving. Winner of 11 All-Breed Bests in Show and four Specialty Bests of Breed, owned by Bonne and Gayle Klompstra, Sheboane Kennels, Sombra, Ontario, Canada.

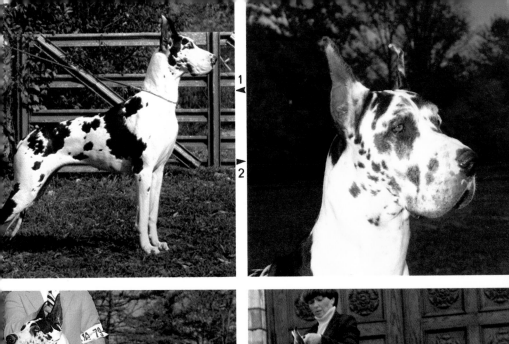

1 ►
2 ►

3 ►
4 ►

5 ►
6 ►

◀Overleaf:

1. Ch. BMW In Vogue, by Ch. BMW Brody ex BMW Socialite, owned by Laura Kiaulenas, Farmingville, N.Y. Photo by Tom Sayvetz.

2. Am. and Can. Ch. Sheboane's Johnnie B. Goode, by Bonne's Adonis Von Sheboane ex Devrok's Windsong Von Sheboane, finished quickly in Canada and the U.S. This Best in Specialty winner is the first Canadian-bred Harlequin in more than 25 years to complete American title. Sire of Best in Show winning Ch. Queststar Valdez of Sheboane. Owners, Bonne and Gayle Klompstra, Sheboane Kennels, Sombra, Ontario.

3. Ch. Zeno's Jedi Master, owned and bred by Barbra Oliva and David Zeno, handled by Joel Rosenblatt.

4. Ch. Davisdane's Double Exposure, C.D., owned by Susan Davis, Hanover, Mass.

5. BMW Calipso, by Ch. BMW Ruffian ex BMW Penumbra, is owned by Mary Ann Zaretos, Columbus, Ohio. Photo by Laura Kiaulenas.

6. Best in Show winning Ch. BMW Bull Lea, by Ch. BMW Ruffian ex Ch. BMW Fantasia. Photo by Laura Kiaulenas.

Overleaf:◗

1. *Left to right*, Ch. BMW Prima Donna, Ch. BMW Ruffian, BMW Mardi Gras, and Ch. BMW Fantasia, four of the outstanding Harlequins owned by Linda Kiaulenas, BMW Kennels, Farmingville, N.Y.

2. Ch. Cyncir Choctaw Chief was bred by Diane Taylor and is owned by Pam and Mark Hendrickson. Linda Springthorpe handled this Great Dane to Best of Opposite Sex at Carroll Kennel Club in 1980.

3. Ch. Dinro What A Charm, famous Harlequin from the Dinro Kennels of the late Rosemarie Robert, Carmel, N.Y. Handled by Ed Lyons to points towards the title.

4. Ch. Dinro Simon Templar, one of Rosemarie Robert's Westchester Best of Breed winners.

5. Aust. Ch. Hildydane Titan King in 1984 is by Aust. Ch. Oby Des Terres De La Rairie (French import) ex Aust. Ch. Hildydane Poppet. Owned by Hildydane Kennels, Hildegarde Mooney, Box Hill, N.S.W., Australia.

6. Ch. Z-Dane's Sounda Music winning points toward the title at Mid-Susquehanna Valley in 1985. Handled by Ed Lyons for owners, Faye and Ric Zahorchak. Photo courtesy of Ed Lyons.

7. Ch. Lancer V. Meistersinger, by Roco Vun Henneberg (Harlequin) ex Ramona V. Meistersinger (black out of Harlequin), at age eight years winning Veterans Dog Class at a Lake Shore Great Dane Club Specialty. Bred by Antonia Pratt. Owned by Francine W. Schwartz, Lake Forest, Ill.

8. Ch. Sounda's Picture Perfect, Winners Dog at the Great Dane Club of Central Pennsylvania Specialty, August 1985. Owned by Dr. Louis Grant Bond and Robert E. Layne, Millbury, Mass.

1

2

3

4

5

6

7

8

1

2

3

4

5

6

7

8

◆Overleaf:

1. Am. and Can. Ch. Vi-Dayne's Pride of Sheboane by Am. and Can. Ch. Queststar Valdez of Sheboane ex Vi-Dayne's Sabrina, at age 11 months winning Best in Show and Best Puppy in Show at Essex County K.C. This youngster was also Best of Winners at the Great Dane Club of America Specialty over 122 dogs and 160 bitches from the Puppy Class. Owners, Bonne and Gayle Klompstra, Sheboane Great Danes, Sombra, Ontario, Canada.

2. BMW Sydney, imported from the U.S.A., by Ch. ZL's BMW Quincy ex BMW Chouette, is owned by Hildegard Mooney, Hildydane Kennels, Box Hill, N.S.W., Australia.

3. World, Intern'l, Am., Can., and Mex. Ch. Zeus Von Meistersinger, by Ch. Lancer Von Meistersinger ex Ch. Timbeleca Von Meistersinger, is the only American-bred Harlequin Great Dane to have attained all five titles. Bred by Francine W. Schwartz and Lee G. Schwartz. Owned by Rafael Gimenez-Valdes in Mexico.

4. Ch. Sounda's Stencil Perfect gaining points at Framingham in 1985. Finished to title by Ed Lyons for owners, Dr. Louis Grant Bond and Robert E. Layne, Dinro-Sounda Danes, Millbury, Mass.

5. BMW Extra Terrestrial, by BMW Ouzo ex BMW Pastel, owned by Laura Kiaulenas, BMW Great Danes, Farmingville, N.Y. Photo by Tom Sayvetz.

6. Aust. Ch. Hildydane Kalinkah, by Hildydane Ali Pasha ex Hildydane Ivy Girl, is a granddaughter of Aust. Ch. Hildydane Lord Thor. A homebred owned by Hildegarde Mooney, Box Hill, N.S.W., Australia.

7. Ch. Dinro's Sociable Charm, Best of Breed at Westminster 1972, another handsome winner from the late Rosemarie Robert's Dinro Danes, Carmel, N.Y.

8. Am. and Can. Ch. Sounda's Marathon Man, outstanding Harlequin who made history when four of his get finished in one year. He was used to illustrate correct movement, and is the first slide in the A.K.C. slides show for the breed. Sounda Great Danes, Dr. Louis Grant Bond and Robert E. Layne, Millbury, Mass.

1. Banachek Morgan, nine months old and just starting his show career in Australia, bred and owned by Mr. L.R. and Mrs. V.E. Hogan, Banachek Great Danes, Kurmond, N.S.W.

2. Ch. Sheridane Iroquois Shenandoah, by Rissone's Super Blu ex Sheridane Iroquois Heather. One of very few blue male champions alive in this country, was bred by Mike Sherman and Pat Wilder and was born Feb. 18, 1980. Owners, Eileen and Mike Sherman, Sheridane Kennels, Hebron, Conn.

3. Ch. Reann's Dark Side of Sounda is a current winner. Pictured taking Best of Winners at Elm City K.C. in 1985. Photo courtesy of Ed Lyons.

4. Ch. Longo's Chief Justice, famous Best in Show winning black Great Dane, owned and bred by Joe and Tootie Longo, Mentor-on-the-Lake, Ohio.

5. Ch. Sheridane Iroquois Hope, handled by owner, Mike Sherman, Sheridane Kennels, Hebron, Ct. This lovely bitch pictured winning in 1979 under judge Ed Dixon, was the first homebred U.S. champion owned by Mike and Eileen Sherman. She finished with a Specialty win over 71 bitches.

6. These two majestic Great Danes are Best in Show winning Ch. Longo's Chief Joseph, handled by Carol Whitney; and Ch. Longo's Double De Luxe handled by Tootie Longo. Joe and Tootie Longo, owners.

WINNERS
DOG

BEST OF
BREED IN VARIETY
SOUTH COUNTY
KENNEL CLUB
1984

GOLDCOAST
KENNEL CLUB
BEST
IN
SHOW
JUDGE
KENNETH PETERSON

BEST OF
OPPOSITE SEX

BEST OF
WINNERS
HUNTERDON HILLS
KENNEL CLUB
1985

OPEN
DOG
HEART OF OHIO
GREAT DANE CLUB

◆Overleaf:

1. Ch. Pinebrook's Blue Magoo in July 1974. This splendid blue dog is owned by Maureen and Anthony Magone and is pictured at the Providence, R.I. Dog Show. Photo courtesy of Ed Lyons.

2. Ch. Janell's Merry Ms. Molly, consistent Group winning black Great Dane bitch, taking Best of Breed at South County K.C. under judge Robert S. Forsyth. Owned by Jane and Lonzie D. Rinker, Jr., Ottsville, Pa.

3. Ch. Longo's Chief Joseph winning Best in Show, Gold Coast Kennel Club 1984, judge Ken Peterson. This magnificent son of Ch. Shadowbrook's Pask ex Longo's Foxxy Lady, was retired following this exciting win. A homebred belonging to Joseph and Tootie Longo, Mentor-on-the-Lake, Ohio.

4. Ch. Longo's Double De Luxe was the first black Great Dane bitch ever to finish from the Bred by Exhibitor Class. Bred, owned, and handled by the Longos.

5. Wildwind Blaze of Glory, owned by Susan Carlin, bred by Jill Ferrera. A lovely example of excellence in a black Dane bitch! Pictured taking Best of Winners at Hunterdon Hills 1985 on the way to her title. Handled by Joel Rosenblatt, Lyndane Kennels, Salem, Conn.

6. Longo's Baby Face Brislyn, by Best in Show winning Ch. Longo's Chief Joseph ex Brislyn's Spirit of Blizzard is just starting his show career in mid-1985. Owned by Joseph and Tootie Longo, Longo's Great Danes, Mentor-on-the-Lake, Ohio.

7. Addidas Friday, by Westwind's Duesenberg ex Addidas Grogheda, age 16 months in photo. Being campaigned in 1985 by Marci Iler, Addidas Great Danes, Boonsboro, Md.

8. Rishmi's Sam A Go Go has a big kiss for his handler, Linda Springthorpe, Ball Ground, Ga. A Go Go is owned by Richard and Mary Ann Kerr.

1. Am. and Can. Ch. Beaucedane's Gent Jr v Mountdania, owned and handled by Ed Lyons, Pride Kennels, Somers, Conn. Shown taking Winners Dog at the Great Dane Club of New England Specialty in 1984.

2. Ch. Windane's Breeze of Stone Valley, by Best in Show winning Am. and Can. Ch. Windane's Zephyr ex Ch. Jeba's Jennifer of Windane, winning Best of Breed at Tualatin in 1983. Bred by Phyllis Ryan. Owned by Darcy Quinlan and June Herbst, Kennesaw, Ga.

3. Ch. Guevric's Dawn's Early Light, owned by Ed and Linda Springthorpe, Thor Dane Kennels, Ball Ground, Georgia. This splendid show and producing bitch, the dam of champions, here is taking Winners Bitch at the Great Dane Club of America National Specialty in May 1981. Linda Springthorpe handled.

4. Ch. Thor Dane's Churchill Downs at age 14 months. Bred by Ed and Linda Springthorpe, this handsome young dog is handled by Linda for Pam Hendrickson.

5. Ch. Edeldane's Celebration taking best of breed first time shown as a special, owner-handled by Janet Quick, Kansas City, Mo.

6. Ch. Temple Dell's Odin v Branstock, by Ch. Edeldane's Wildfire ex Ch. Sarah Davis of Temple Dell. A Best in Show and top winning Great Dane in 1985. Photo courtesy of Mr. and Mrs. Lowell K. Davis, Covina, Calif.

151

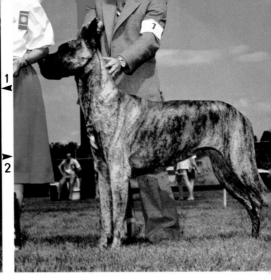

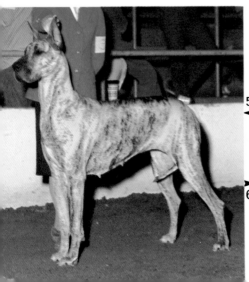

1 ◄

2 ◄

3 ◄

4 ◄

5 ◄

6 ◄

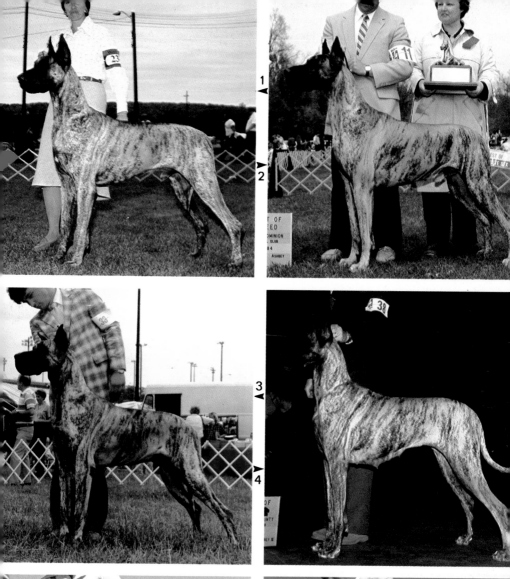

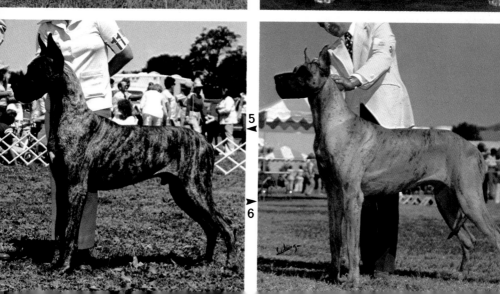

◀Overleaf:

1. Ch. Sounda Flash Gordon taking Best of Breed at Windham County in 1982. Sounda Danes owned by Louis Grant Bond and Robert E. Layne, Millbury, Mass.

2. Ch. Darrdane's Opening Bid finished title in 15 shows at the age of nine months, to become a multi-Group and Specialty winner and #3 Great Dane in the U.S. in 1983. Owned and bred by Dr. and Mrs. Robert Rothenberg, Avon, Connecticut. Handled and co-bred by Joel Rosenblatt, Lyndane Kennels, Salem, Conn.

3. Stone Valley's Dream Hustler, born September 6, 1981, by Best in Show winning Am. and Can. Ch. Windane's Zephyr ex Stone Valley's Dream Weaver. Bred and owned by Chuck and Darcy Weaver, Stone Valley Kennels, Kennesaw, Ga.

4. Am. and Can. Illiads Artemus winning at the Windham County K.C. in 1982, owned by Ed Lyons and Regine Dionne. Lyons Pride Kennels, Sommers, Conn.

5. Ch. Sounda's Duke of Earl at Wallkill K.C. in 1983. Sounda Great Danes, Dr. Louis Grant Bone and Robert E. Layne, Millbury, Mass.

6. Ch. Stockdales Rory O'More, owned by Larry and Carleen Radanovich, Stockdale Kennels, Bakersfield, Calif.

154

1. Ch. Shadam's Brooke, a "Charlie" daughter bred, owned and handled by Arthur and June Shafer, Shadam Great Danes, Ft. Wayne, Ind.

2. Ch. Hallmarks Jody Davis, by Ch. Temple Dell's Odin v Branstock ex Ch. Joanne Davis. Breeders-owners, Peggy McQuillon and Arlene and Lowell Davis, Covina, Calif.

3. Ch. Joanne Davis, by Ch. Mountdania's Ashley ex Ch. Jessica Davis, pictured with handler Doug Toomey in 1982. Bred and owned by Arlene and Lowell Davis, Covina, Calif.

4. Ch. Addidas Andiamo winning a major. Born May 1977, by Ch. Von Raseac Westwind ex Monsey Abiding Affection, C.D. Owned by Carol Lamberto and Nancy Welsh, this dog is the sire of champions and others with points.

5. Ch. Woodcliff's Sweet Rebecca going Best of Winners at Bucks County in 1984. Agent, Barbara Waldkirch, handled for owner, Richard E. Nelson, Woodcliff Lake, N.J.

6. Ch. Fahmie's Golden Vulcan v Fury winning a 4-point major under Mrs. Dona Hausman en route to his title. Next time out, as a special, he took Best of Breed under Helen Fisher and Group 1st under Louis Murr. Owned by Mr. and Mrs. John Fahmie, Miami, Fla. Handled by Linda Springthorpe.

7. Ch. Lady Shauntell Thrall McDavis, by Ch. Temple Dell's Odin v Branstock ex Ch. Joanne Davis, winning at Greater Daytona in 1984. Bred by Peggy McQuillon and Arlene and Lowell K. Davis.

8. A Rochford Great Dane with her seven weeks old litter. Owned by Janet Quick, Kansas City, Mo.

155

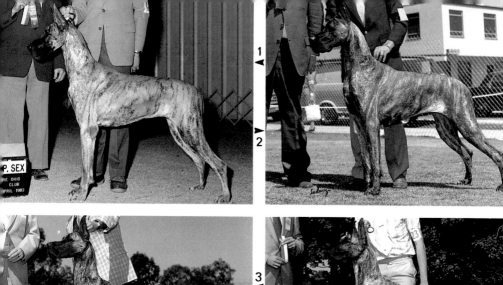

1 ►

2 ►

3 ►

4 ►

5 ►

6 ►

7 ►

8 ►

◀Overleaf:

1. Ch. Woodcliff's Sister Carrie triumphing over 140 bitches at the National Specialty at Westchester in 1981 under judge Kittie Kolyer. Handled by Dan Lasky for owner Richard L. Nelson, Woodcliff Great Danes, Woodcliff Lake, N.J.

2. Ch. Shadam's Chessa, born January 1982 in Shadam Kennels, Ft. Wayne, Indiana, by Best in Show winning Am. and Can. Ch. Windane's Zephyr ex Ch. Shadam Aboard the Merrimac (Ch. Windane's Zephyr-Ch. A Girl Called Charlie). Pictured taking Best of Opposite Sex at the Vancouver K.C. in 1985. Nancy L. Gilbert and June Herbst, owners, are from Everett, Wash. and Albany, Ore., respectively.

3. Am. and Can. Ch. Dionne's Aphrodite finished in six consecutive shows from the Bred-by Exhibitor Class. Owned by Ed Lyons and Regene Dionne, handled by Mr. Lyons. Pictured here winning at Tuxedo Park in 1984.

4. Ch. Live Wire Dorridane Voyager, a Group winning homebred owned by Dr. and Mrs. Robert J. Crawley, Folsom, La.

5. Ch. Tallbrook's Wild Chile, a current winner by Ch. Edeldane's Wildfire ex Ch. Bit O'Tallbrook's Honey Chile is pictured winning the Great Dane Club of California Second Specialty in 1983. Bred by Kathleen Twaits and Jacqueline F. White; owned by Jacqueline F. White, Kathleen Twaits and Cathy Schaefer.

6. Ch. Dorridane's Sweet Molly, a homebred owned by Dorridane Kennels, Dr. Robert and Patricia Crawley, Folsom, La. the Dam of seven champions including Ch. Tomike's Ringer of Dorridane.

7. Winning Best in Specialty Show, Greater Cincinnati Great Dane Club, May 1981. Ch. Shadam's Aliage, a "Charlie" daughter, bred and owned by Arthur and June Shafer, Ft. Wayne, Ind. Handled by George Rood.

8. A very famous dog from the 1960's, Ch. Nandane's Tamanaco, bred by Nandane Kennels, co-owned by Lyn Fuhrman and Carnell Gurrath (handling). This handsome big brindle was sire of at least 35 American Champions, four Canadian Champions, and two Champions of India, among them three Best in Show winners including Ch. Big Kim of Belladane. Years after his death his grandsons continue making history, among them Am. and Can. Ch. Heidere's Kolyers Kimbayh and Champion Tomike's Ringer of Dorridane. For many years Tamo was unchallenged as the breed's Top Producing sire. It was not until the 1980's that his record was surpassed by a fawn dog. At time of writing, Tamo remains the top brindle sire in breed history. Tamo lived to within a few weeks of his 11th birthday.

1. Ch. Gary Davis, by Ch. Mountdania's Ashley ex Ch. Jessica Davis, pictured with handler, Pete Gaete, in 1982. A homebred owned by Arlene and Lowell K. Davis, Covina, Calif.

2. Monsey Abiding Affection, C.D., dam of champions and pointed get, with Addidas Chamomile, C.D. (dam of champions and pointed get) on the *left*, and Addidas Orange Pekoe. The foundation stock of Addidas Kennels, Marci Iler, Boonsboro, Md.

3. Headstudy of Am., Can., and Mex. Ch. Stockdale's King's Ransom owned by Larry and Carleen Radanovich, Bakersfield, California. From the first litter bred by this kennel. By Ch. Von Raseac's Great Caesar Quote from a Dinro-Lovett bred dam. Littermate to Ch. Stockdales Rudolph V Raesac and Ch. Stockdales Twilight Twinkle.

4. Best in Show winning Can. Ch. Davos Deacon, C.D., T.T., pictured winning Best Canadian Bred in Show at the Great Dane Club of Canada Specialty on September 15, 1984. Judge, Amos Le Jeune. Owned by Hannadale Great Danes, Bill and Aila Treloar, Mississauga, Ontario, Canada.

5. Ch. Addida's Amtrak, by Ch. Addida's Andiamo ex Addida's Autumn Acorn. Bred by Marci Iler, owned by Jim Iler, Boonsboro, Md. Taking points en route to the title at Bald Eagle in 1984. Handled by Marci Iler.

6. Ch. Shadam's Aliage finishing title at less than one year old, St. Petersburg, 1981. A Charlie daughter bred and owned by M. Arthur and Jane Shafer, Ft. Wayne, Ind. Handled by George Rood.

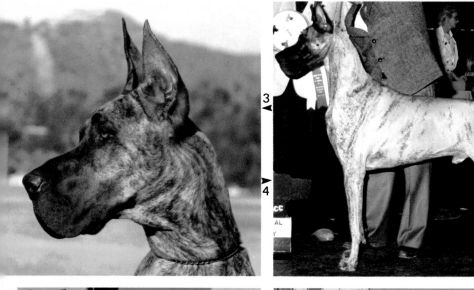

1 ◄

2 ◄

3 ◄

4 ◄

5 ◄

6 ◄

◀Overleaf:

1. Linda Springthorpe winning Group 1st at Tampa Bay in 1976 with Ch. Fahmie's Golden Vulcan v Fury.

2. Sargon Chadsworth v Shadam at 12 months. A "Charlie" great grandson. Owned by M. Arthur and June Shafer, Shadam Kennels, Ft. Wayne, Ind.

3. Ch. Bit O'Tallbrook's Honey Chile accepts congratulations for a nice win. Kathleen Twaits and Jacqueline White, owners, Los Angeles, Calif.

4. Am. and Mex. Ch. Tydwinds Sail Maker, by Ch. Temple Dell's Odin V Branstock ex Ch. Von Raseac's Whirlwind v Tybo, bred by the owners and Elizabeth Mitchell. Owned by Dennis and Joy De Gruccio, Orange, Calif.

5. Chelshar Claim To Fame at 12 months. Sired by Dharug Edric ex Aust. Ch. Chelshar Cabaret. Brindle homebred owned by Mrs. S. Wright, Schofield, Sydney, Australia.

6. Ch. Winfall's Papillon v Mako, by Ch. Castile's Gent of Mountdania ex Ch. Sunridge's Butterfly McQueen, taking points towards the title for owner, Kathy Varian, Rika Kennels, Reseda, Calif. Handler, Doug Toomey.

1. A lovely informal front view of the beautiful Great Dane, Ch. Shadam's Chessa owned by Nancy Gilbert, Everett, Wash.

2. Ch. Sheenwater Ace In The Hole, by Ch. Bodane Tourister ex Sheenwater X-Clamation. This splendid dog, bred and owned by Sally Chandler, died of cancer when still under three years of age. He has left one champion son and two others close to finishing. Sheenwater Kennels are at Loganville, Ga.

3. Headstudy of Ch. Edeldane's Celebration in 1983. By Lazycroft Murlo Harris ex Edeldane's Lothario. Owners, Gary and Janet Quick, Rochford Great Danes, Kansas City, Mo.

4. Ch. Ardlyn's Adam of Marydane was the first champion owned by H. Arthur and June Shafer, and the "backbone" of their Shadam Great Danes. Handled by George Rood.

5. Ch. Stockdale's Rudolph V Raseac, litter brother to Am., Can., and Mex. Ch. Stockdales King's Ransom and Ch. Stockdales Twilight Twinkle.

6. Rochford's Devon, brindle bitch at age 11 months in 1984. Owned by Lourdes Carvajal, Kansas City, Mo. Bred by Gary and Janet Quick, Rochford Great Danes.

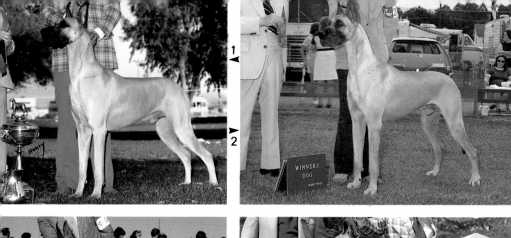

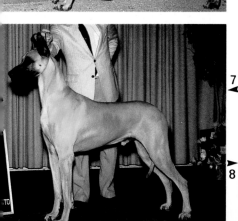

1

2

3

4

5

6

7

8

1. Ch. Von Raseac's Tyro O'Lorcain, multi-Group winner and the sire of 21 champions. By Ch. Sunridge's Chief Justice ex Ch. Von Raseac's Quintessence, Tybo was bred by Harriet Larkin and Brucie Mitchell, San Luis Rey, Calif., and is owned by Dennis and Joy DeGruccio.

2. Dinro Laramie owned by Dinro-Sounda Great Danes, Millbury, Mass.

3. Ch. Desert Springs Cynthia Davis pictured in 1982. By Ch. Mountdania's Ashley ex Ch. Jessica Davis, Cynthia was bred by Arlene and Lowell K. Davis who co-own her with Peggy McQuillan. Handled by Doug Toomey.

4. Ch. Von Raseac's County Cork, by Ch. Von Raseac's Valor of Tybo ex Ch. Von Raseac's Windsong. Noted breed and Specialty winner and the sire of champions, bred and owned by Brucie Mitchell and Linda Welsh.

5. Ch. Sheenwater Phoenix, by Ch. Sheenwater Jokers Wild ex Ch. Sheenwater Heat Wave, handled by Vic Capone to Best of Opposite Sex at Clearwater in 1980 for owner, Sally Chandler, Sheenwater Great Danes, Loganville, Ga.

6. Ch. Sheenwater Joker's Wild by Ch. Ashburn Acres Avant Garde ex Sheenwater Grassfire pictured winning the breed at Somerset Hills in Sept. 1977. The next day he won the Great Dane Club of America National Specialty at Westchester under breeder-judge Ruth Allen.

7. Ch. Von Raseac's Chaz of Hillview, by Ch. Reann's French Aristocrat ex Ch. Von Raseac's Cerissa V Song, bred by Linda Epperson Welsh and Wanda Needels, this is the most recent show and stud dog at Von Raseac Kennels. Pictured winning the Arizona Specialty in 1985. Owned by Donald Salyers and Gene Mitchells.

8. Ch. Rochford's Essex taking his first major at age 11 months in 1984, at the Great Dane Club of Greater Kansas City Specialty. Completed his title prior to reaching two years' age, owner-handled all the way. Owners, Jerry and Valerie Parsons, De Soto Kennels. Breeders, Gary and Janet Quick.

1. Ch. Stockdales Corporate Dividend, successful winner as a special with Bests of Breed and Group wins to his credit is also producing outstanding youngsters. Co-owned by Chuck and Pam Richter with Larry and Carleen Radanovich.

2. Amasa Chardonnay, sister to Amasa Cygnus, and also doing well at the shows. Owned by Sue and Alan Whyte, Denise and Fred Bennett, Amasa Kennels, Schofields, N.S.W., Australia.

3. Ch. Dinro Taboo's Voodoo was bred by Rosemarie Roberts at Dinro Danes, Carmel, N.Y.

4. Ch. Almisilvers Kojak Groski making an impressive win at the Exposition in September 1982 for owner Alfredo Vargas. Mrs. Jane Forsyth is the judge.

5. The noted Specialty Best in Show winner, Ch. Sheridane Prince Valiant, bred and owned and handled by Eileen and Mike Sherman, Sheridane Kennels, Hebron, Connecticut. Winner of two Specialty Bests in Show, close to 100 Bests of Breed, and 25 Group placements, the current special being shown by the Shermans, who will be retired during 1986.

6. Ch. Addidas Up N Coming Star, by Ch Wynkist's Mountaintop Rascal ex Addidas Penn Central, born Nov. 16, 1984. Bred by M. Iler and N. Davis. Owned by Marci Iler and Corinne Witt. Best of Breed at his first show when only nine months of age over nationally ranked special. Finished with ease, owner-handled, at 16 months.

1

2

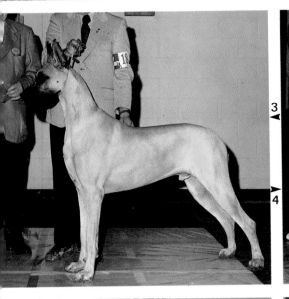

3

4

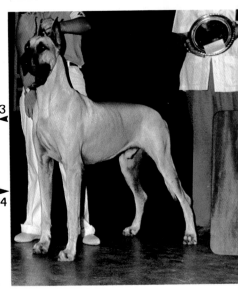

5

6

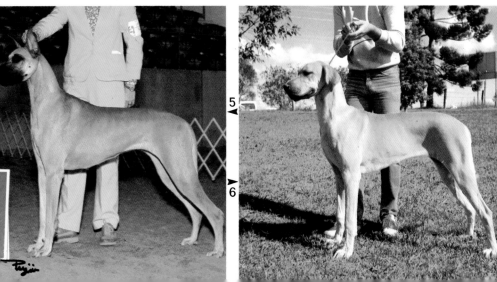

◆Overleaf:

1. Ch. Stone River's Delta Dawn, by Sheenwater Open Sesame ex Rockbridge's Texas Lady was bred by Tom Wilson and Bob Smithson. A great show bitch as well as a superior brood bitch, she has three champion get to date with others pointed. Owned by Sally Chandler and C.A. O'Connell, Sheenwater Great Danes, Loganville, Ga. Here taking Best of Breed at Rochester Specialty Ass'n in July 1983.

2. Ch. Dinro Tosca Too at Manatee in 1980. Dr. Louis Grant Bond and Robert E. Layne, owners, Millbury, Mass.

3. Ch. Viking's Vaquero V Stockdale, owned by Larry and Carleen Radanovich, Bakersfield, Calif.

4. Am. and Can. Ch. Dinro Diplomat, a fine representative of the Dinro breeding program of the late Mrs. Rosemarie Robert, owned by Robert Heal. A very important Best in Show winning Dane of the late 1970's. Photo courtesy of Ed Lyons.

5. Ch. Tara's Wonder Woman v Horizon's winning the Working Group at Beaumont K.C. in 1983. Owners, C. and D. Kirksey, Marilyn Riggins, and Sharon Fulford, Houston, Tex.

6. Banachek Peter, promising seven-month-old homebred owned by Mr. L.R. and Mrs. V.E. Hogan, Banachek Great Danes, Kurmond, N.S.W., Australia.

170

1. Ch. Von Raseac's Windsong, by Ch. Von Raseac's Tybo O'Lorcain ex Am. and Can. Ch. Von Raseac's Quite A Gal. Bred by Brucie Mitchell and Clare Lincoln; co-owned by Mrs. Mitchell with Linda Epperson Welsh. Multi-breed and Specialty winner; the dam of 3 champions.

2. Ch. Woodcliff's Gentle Greaves finishing title at Mason and Dixon K.C. in 1979 for owner Richard L. Nelson, Woodcliff Lake, N.J.

3. Ch. Tyler Lovett of Falconroc by Ch. Dinno H. Lovett ex Dante's Lucky Lady, fawn male born March 28, 1978. Bred by Marilyn S. Lovett and Janet Purdy. The sire of 10 champions as of mid-1985. Owned by Marilyn Lovett, Schodack Landing, N.Y.

4. Ch. Kolyer's Dame Daphne, C.D., going Best of Winners under judge Geraldine Parks at 1st Company Governor's Foot Guard in 1975. Joseph Fiducia handled for owner, Richard L. Nelson, Woodcliff Lake, N.J.

5. Ch. Rika's Plain Jane v Hauer, by Best in Specialty Show winning Ch. Hauerdane's War Bonnet ex Ch. Kingswood Phoebe Snow. Owned by Beve Hauer, Kathy Varian and Treasure Hauer, the latter handled as Plain Jane took Best Puppy at the Great Dane Club of California at seven months old.

6. Ch. MJM's Class Act of Lyndane, by Ch. Darrdane's Opening Bid ex Ch. Murlo Scarlett O'Harris. A leading winner for 1985, with Group and Specialty victories. Owned by Laurie and Michael Maulucci, Avon, Conn. Handled by Joel Rosenblatt.

7. Ch. Rochford's Cumbria taking Best of Breed at Nebraska K.C., May 1985. Owned by Gary and Janet Quick, handled by Janet. By Ch. Temple Dell's Odin v Branstock ex Ch. Edeldane's Celebration.

8. Ch. Dinro/Sounda Good Luck Charm owned by Dinro-Sounda Great Danes, of Dr. Louis Grant Bond and Robert E. Layne, Millbury, Massachusetts. Taking Winners Bitch at Land O'Lakes Kennel Club, June 1983. Ed Lyons handled.

171

1

2

BEST OF
WINNERS
MASON AND DIXON
KENNEL CLUB
1979
SHERRY PHOTO

3

4

BEST OF
WINNERS
STATEN ISLAND
KENNEL CLUB

BEST OF
WINNERS
ASHBEY PHOTO

5

6

BEST OF
BREED
PENN TREATY
KENNEL CLUB
1985
ASHBEY

7

8

WINNERS BITCH
LAND O' LAKES K.C.
JUNE 15, 1983
OLSON PHOTO

1

2

3

4

5

6

7

8

◆Overleaf:

1. Ch. Von Raseac's County Cork and daughter, Ch. Kingwood's Irish Rose of Hillview won together at this San Diego Great Dane Club Specialty. The bitch owned by Don and Chris Salyers; the dog by Brucie Mitchell and Linda Welsh.

2. Ch. Rika's Rendition of Kingswood with owner Kathy Varian. This famed sire and Best in Show winner belongs to the Varians in co-ownership with Richard N. Gebhart and was bred by Evelyn Porter and Gary Catron.

3. Ch. Dinro De Wolf ("Big Red") taking points along the way to title at the Great Dane Club of Central Pennsylvania Dog Show in 1975. Mrs. Rosemarie Robert, Dinro Danes, Carmel, N.Y.

4. Aust. Ch. Chelshar Vashti, by Chelshar Brook ex Chelshar Saffron, photographed in 1982, age two years. A homebred owned by Mrs. S. Wright, Schofields, Sydney, Australia.

5. Ch. Brandelyn Derek of Woodcliff taking Winners Dog at Penn Treaty in 1978 for Richard L. Nelson, Woodcliff Great Danes, handled by Dan Lasky. Derek was from one of the most successful Dane litters in memory, six or seven of the eight puppies having gained championship. They were bred by Andrea Haworth of Pennsylvania, and the dam, Ch. Brandelyn's Rhiannon was still living in 1985.

6. Airways Adrian, fawn Swedish import by Swedish and Finnish Ch. Gerjo's Shilo of Airways ex Swedish and Finnish Ch. Airways Lemona, is descended from several American champions from Harmony Hill, Timberlake, Gilberts, and Dinro bloodlines. Adrian is a multi-All Breed Best in Show winner owned by Mr. S. and Mrs. L. Arrowsmith, Cooroy, Queensland, Australia.

7. Ch. Sheenwater Joker's Wild and Ch. Sheenwater Joie de Vivre in Autumn 1974. By Ch. Asburn Acres Avant Garde ex Sheenwater Grassfire. Bred and owned by Sally Chandler, Sheenwater Great Danes, Loganville, Georgia. Both Joker and Joy finished easily, and both won their first majors from the puppy class. Joker finished at 13 months, the day after winning Best of Breed at the Great Dane Club of Maryland from the classes.

8. Aust. Ch. Amasa The Enchantress, by Danewindsor Drummond ex Ch. Amasa Honey Amber is currently (mid-1985) the top winning Great Dane bitch in Australia. At only three years of age, has amassed more than 20 In Show awards in All Breed competition. Dane of the Year 1983-84 and 1984-85. Owned by Amasa Great Danes, Sue and Alan Whyte and Denice and Fred Bennett, Schofields, N.S.W., Australia.

1. Am. and Can. Ch. Illiad's Bolonia, owned by Eric and Hillary Sallisbury, handled by Ed Lyons to Best of Opposite Sex under noted Great Dane specialist judge Donald Booxbaum.

2. Ch. Von Raseac's Valor of Tybo, by Ch. Von Raseac's Tybo O'Lorcain ex Ch. Von Raseac's Sierra v Lincoln, is a noted sire of champions. Bred by Brucie Mitchell and Harriet Spertus, he is owned by Linda Epperson Welsh. Photo courtesy of Brucie Mitchell.

3. Ch. Von Raseac's Sierra v Lincoln, by Handsomes Hundchen Jetzt ex Am. and Can. Ch. Von Raseac's Quite A Gal. The dam of champions, she was bred by Brucie Mitchell and Clare Lincoln and is co-owned by Mrs. Mitchell and Harriet Spertus.

4. Ch. Shadam's A Girl Called Charlie winning the Working Group at Crawford County in 1980, Lina Basquette handling for owners M. Arthur and June Shafer, Shadam Great Danes, Fort Wayne, Ind.

5. Ch. Tallbrook's Akamai of Alii was bred by Kathleen Twaits and Jackie White by Ch. Tallbrook's Dapper Dan ex Ch. Tallbrook Farms Taly Overcup. Finished easily in California. Owned by Pat Adameck of Kailua, Hawaii.

6. Famous star of stage and screen and of the dog show rings, Lina Basquette, in an informal pose with the Great Dane she considers to be "The love of my long life," America's #1 winning Dane in breed history, Ch. C. and B's Special-K Gribbon. Lina and K. made a winning team that accounted for 29 Bests in Show (breed record), 103 times first in the Working Group, and 286 times Best of Breed. K owned by J. & F. Campbell.

1

2

3

4

5

6

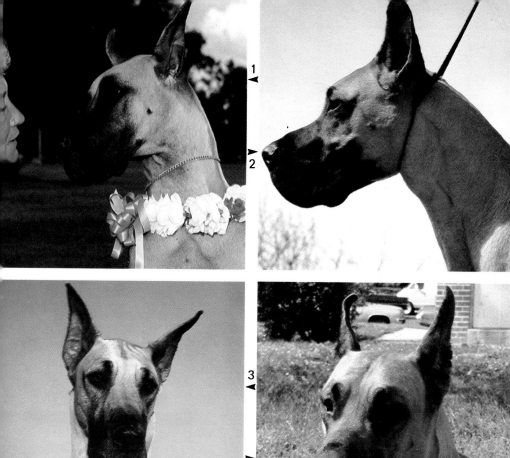

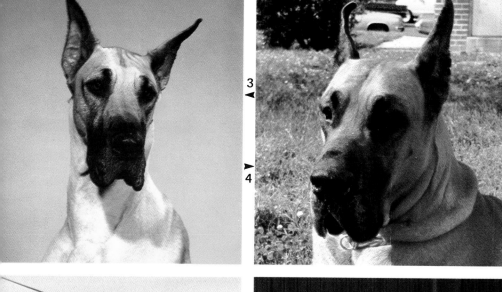

1

2

3

4

5

6

◆Overleaf:

1. "Mutual admiration." Best in Show winning Ch. Brierdane's Indian Amber and his handler, Sylvia Rodwell, exchange admiring glances. Amber, by Ch. Hauerdane's War Bonnet ex Mirando's Match Point Mandy, was bred by Karen M. Lindsay and Beve Hauer. Co-owned by Karen Lindsay with Richard E. and Kathy Varian, Rika Danes, Reseda, Calif.

2. Rochford's Buckingham, fawn dog, at age 11 months, by Ch. Temple Dell's Odin v Branstock ex Ch. Edeldane's Celebration. Bred by Gary and Janet Quick, Kansas City, Missouri. Owners, George and Nancy Burget, Independence, Mo.

3. Headstudy of Can. Ch. Hannadale's Deacon's Treasure, by Best in Show winning Ch. Davos Deacon, C.D., TT, ex Ch. Davos Isle Hannadale. Bred and owned by Bill and Aila Treloar, Mississauga, Ontario, Canada.

4. Addida's Jovan, by Ch. Von Raseac Westwind ex Addidas Chamomile, C.D., born in 1977. Bred by Marci Iler and Deena Bronstein, owned by Marci Iler, Addidas Great Danes, Boonsboro, Md.

5. Ch. Dinro Legend, who appears in the A.K.C. slide show featuring Great Danes, is owned by Dr. Louis Grant Bond and Robert E. Layne, Dinro-Sounda Kennels, Millbury, Mass.

6. "The Winners." Sylvia Rodwell hugs Ch. Brierdane's Indian Amber, whom she has just piloted to a Group 1st at Ventura County, for owners Richard E. and Kathy Varian and Karen M. Lindsay, and co-owner co-breeder (with Beve Hauer) Karen M. Lindsay. A multiple Best in Show and Multiple Specialty winner; ranked in the Top Ten Danes, both breed and Group, 1983, 1984 and 1985.

1. Ch. Hauerdane Bendigo Sutton handled by Joseph Napolitano for owner Shirley Sutton winning Working Group 1st at Jupiter-Tequesta K.C., October 1983.

2. Shadam's Hillary, a typical six-month female from this kennel winning her 6-9 Month Sweepstakes Class at the Heart of Ohio Great Dane Club Specialty, June 1985. Owned by Arthur and June Shafer, Fort Wayne, Ind.

3. Ch. Tomike's Ringer of Dorridane, bred and co-owned by Pat Crawley, Folsom, Louisiana; owned by Tom and Mike Johnson, Shreveport, Louisiana. #2 Great Dane in 1977; #3 in 1978; and #8 in 1979, shown only four times during the latter year. Pictured winning one of his nine Working Group 1sts during a career which included 60 times Best of Breed, a Specialty Best in Show, and 22 Group placements.

4. Ch. Broadway's Handsome Harry taking points towards the title. Handled by Jane Forsyth for Mr. and Mrs. John Morris, Broadway Kennels, West Nyack, N.Y.

5. Ch. Broadway Tabitha Cass Romano, owned and handled by Pat Morris, Broadway Great Danes, West Nyack, New York, taking Best of Breed at Middlesex County 1979.

6. Shadam's Gideon, the exciting new puppy for whom hopes are high at this kennel. He has 12 points, including a major, plus a Best of Breed from the classes. Arthur and June Shafer, Shadam Great Danes, Ft. Wayne, Ind.

7. Ch. Thor Dane's Butterfly, bred and handled by Linda Springthorpe, is owned by Sally Chandler. Winning points towards title at Classic City K.C., May 1982.

8. Stone Valley Dream Weaver, by Ch. Wallach's Gordie Howe, C.D. ex Fanta's Echo of Stone Valley, bred and owned by Darcy Quinlan, is the foundation bitch at Stone Valley Kennels. Chuck and Darcy Quinlan, Kennesaw, Ga.

◀Overleaf:

1. Ch. Don Lu's Maggie Davis, by Ch. Mountdania's Ashley ex Ch. Jessica Davis, was bred by Arlene and Lowell K. Davis and is owned by Don and Mary Lou Carmody. #10 Great Dane in 1980; #2 Great Dane in 1981. Shown only one year as a special before cancer claimed her young life at only three years old. The winner of four all breed Bests in Show and 13 Group 1sts.

2. Winning one of his Bests in Show, Am. and Can. Ch. Dinro Diplomat, owned by the late Mrs. Rosemarie Robert, later by Robert Heal, this dog handled by Ed Lyons was a "star" of the late 1970's, and a very famous Best in Show Dane.

3. Ch. Sheenwater Jump for Joy, by Ch. Reann's French Aristocrat ex Ch. Stone River's Delta Dawn, is a full sister from a repeat breeding of that which produced Gamble On Me and Georgia Pacific. This bitch (18 months old) will be heavily campaigned in the show ring. Owned by C.A. O'Connell and Sally Chandler.

4. Ch. Sheerwater Gamble On Me, by Ch. Reann's French Aristocrat ex Ch. Storm River's Delta Dawn, bred and owned by Sally Chandler and Chris O'Connell, Loganville, Ga.

5. The handsome Ch. Homewood Holly taking points towards her title, handled by Ed Lyons. Owned by Nancy Welsh.

6. The noted Best in Show winner, Ch. Brierdane's Indian Amber, winning a Working Group in 1984. Amber has been Best in Show (all breeds) on four occasions; has 52 Group placements including 20 Group 1sts; and 80 times Best of Breed, including eight Specialty Shows. Youngest Great Dane bitch owned in California to complete a championship, finishing at 12 months with four majors. #1 Great Dane, Best of Breed System, year end 1984. #2 Great Dane, Group System, year end 1984. Owned by Richard E. and Kathy Varian, Rika Danes, Reseda, Calif., and Karen M. Lindsay, the latter with Beve Hauer, breeders of this magnificent bitch. Sylvia Rodwell, handler.

7. Ch. Temple Dell's Fleetwood v Alii, Hawaii's #1 Great Dane since 1981; #1 Dog All Breeds 1983; #2 All Breeds 1984. Sired by Ch. Edeldane's Wildfire ex Ch. Sarah Davis of Temple Dell. Owned by Pat (Valdez) Adameck, Kailua, Hawaii; co-owned by Paula Schmidy. Trained and always handled by Dick Schaefer.

8. Ch. Rika Rumor Has It Merry Meadows, by Ch. Rika's Rendition of Kingswood ex MTC Madame. Bred by Floyd and Nicole McGinnis. Owned by Kathy Jacobs and Kathy Varian. Taking Best of Winners at the Great Dane Club of California Winter Specialty. Handled by Jane Chopson.

Overleaf:▶

1. Ch. Kim's Sabu of Lyndane winning Best of Breed. Jane Forsyth handled for Dr. Anthony DiNardo and Mrs. Sheila DiNardo, West Hartford, Connecticut. A highly successful winner of the early 1970's. Sabu, born in February 1970, was by Ch. Big Kim of Bella Dane ex Susie of Breezydane, and was bred by Lynn Rosenblatt.

2. Ch. Shadam's A Girl Called Charlie, by Ch. Ardlyn's Adam of Marydane ex Devrok's Tender N Trouble, taking Best of Opposite Sex at the Great Dane Club of Pennsylvania in 1980. #1 Producing Bitch, the dam of nine champions, who now at age eight and a half years rules her owners' home in happy good health. Handled by Lina Basquette for owners M. Arthur and June Shafer, Fort Wayne, Ind.

3. Ch. Rika's Rendition of Kingswood, handled by D. Toomey, making a nice win for owners Richard E. and Kathy Varian, Rika Danes, Reseda, Calif. and co-owner Richard N. Gebhart.

4. Ch. Stone Valley's Midnight Dream, by Brays Waldorf V. Lesliedane ex Stone Valley's Dream Weaver, taking Winners at Atlanta in May 1980. Homebred by owner, Darcy Quinlan, Kennesaw, Ga.

5. Ch. Sheridane Apricot Brandy, owned by Kathy Germond, handled by co-breeder Mike Sherman, Sheridane Kennels, Hebron, Conn.

6. Ch. Von Raseac's Tybo O'Lorcain, by Ch. Sunridge's Chief Justice ex Am., Mex., and Can. Ch. Von Raseac's Quintessence, is the sire of 21 champions. Bred by K. and H. Larkin and E. Mitchell, owned by Dennis and Joy De Gruccio, Orange, Calif. Outstanding as a stud dog and in the show ring.

7. Ch. Bing's Impulse of Dorridane taking Best of Opposite Sex at the first Regional National Specialty of the Great Dane Club of America. A homebred owned by Dr. and Mrs. Robert J. Crawley, Folsom, La.

8. Ch. Von Raseac's Vigilante, by Ch. Von Raseac's Tybo O'Lorcain ex Ch. Von Raseac's Sierra v Lincoln. Bred by Gene and Brucie Mitchell, Von Raseac Great Danes, San Luis Rey, Calif. Owned by Brucie Mitchell and Harriet Spertus. One of Brucie Mitchell's favorite Danes!

183

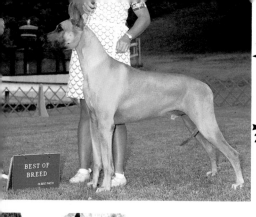

1

2

3

4

5

6

7

8

1

2

3

4

5

6

1. Ch. Rika's Rendition of Kingswood with his handler Doug Toomey. This noted Best in Show winner is owned by Richard E. and Kathy Varian and by Richard N. Gebhart.

2. Sheenwater Jurisprudence, by Ch. Reann's French Aristocrat ex Ch. Stone River's Delta Dawn, was bred by Sally Chandler and C.A. O'Connell, Loganville, Ga., and is owned by Ed and Linda Springthorpe.

3. Ch. Can't Miss of Tamerlane here is winning a Working Group for owner Marvin Dipsinki.

4. This elegant Dane bitch is Ch. Kingswood Phoebe Snow, by Am. and Mex. Ch. Jecamo's Aalborg v Dibo ex Ch. Kingswood Lily Langtry. Bred by Evelyn Porter and Gary Catron, she is owned by Richard E. and Kathy Varian, Rika Danes, Reseda, Calif. Agent/handler, Eric Ringle, PHA. A multiple Best of Breed winner although shown for only three months after completing championship. The dam of Ch. Rika's Plain Jane v Hauer and Ch. Rikas Putn On The Ritz M'Mdws; both in her first litter.

5. Am. and Can. Ch. Sounda's Fortune Hunter winning Best of Breed at Central New York in 1977. Owned by Sounda Great Danes (now Dinro-Sounda), Dr. Louis Grant Bond and Robert E. Layne, Millbury, Mass.

6. Ch. Stockdales Savannah was #1 Great Dane Bitch in the Nation in November 1985. Winner of 29 times Best of Breed, including the Great Dane Club of America Regional National. She has 6 Group 1sts to her credit and ten additional placements, plus 24 times Best of Opposite Sex. Handled by Eric Ringle for owners, Larry and Carleen Radanovich, Stockdale Kennels, Bakersfield, Calif.

1. Ch. Von Raseac's Lyric of Song, an inbred winner from the Northwest, was sired by Ch. Von Raseac's Valor of Tybo ex Von Raseac's Windsong. Co-owned by Larry Bright and Brucie Mitchell; bred by Mrs. Mitchell and Linda Epperson Welsh.

2. Ch. Sheenwater Jump for Joy, bred and owned by Sally Chandler and C.A. O'Connell, Loganville, Ga. By Ch. Reann's French Aristocrat ex Ch. Stone River's Delta Dawn, Joy finished with three majors including a Specialty Best of Opposite Sex from the puppy class and a Best of Breed over specials. Pictured winning under Michele Billings in April 1985.

3. Ch. Lyndane's Special Edition, bred by Joel and Lynn Rosenblatt, owned by Henry Thunhorst. "Eddy" was one of the leading Dane winners during 1981-1982, with multi-Group and Specialty wins to his credit. Here winning the Working Group at Westbury in 1982.

4. Ch. Barbara Ann Davis, by Bit of Cinnamon's Firechief ex Ch. Jessica Davis. A double granddaughter of Ch. Abner Lowell Davis. Pictured in 1979 at age 10 months. Breeder-owner, Lowell Davis of Covina, Calif.

5. Jodi Sherman, well-known junior handler, with Sheridane Elysse v Sharwell, by Ch. Sheridane Prince Valiant ex Sheridane Amber of Antiquity. Jodi is a very successful young lady in Junior Showmanship Competition, and is pictured winning first at Ladies Dog Club, judge Mrs. Lynette Pazzino.

6. Ch. Tallbrook's Bit O'Honey, by Ch. Abner Lowell Davis ex Ch. Brenda Von Overcup, bred by Tallbrook Great Danes, Kathleen Twaits and Jacqueline White. Owned by Susan McCarthy and Herb Twaits, Los Angeles, Calif. A Group and Specialty winner and the dam of six champions.

7. Ch. Sheridane Easy Money, owned by Hilda Ballero, bred and handled by Mike Sherman, at the Hatboro Dog Club in 1984. One of the handsome Danes bred at Sheridane Kennels.

8. Ch. Sheenwater Georgia Pacific, by Ch. Reann's French Aristocrat ex Ch. Stone River's Delta Dawn, owned by C.A. O'Connell and Sally Chandler, Sheenwater Kennels. Litter brother to Ch. Sheenwater Gamble On Me. Owned by C.A. O'Connell and Sally Chandler.

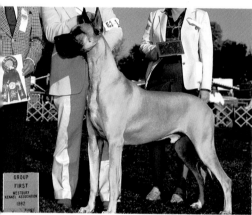

1
2

3
4

5
6

7
8

◀Overleaf:

1. Ch. Rochford's Essex in 1984. By Ch. Temple Dell's Odin v Branstock ex Ch. Edeldane's Celebration. Owned by Jerry and Valerie Parsons, De Soto, Kans. Bred by Janet Quick, Rochford Great Danes.

2. Thor Dane's Class Action, handsome young bitch on way to the title, taking Best of Winners and Best of Opposite Sex at Tuscaloosa K.C. in 1984. Linda Springthorpe handling, co-breeder-owner with husband, Ed Springthorpe, Thor Dane Kennels, Ball Ground, Ga.

3. Am. and Can. Ch. O'Lorcain's Too Much Von Raseac by Ch. Sunridge's Chief Justice ex Ch. Von Raseac's Quintessence, a Group winner and dam of five champions, pictured at seven years of age. Bred by Harriet Larkin and Brucie Mitchell; owned by Steven and Linda Talkington.

4. Ch. C. and B's Special-K winning one of her many Groups before the age of two years. Handler, as always, Lina Basquette. K owned by J. and F. Campbell and J. and M. Benjamin.

5. Can. Ch. Merry Meadows Carmina, by Ch. Jecamo's Johnny Walker ex Merry Meadows Melissa. Breeders/owners/handlers, Kathy Jacobs and Kathy Varian, Reseda, Calif. Kathy Jacobs owner-handled to Best of Opposite Sex.

6. Ch. Dinro Detente of Sylvan, owned by Ed Lyons, Ron and Mary Patrucci, taking Best of Breed. Mr. Lyons handled, at Central Maine K.C. in 1979.

7. At home in England! Lincoln's Winstead Von Raseac, by Am. Ch. Von Raseac's Tybo O'Lorcain ex Am. and Can. Ch. Von Raseac's Quite A Gal was bred by Brucie Mitchell and Clare Lincoln and sold to Sheila Edmunds in England, where he became one of the top all-time producers of Great Dane champions in the United Kingdom; thus he as been very influential on the breed there.

8. Ch. Sarah Davis of Temple Dell, by Ch. Sunridge's Chief Justice ex Ch. Abigail Davis of Tallbrook. Breeders, Arlene and Lowell K. Davis; owners, Stephen and Betty Temple. The dam of four champions including two Best in Show winners. Photographed in 1976.

Overleaf:➧

1. Ch. Sheenwater Heat Wave, by Ch. Mr. Pacific of Marydane ex Sheenwater Grassfire, was the Chandlers' first American champion. Please note the elegant head quality of this exquisite bitch. Handled by Stanley Flowers.

2. Ch. Broadway Sunshine, owned by Pat Morris, taking points under Bob Forsyth. Vic Capone handled.

3. Ch. Broadway Annie Oakley in 1973, handled by Bob Forsyth for John and Patricia Morris, West Nyack, N.Y. This famous bitch sired by Ch. Big Kim of Bella Dane ex Broadway Princess Pat was born in April 1970 and had an enviable record in the show ring.

4. Ch. Stone River's Delta Dawn, owned by C.G. O'Connell and Sally Chandler, handled by Victor Capone to Best of Breed, Delaware Water Gap 1982, under Robert S. Forsyth.

5. Ch. Aomi of Marydane, handled by Jane Forsyth to points towards her title for Mr. and Mrs. Gerard Johnston, Wilton, Conn. One of many outstanding champions owned by the famed Marydane Kennels.

6. Ch. Sheenwater Joie de Vivre, by Ch. Ashbun Acres Avant Garde ex Sheenwater Grassfire. Bred and owned by Sally Chandler, Sheenwater Kennels, Logansville, Ga.

7. Ch. Sheenwater Georgia Pacific, by Ch. Reann's French Aristocrat ex Ch. Stone River's Delta Dawn, taking points towards title at Vacationland Dog Club in 1984. Bred and owned by Sally Chandler and C.A. O'Connell, Loganville, Ga.

8. Rochford's Essex at age 10 months. By Ch. Temple Dell's Odin v Branstock ex Ch. Edeldane's Celebration. Owners, Jerry and Valerie Parsons. Bred by Rochford Great Danes, Kansas City, Mo.

1

2

3

4

5

6

7

8

Chapter 8

Talk about Danes and Comments on the Breed
by Lina Basquette

AUTHOR'S NOTE: Words could not possibly express our pleasure at receiving the following from the incomparable Lina Basquette which she so kindly got together for this book. As a breeder-exhibitor-professional handler of several decades' experience in the Dane world, and as a prospective judge, Lina is one of the most knowledgeable persons to be found anywhere in our Fancy. The Danes she talks about are world famous; and her comments on them should give the newer fanciers, who may not be personally familiar with them, an insight into how they achieved greatness and contributed to the breed. It is hard to believe that so glamourous, vibrant, and energetic a lady is now 78½ years of age at time of writing. Her appearance and attitude deny it, even though her words do not! To see her literally fly around the ring with Special K these past few years would make many a 25-year-old green with envy! I turn these next few pages over to Lina with full confidence that her remarks will add tremendously to this book's value.

A.K.N.

To be a Great Dane fancier, one must be prepared to give one's whole life and *love* to the breed. These are most demanding dogs, and until one becomes a privileged owner of a Great Dane (or a dozen or more) one cannot conceive of how seductively they take over one's entire existence.

Throughout the history of the breed, although it is a popular one in comparison to many others, there have been few Danes who have attained the ultimate Best in Show heights, and, to be blatantly truthful, this has been mainly the fault of those who have failed to go beyond *head* and *size* in developing their dogs. Movement, and overall soundness, which in other breeds (especially those of the Working Group) have proven that these attributes are those which make an outstanding show dog.

For more than three decades, as a breeder and handler, I have tried to "educate" my colleagues that structure and anatomical soundness are of primary importance. Yes, there must be breed type. But unfortunately "type" has become ambivaleñt, despite a breed Standard that is excessively written and actually could be cut in half and still give prospective breeders and judges a clear insight as to the *ideal* Great Dane.

There is more speculation than fact as to how Great Danes were developed through the centuries. We do know that in Germany (Prussia) they were maintained as guard, fighting, and hunting dogs, and probably were originally developed from Mastiffs, Greyhounds, and other Teutonic breeds. Today, according to the A.K.C. approved standard, we do not want them to resemble either a Mastiff or a Greyhound, although too often we see them judged as though this were not the case. Neither the Mastiff nor the Greyhound resemblance is correct. There must be elegance and nobility with substance; size with agility; tremendous muscle tone to support strong bone and height.

Until Harlequins are judged on a separate standard, they, too, must conform to the all over *type* of other colors. This applies to blacks and blues as well. And the latter, by the way, is seldom seen in the true blue color.

The male "stand-outs" in this breed to this old-timer have been:

GREGORY OF KENT, red golden brindle. A superb sire of dozens of worthwhile champions. Gregory, lovingly known as Jason, survived a tragic accident at seven months of age during

Ch. C. and B's Special-K Gribbin winning one of her 29 Bests in Show. Lina Basquette handling for J. and F. Campbell and J. and M. Benjamin.

which his leg was completely crushed, the result of being hit by a truck. Several judges, along with me, seeing this youngster with, at the time, the greatest head, neck, eyes, expression, color, and over-all conformation at seven months, felt that despite the crippled leg, for the advancement of the breed, which is the primary goal in all purebred dog activities, Jason must be saved and somehow be "put back together," if for no other reason than breeding purposes.

I took on the challenge, and practically mortgaged Honey Hollow in order for the incredible orthopedic miracles which were performed at the University of Pennsylvania Veterinary Hospital to take place. The determined genius of Dr. Jenny, formerly of Austria, who loved this dog almost as much as I did, in about a year accomplished what was indeed a miracle.

Gregory went on to win 12 points (three majors) towards his championship, also winning Best of Breed over contemporary specials, but due to a small calcium deposit above his pastern, he was taken out of competition. It was really a crime against the breed, although his genetic qualities went on to produce, subsequently, some of the *greatest* that have ever been seen in Great Danes. In my humble opinion, Gregory of Kent had just about everything. The most magnificent red-golden brindle coloring, terrific temperament, about 36 inches tall, excellent conformation fore and aft. A *square* dog, as Danes should be, level topline, and he could move out with the best of the Working dogs. Plus a head that was perfectly balanced with proper planes, clean, and a true noble expression enhanced by perfectly shaped dark eyes. All in all, a fancier's dream of a male Great Dane.

Gregory was bred by Marian Rankin of Knoxville, Tennessee. His sire, Champion Duyster's Lord Jim. His dam, Champion Diana of Kent, brindle and fawn respectively.

CHAMPION DION OF KENT, golden fawn, also bred by Marian Rankin, in the early 1950's was one of the rare Great Danes of that era to win Best in Show. Also, as a professional handler, my own first Best in Show, at Union County under Laura Delano (Franklin Delano Roosevelt's cousin) who remarked afterwards that this was the first of the breed to whom she had ever awarded a Best in Show and the first she had seen who could

196

move without falling apart. Dion also won the breed at Westminster and Morris and Essex back when the Dane entries were exceptionally large.

CHAMPION HONEY HOLLOW STORMI RUDIO, "orange" golden fawn, he was MY "Honey Hollow" homebred. His story is in the Honey Hollow kennel resume section of this book. Never shown more than 200 miles from home, Stormi, owned by Kay and Bill Clarke of Medford Lakes, New Jersey, was breeder-handled by me to eight Bests in Show and many other prestigious wins, including first in the Working Group at Westminster under John Cross in 1959. In the history of Great Danes, only four of them to date have won this award at Westminster, two of which it was "yours truly's" pleasure to handle.

CHAMPION DANE EDEN'S SAMSON: biscuit fawn and one of the greatest Great Danes to move like a Working dog should. Bred by Jack and Lillian McEdward and their son Blake Edwards (now the famous director of big hit movies and the husband of Julie Andrews) of Hollywood, California. Samson was from the well-known legendary litter that produced seven champions, including Samson, Delilah, etc. After achieving this outstanding accomplishment, the McEdwards never bred Danes again and got out of the breed except for their house pets and their activity in the Southern California Specialty clubs. Sire of this fabulous litter was Champion Faecarl's Brendo; the dam Champion Duchess of Zel-Thor. Samson was shipped to me from California, not only to be shown but to improve conformation and "running gear" of the Eastern bloodlines. Many fanciers failed to see "the forest for the trees" and missed the opportunity offered by the McEdwards. "Yours truly," practically a novice at the time, used Samson with almost every brood bitch at Honey Hollow, and for many years reaped the harvest of having done so. Authoritative judges of that period (1952) felt that Samson and his bloodlines were desperately needed, for, although many of the East Coast Danes were statuesque and elegant, sadly they were slung together with "piano wire" and could not move their way out of a paper bag. Mainly through Champion Dane Eden's Samson, Honey Hollow went zooming to the top, and I shall be forever grateful to the McEdwards.

CHAMPION BIG KIM OF BELLA DANE: golden fawn, certainly one of the greatest sires in the breed, stamping his exceptionally ideal type and over-all eye-filling elegance—a sound and substantial dog with an expression of true regal nobility that is rarely seen these days. His background included the immortal Gregory of Kent, Champion Honey Hollow Great Dion, Champion Rori of Noblebrook, and Champion Nandane's Tamanaco with his dam's background of the very fine bloodlines collected by Connie Bosold. Known as a judge of many groups, Mrs. Bosold is a conscientious and gifted breeder of Sporting and Working dogs.

Big Kim was bred by Kay Stebnitz of Milwaukee, Wisconsin, owned by her and Mrs. Mabel Sheppard (now Mrs. Gunville), a most authoritative judge of several groups.

Big Kim won countless Bests of Breed and Specialties, plus first in the Working Group on 90 occasions and 24 times Best in Show. Also he is the only Great Dane in history to have won the Quaker Oats Award for the Working Group.

Through the prodding of Alva Rosenberg, Peter Knoop, Percy Roberts, and other "greats" of the past, Big Kim was turned over to yours truly and I not only had the honor of presenting this magnificent dog in the show rings, but was permitted to have him as my superior stud dog at Honey Hollow. Big Kim's record of 24 Bests in Show was surpassed only, in males, by his own son, Champion Heidere-Kolyer Kimbayh that I piloted to 28 Bests in Show.

It should be mentioned here that only *four* Great Danes in the annals of the breed have ever had more than 24 Bests in Show. Champion Reggen's Madas-L of Marydane, 25 Bests in Show, was bred by Genevieve Parks and owned by Gerard and Mary Johnston. Big Kim had 24, Kimbayh 28; and the top winning Great Dane of all time, the bitch Champion C. and B.'s Special-K Gribben had 29.

CHAMPION LESLIE'S THUMPER V. BARNHARDT: orange fawn, a superb showman who was fun to handle. He literally "chewed up the scenery" in Groups and Best in Show and hammed his way to 18 Best in Show awards.

CHAMPION MR. PACIFIC OF MARYDANE: fawn male owned and bred by Mary and Gerard Johnston. An elegant dog with a classic head, a beautiful dog who contributed much to the breed.

CHAMPION HEIDERE-KOLYER KIMBAYH: golden fawn, until his great-granddaughter, Champion Special-K surpassed him, was the Top Winning Great Dane (male or female) in breed history. Bred by Erna Heidere and Kitty Kolyer and owned by Dr. James and Elizabeth Gribbin, this lovely dog brought great respect to the breed.

CHAMPION ABNER LOWELL DAVIS: fawn male owned and bred by Arlene and Lowell Davis, mainly pursued his highly successful winning career on the West Coast, and in the Southwest. Was beautifully handled by Jack Dexter (now a renowned judge). Abner was a popular stud, did much to enhance the breeding programs of many fanciers throughout the country.

CHAMPION HONEY HOLLOW GREAT DONNER: solid black from the Great Dane Club of America outlawed mixed color breeding. To the present day, 1985, he remains the top winning *black* Great Dane of all time, achieved with a relatively limited career. Four Bests in Show, 45 Group 1sts, 90 times Best of Breed. Owned by Dr. and Mrs. James Childress of Wexford, Pennsylvania.

CHAMPION HONEY HOLLOW RAMESES: black, owned by J. Council Parker. In any color there has seldom been a more *classic* head. He eventually was sold to Argentina, where Rameses lived in princely luxury. Unfortunately at the same time he was lost here to what could have been the betterment of the breed. A dog I shall never forget for sheer beauty and glorious temperament.

CHAMPION HONEY HOLLOW GREAT DION: golden fawn who probably did more for the breed as a stud with few litters than any other of his time. Owned by Virginia and Garnett Matthews of Kirkwood, Missouri, Dion always lived at Honey Hollow. He completed his championship in record time, but Dion hated dog shows and the show ring so was never campaigned as a special.

I am omitting Harlequins, beyond commenting that Antonia Pratt of Meistersinger Kennels, Louisville, Kentucky, has imported many and her homebreds have made Harlequin history.

Now—the bitches.

CHAMPION SENTA: I shall never forget her. She was the first Great Dane whom I ever saw take a Best in Show, when I had been in the breed less than a year. Senta was my inspiration. Believe she was bred by William Gilbert, and always shown by him. Completely devoid of a black mask, yet had a divine head and was one of the very few Great Danes of her time that could *move*. In those days there were few around who recognized her potential. In the 1940's and 1950's, Great Dane-ites were satisfied if their dogs had size, heads, and could be molded into shape.

CHAMPION SHALOTT'S LADY ALICIA: fawn bitch, sister of Champion Shalott's Sir Allistair. Alicia won 25 Bests of Breed, firsts in ten Working Groups, and three Bests in Show, after which her owners pulled her from competition. She was one of the best Danes I have ever handled. It should be noted that she gave birth to 16 puppies in *one* litter and raised them all!

CHAMPION HEATHER OF BRAESIFE: one of the finest bitches ever bred, whose main fault was "lack of attitude towards the show ring." However, she did win eight Bests of Show when breed and Group competition was mighty tough.

CHAMPION A GIRL NAMED CHARLIE: was probably one of the greatest brood matrons in the breed, and a most lovable companion. She was owned, bred, and loved by June and Arthur Shafer of Shadam Kennels in Fort Wayne, Indiana.

There have been several bitches during the 1970's and 1980's who have been outstanding, especially those on the West Coast.

CHAMPION C. AND B's SPECIAL-K GRIBBON: for fear of "running off at the mouth" I almost hesitate to speak of this magnificent bitch. May I say that I doubt that I would be hale and hearty at my present age had it not been for this "wonder girl" having come into my life during the Spring of 1981, at six months of age. I knew she was a *star* then, and in four years she never let me down, attaining Top Winning Great Dane in History in so many categories: breeds, Groups, Bests in Show! She won the breed three times at Westminster, including first in the 1983 Working Group. She won her first major at age six and a half months, completing her championship at ten months, taking her first Best in Show at 13 months.

Owned and dearly loved by Dr. and Mrs. Campbell and J. and M. Benjamin of Darnestown, Maryland, she is also the "love of

The immortal Gregory of Kent, son of Ch. Lord Jim, was sire and grandsire of many Honey Hollow champions, the dog Lina Basquette has described as having, in her opinion, "just about everything." Study the photo well as you read her comments on him!

my long life." To me, K is the God-given reward for all my years of devotion, hard work, and investment in the breed. A dream to handle, to me she represents the epitome of what a Great Dane bitch should be. She was bred by Elaine Sauerman of York, Pennsylvania. Sired by Champion Von Raseac's West Wind ex Deer Run's Almost Heaven. She is one of those examples truly heaven sent and sprinkled with stardust. If she can only produce her superb type, soundness, and showmanship in her puppies that are due in October 1985 bred to the outstanding fawn male from San Diego, Champion Aquino's Little Dooz Coupe, S.D.H.!

Due to time and space there have been many dogs and bitches— breeders, owners, devoted fanciers, that have been omitted. Today the breed is in better shape than it has been for a long time. There are several youngsters coming along that show enormous potential. The most important thing is, people must *care* for them—keep them in top condition, not let them become "show-worn," calloused, or burnt-out. It is not easy, and requires an enormous amount of time, energy and common sense to maintain this breed properly. In more than three decades, I have found out that there are no short cuts.

201

Am. and Can. Ch. Aquehonga All Spice, by Champuss von Wiesengrund Unterhorr ex Pepper V, was bred by Ben Shalom and owned by Anthony Hodges, noted multiple breed judge, and is pictured with his daughter Andrea Jane Hodges.

Chapter 9

The Harlequin Great Dane

As a tremendous admirer of the Harlequin Great Dane, one of the first things I did when planning for this book was to consider how best to present the subject, and these magnificent dogs, through its pages in hopes of spreading further appreciation and admiration of this coloring among new owners and new fanciers of Great Danes.

How to go about it? When one sees as frequently as we do here in the East a fancier who is breeding and showing and winning spectacularly weekend after weekend with Harlequins in strongest Eastern competition, one figures her to be someone thoroughly familiar with and knowledgeable about all phases of the Harlequin, thus the most logical person with whom to discuss them for our readers. This is how I came to approach Laura Kiaulenas for some of her thoughts about the Harlequins, which she has very graciously shared with us.

Laura feels strongly that the Harlequin is an original wild dog color because it cannot be created from any of the other coat colors and is dominant to all of them. Great Danes are the only domesticated dogs carrying these ancient genes. Should Harlequins disappear, then the color would be forever lost.

Australia Day International — history made! Not only was the Challenge Certificate line-up all of Harlequin bitches, but with the same kennel prefix! *From left to right:*, Ch. Hildy-dane Janushka (Best Open), Aust. Ch. Hildydane Poppet (Best Intermediate), Aust. Ch. Hildydane Quelle, C.D. (Best Junior); and Hildydane Tiffany (Best Puppy). The judge was John Patterson from the U.S.A. The Hildydane Great Danes owned by Hildegarde Mooney, Box Hill, N.S.W., Australia.

Can. Ch. Alexis McDavis of Rika and Daneridge's Knickknack of Kimo at eight weeks of age. Owned by Richard E. and Kathy Varian, Rika Great Danes, Reseda, Calif.

It was an interesting experience for Laura, visiting Crete when traveling with her Mother some years back, to see a most glorious Assyrian mural depicting a hunt with three large very Dane-like hounds chasing a deer, particularly so since the dogs were very attractively spotted with torn patches on white base coats. One dog had red-brown patches; another, blue patches; and the third was spotted in black patches. This mural had originated several thousand years B.C., during the time of the Pharoahs in Egypt.

A Harlequin is assumed to be a white dog with black spotting, at least in the minds of many people. To one well versed in Harlequin genetics, however, it is more sensible to regard the Harlequin color as a white overcoat on which irregular cutouts or holes have been superimposed on the background color as irregular spots or patches. The only currently accepted base color for a Harlequin is black, although definitely any of the other Dane colors could be present, and were until about a century ago. The reason for this is that the Harlequin white will often overlay or restrict any of the others, to the extent that it frequently is referred to as a "restrictor gene."

Laura points out that there are four basic colors in Harlequin litters, which on the average occur in fairly equal proportions. The percentage of Harlequin is the same whether one breeds Harlequin to Harlequin; Harlequin to merle; or Harlequin to black. Merle to merle; merle to black; and black to black will *never* produce Harlequins. Certain whites bred to blacks *may* produce Harlequins; these whites are not always pure white, but may have some spots or patches of merle or black, Laura points out.

To pause a moment and consider these whites, there is an unfortunate chance of white puppies also being entirely or partially deaf or blind. Happily this weakness cannot and does not appear in the other colors which are components of the Harlequin.

It is a mistaken tendency among some to consider color genes to be something mixed like paints on an artist's palette, which dilute when blended together. This is not the case at all; rather, it is like mixing a handful of marbles, rolling them around together, thus creating a mixture of colors, one of which in no way dilutes the others, but which instead creates a mixture that in no way dilutes or alters the depth of color of any individual marble. That is how it works with regard to the Harlequin color components in

Famous Great Dane of the past. Int. Ch. Dinro's Lucky Charm, noted Harlequin owned by Rosemarie Robert, Dinro Danes, Carmel, N.Y. Lucky Charm was sired by Ch. Umpachne Sir Van v Edelherz, C.D. (by Ch. I.W. Harper von der Stadt Hamburg) ex Dinro's Unlimited Charm (Ch. Herold v St. Magn. Obertraubling ex Ch. Brandy's Charm of Lidgerwood). Photo courtesy of Ed Lyons.

This litter of Harlequins by BMW Ouzo ex BMW Vanilla, is from BMW Kennels, Laura Kiaulenas, Farmingville, N.Y. *Left to right:* the puppies became BMW Starlight, Ch. BMW Prima Donna, BMW Celebration, Can. Ch. BMW Caprice, BMW Vito, BMW Danskin, and Ch. BMW Fantasia. This shows the random Harlequin color variations in a litter.

breeding Harlequin Danes. Proper use of these genes in a breeding program definitely does *not* lead to deterioration of the quality of the Harlequin color. On the contrary, color variants bred from well-marked Harlequins carry the genes to produce other well-marked Harlequins. Laura comments that breeders have bred all the Harlequin components successfully without any increase or decrease in the percent of Harlequin puppies produced, adding that one hundred years of culling has made absolutely no difference.

Two of the principal difficulties in breeding Harlequins, we understand, are the facts that only a small minority of puppies inherit the correct combination of genes that produce the Harlequin markings; and the irregularities that can occur in these markings brought about by the lack of control over the placement of the pattern created by the white restrictor gene on the basic color. Laura calls attention to the phenomena of blue eyes and pink noses, acknowledged by the Standard as "permissable but not desirable," calling these "simple specific expressions of haphazard pigment distribution." The nose being hairless is colored by either black or pink skin or both. The eyes may both be blue or brown or one may be blue and the other brown or both colors may be present in a single eye. This is due to the fact that basically the eyes are not genetic blue or the noses genetic pink, but rather they are, in Harlequins, *spotted* eyes and *spotted* noses. To control pigment in these anatomical areas in an individual dog is no more possible than to control the exact placement of a given marking or spot on the other areas of the dog. Every effort is made to encourage the presence of strong facial markings in hopes of getting more brown eyes and black noses, but even so, the element of unpredictability remains.

Laura refers to the "Boston pattern," which we frequently hear mentioned, which, as she points out and with which we agree, is actually a misnomer. The word was adopted in connection with Harlequin Great Danes for the obvious reason that it describes a similarity in coat pattern between certain Danes and the Boston Terrier. Yet no such expression is used anywhere else in American Kennel Club terminology nor in any breed standard to depict coat color. This type of marking is familiar and common to many breeds, the usual wording for it being "black and white," "black with white markings," "parti-colored," or "piebald." By using the word "Boston," Great Dane fanciers may be creating a problem for the future, particularly where American Kennel Club acceptance of the description is concerned.

Continuing on the subject of this color pattern, Laura comments that it can be chosen to be more rather than less extensive, which limits the area of distribution of black pigment. Breeders can select for cleanness of color, i.e., a truly *white* white, free of ticking; and sharply defined black with as few gray hairs as possible. Thus, in summation, it is possible to exert control over quality of color even though not over the quantity. The difficulties of breeding Harlequins can be very tedious when one stops to consider that probably only a tenth of Harlequin puppies born ever make it to the show ring in classic markings; and that out of every litter, no matter what its size, breeders are fortunate if they find themselves with a puppy or two of the desired Harlequin color distribution.

Laura comments that, when one considers the small percentage of show Harlequin puppies, every effort must be made to breed so that these dogs will be of true excellence in all respects. In other words, they cannot be common animals with nothing distinguished but their markings; they must be outstandingly high quality, sound, well structured, of good temperament, and strong in breed type if they are to fulfill the breeder's hopes. Thus overall quality is of greater than average importance in these litters, for without them in addition to the desired coloring, a Harlequin will find it rough going in the show ring. To achieve this consistency in quality, a broad breeding program is essential, where *all* of the basic qualities are highly valued. In breeding stock, the most attractively marked is not always the best choice; and there are cases when the animal of closest overall adherence to the standard should take preference.

To this Laura adds the observation, "Breeding Harlequins is rather like running a race with a handicap. No matter how good the overall quality of the litter may be, there will only be one or two puppies to choose from for the show ring."

Another well-known breeder of Harlequins, Fran W. Schwartz, has this to say about breeding them. "For the average person,

208

color genetics can be confusing and difficult. To put it very simply: Fawn bred to Fawn will produce only Fawn; Fawn bred to Brindle can produce both Fawn and Brindle; Brindle bred to Brindle can produce both Fawn and Brindle if there is fawn in the background; Blacks with Blue in the background can produce both Blue and Black; breeders of Black Great Danes do not as a rule breed to blacks out of Harlequin breeding because of the white factor.

"Harlequin breeding follows no set genetic pattern. Some breeders feel that the true color is Merle (gray base with black patches). Harlequin bred to Harlequin can produce White, Albino, Merle, Black, Mis-marked (white base coat with gray patches), or the much sought Harlequin. Most breeders of Harlequins will introduce black out of Harlequin into their breeding program at some time, feeling that the amount of black can diminish with only straight Harlequin to Harlequin breeding for too long a time. Harlequin breeding is not for the faint of heart, since there can be litters with not even a single puppy with acceptable Harlequin markings.

"Please bear in mind that Harlequins with a few patches, or all pink noses are not what is considered acceptable for the show ring. Fawns too light in color, or of a muddy color are not desirable. Brindles with insufficient markings, or color which prompt one to wonder if it may not be a Fawn with black stripes or a Black with fawn stripes are also incorrect."

Mrs. Schwartz advises all who are contemplating becoming breeders of Great Danes to read and follow the Breeders Code of Ethics of the Great Dane Club of America. The purpose of this Code of Ethics is to point out that there is a proper, and an improper, way of breeding Great Danes from the point of view of color; at the same time attempting to assure that these colors would be properly bred. A great deal of emphasis is accorded color in the Standard of the Great Dane Club of America which appears in this book, as does the Code of Ethics. Some latitude is allowed in shades of color; but one should read carefully the undesirable factors in each color.

Our thanks to Laura Kiaulenas and to Fran W. Schwartz for sharing their views with us on the very important color issue which exists in Great Danes.

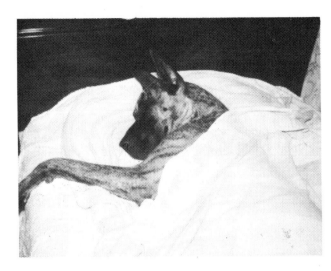

Ch. Honey Hollow Wickm's Whim, two-year-old brindle bitch, loves nothing more than to relax in bed and under the covers. Mrs. Mathews, owner. Photo courtesy of Lina Basquette.

Ch. Castile's Carousel with family. Shown are the DiNardo youngsters, Toni Leigh, Cheri and Gina, with their mother, Mrs. Sheila DiNardo, and the Best in Show winning Dane, Carousel. Dr. and Mrs. Anthony DiNardo, West Hartford, Conn.

Chapter 10

The Great Dane as a Family Dog

Asking the man who owns one has always been my theory about learning the truth of what a breed is like to live with; and so I have followed that pattern with the Danes and to say the least, am overwhelmed by the enthusiasm with which the question is answered by those who have experienced it.

Without qualification, Dane owners agree that Danes make ideal house dogs; they are clean and pleasant to have around; they are quiet and not destructive; and that boils down to their being an utter delight. Their actions give credence to their words in this regard, for I have noted sometimes almost with surprise how very many show dogs in this breed live as house pets; how many accompany their owners practically everywhere; and how they thrive best of all in a home atmosphere. Most of our prominent Dane breeders tell us that they limit themselves to the number of dogs they can keep in the house, (somewhere in the area of four or five), then make arrangements for co-ownership under similar circumstances for any others they may own an interest in rather than relegate dogs of this breed to kennels. Danes crave human companionship and are happiest when they can spend all 24 hours of every day with the people they love. They are quiet dogs, never

211

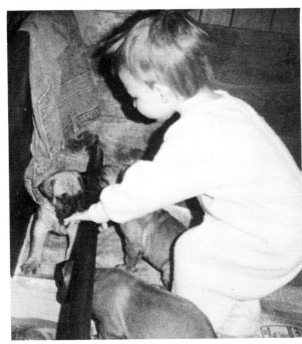

A happy family group as Marci Iler's baby enjoys a bit of socialization with some of the Great Dane puppies at Addidas Kennels owned by her parents.

Ch. Rika's Rendition of Kingswood, now a Best in Show winner, at age seven weeks. Owned by Richard Gebhart. Inset, D. Toomey, also as a youngster.

"yappy" nor given to pointless barking, thus do not cause a noise disturbance. They are calm, relaxed dogs, not hyper-active, constantly chewing, or "destructive." When nothing is going on, they think it fine to stretch out and take a nap. Their only destructiveness actually is caused by their size. A wagging Great Dane tail can take its toll of bric-a-brac, as can a Dane-sized dog making his way around a room. Dane owners soon learn to cope with this, and keep their inanimate treasures out of tail's reach.

The presence of a Great Dane or two certainly can add to the safety of your home or property, many people being scared stiff of a dog that big without realizing that this breed is a gentle one. After all, outsiders do not need to know that your Dane adores the children, considers himself a lap dog where sofas and beds are concerned, and takes an entirely friendly view of the world. He is a perfect combination of a reliable family member with a dog who, to the uninitiated, looks forbidding.

It is really unfair to keep a Great Dane sized dog confined to an apartment, although I know that some can adjust under proper circumstances—the latter, in this case, meaning your willingness to provide adequate exercise for your pet with long walks on a steady basis regardless of the weather. A dog cannot be well if not permitted adequate exercise, and in the case of such a large dog, "adequate" means considerable. A Dane should have a fenced yard of sufficient size to permit him to move about freely, in addition to a supervised walk with you at least once daily.

If you have toddlers in your family, or older people not in the best of health, remember that a Dane is big and heavy and that there is a chance of danger to the person just from his sheer weight. Someone unsteady on their feet, or with other health or age problems, should not be subjected to any big dog unless accustomed to that way of life. If you have always had them around, you know how to manage; but the introduction of one to somebody who is used only to Toy breeds or dogs of similar size may not work out.

Be aware that Danes are big eaters and need ample, nourishing food to keep in good health. Thus they are a fairly expensive breed to maintain. But so very well worth it!

Ch. Grenada's Bit O'Tallbrook, owned by Kioko Wylie and Herb Twaits. This handsome son of Tallbrook's Darby Dan ex Ch. Tallbrook's Bit O'Honey is the sire of 12 champions. Tallbrook Kennels are at Los Angeles, Calif.

Chapter 11

The Purchase of Your Great Dane

Careful consideration should be given to what breed of dog you wish to own prior to your purchase of one. If several breeds are attractive to you, and you are undecided as to which you prefer, learn all you can about the characteristics of each before making your decision. As you do so, you are thus preparing yourself to make an intelligent choice; and this is very important when buying a dog who will be, with reasonable luck, a member of your household for at least a dozen years or more. Obviously since you are reading this book, you have decided on the breed—so now all that remains is to make a good choice.

It is never wise to just rush out and buy the first cute puppy who catches your eye. Whether you wish a dog to show, one with whom to compete in obedience, or one as a family dog purely for his (or her) companionship, the more time and thought you invest as you plan the purchase, the more likely you are to meet with complete satisfaction. The background and early care behind your pet will reflect in the dog's future health and temperament. Even if you are planning the purchase purely as a pet, with no thoughts of showing or breeding in the dog's or puppy's future, it is essential that if the dog is to enjoy a trouble-free future you assure yourself of a healthy, properly raised puppy or adult from sturdy, well-bred stock.

Throughout the pages of this book you will find the names and locations of many well-known and well-established kennels in various areas. Another source of information is the American Kennel Club (51 Madison Avenue, New York, New York 10010) from whom you can obtain a list of recognized breeders in the vicinity of your home. If you plan to have your dog campaigned by a professional handler, by all means let the handler help you locate and select a good dog. Through their numerous clients, handlers have access to a variety of interesting show prospects; and the usual arrangement is that the handler re-sells the dog to you for what his cost has been, with the agreement that the dog be campaigned for you by him throughout the dog's career. It is most strongly recommended that prospective purchasers follow these suggestions, as you thus will be better able to locate and select a satisfactory puppy or dog.

Your first step in searching for your puppy is to make appointments at kennels specializing in your breed, where you can visit and inspect the dogs, both those available for sale and the kennel's basic breeding stock. You are looking for an active, sturdy puppy with bright eyes and intelligent expression and who is friendly and alert; avoid puppies who are hyperactive, dull, or listless. The coat should be clean and thick, with no sign of parasites. The premises on which he was raised should look (and smell) clean and be tidy, making it obvious that the puppies and their surroundings are in capable hands. Should the kennels featuring the breed you intend owning be sparse in your area or not have what you consider attractive, do not hesitate to contact others at a distance and purchase from them if they seem better able to supply a puppy or dog who will please you *so long as it is a recognized breeding kennel of that breed.* Shipping dogs is a regular practice nowadays, with comparatively few problems when one considers the number of dogs shipped each year. A reputable, well-known breeder wants the customer to be satisfied; thus he will represent the puppy fairly. Should you not be pleased with the puppy upon arrival, a breeder such as described will almost certainly permit its return. A conscientious breeder takes real interest and concern in the welfare of the dogs he or she causes to be brought into the world.

216

Ch. Cinderella of Tamerlane, owned by Dr. and Mrs. Taylor, an outstanding puppy pictured here at the Lakeshore Great Dane Club Specialty.

Ch. Murphy's Mr. Dubh winning at Suffolk County K.C. in 1970. Robert Forsyth handling for owner, Robert T. Murphy, Clinton Corners, N.Y.

"Planning for the future." Beautiful eight-week male and female puppies owned by Rochford Kennels, Janet Quick, Kansas City, Mo.

Ch. Tiara Terry's Shanee of Caesar, handled by Jane Forsyth for owner Terry Goldman during the early 1970's. Winning under famous judge, the late Louis Murr.

Such a breeder also is proud of a reputation for integrity. Thus on two counts, for the sake of the dog's future and the breeder's reputation, to such a person a *satisfied* customer takes precedence over a sale at any cost.

If your puppy is to be a pet or "family dog," the earlier the age at which it joins your household the better. Puppies are weaned and ready to start out on their own, under the care of a sensible new owner, at about six weeks old; and if you take a young one, it is often easier to train it to the routine of your household and to your requirements of it than is the case with an older dog which, even though still a puppy technically, may have already started habits you will find difficult to change. The younger puppy is usually less costly, too, as it stands to reason the breeder will not have as much expense invested in it. Obviously, a puppy that has been raised to five or six months old represents more in care and cash expenditure on the breeder's part than one sold earlier and therefore should be and generally is priced accordingly.

There is an enormous amount of truth in the statement that "bargain" puppies seldom turn out to be that. A "cheap" puppy, cheaply raised purely for sale and profit, can and often does lead to great heartbreak including problems and veterinarian's bills which can add up to many times the initial cost of a properly reared dog. On the other hand, just because a puppy is expensive does not assure one that is healthy and well reared. There have been numerous cases where unscrupulous dealers have sold for several hundred dollars puppies that were sickly, in poor condition, and such poor specimens that the breed of which they were supposedly members was barely recognizable. So one cannot always judge a puppy by price alone. Common sense must guide a prospective purchaser, plus the selection of a *reliable,* well-recommended dealer whom you know to have well satisfied customers or, best of all, a specialized breeder. You will probably find the fairest pricing at the kennel of a breeder. Such a person, experienced with the breed in general and with his or her own stock in particular, through extensive association with these dogs has watched enough of them mature to have obviously learned to assess quite accurately each puppy's potential—something impossible where such background is non-existent.

One more word on the subject of pets. Bitches make a fine choice for this purpose as they are usually quieter and more gentle than the males, easier to house train, more affectionate, and less inclined to roam. If you do select a bitch and have no intention of breeding or showing her, by all means have her spayed, for your sake and for hers. The advantages to the owner of a spayed bitch include avoiding the nuisance of "in season" periods which normally occur twice yearly, with the accompanying eager canine swains haunting your premises in an effort to get close to your female, plus the unavoidable messiness and spotting of furniture and rugs at this time, which can be annoying if she is a household companion in the habit of sharing your sofa or bed. As for the spayed bitch, she benefits as she grows older because this simple operation almost entirely eliminates the possibility of breast cancer ever occurring. It is recommended that all bitches eventually be spayed—even those used for show or breeding when their careers have ended—in order that they may enjoy a happier, healthier old age. Please take note, however, that a bitch who has been spayed (or an altered dog) *cannot be shown at American Kennel Club dog shows once this operation has been performed.* Be certain that you are *not* interested in showing her before taking this step.

Also, in selecting a pet, never underestimate the advantages of an older dog, perhaps a retired show dog or a bitch no longer needed for breeding, who may be available quite reasonably priced by a breeder anxious to place such a dog in a loving home. These dogs are settled and can be a delight to own, as they make wonderful companions, especially in a household of adults where raising a puppy can sometimes be a trial.

Everything that has been said about careful selection of your pet puppy and its place of purchase applies, but with many further considerations, when you plan to buy a show dog or foundation stock for a future breeding program. Now is the time for an indepth study of the breed, starting with every word and every illustration in this book and all others you can find written on the subject. The Standard of the breed now has become your guide, and you must learn not only the words but also how to interpret them and how they are applicable in actual dogs before you are ready to make an intelligent selection of a show dog.

Ch. Honey Hollow Great Donner, noted early black Dane winner, handled by Lina Basquette to a Group 1st (one of many) under the late Dr. Mitten.

Ch. Dinro Kimberly among the many splendid Great Danes owned by the late Rosemarie Robert, Carmel, N.Y.

Ch. Dinro Don owned by the late Rosemarie Robert, Carmel, N.Y. Photo courtesy of Ed Lyons.

1952 at the Eastern Dog Club. A priceless picture of *(left)* Jane K. Forsyth handling Ch. Illiance of Marydane and Lina Basquette *(right)* handling Ch. Dinro Aslan. The judge *(center)* is Mrs. Harry (Florence) Warren, who, with her husband, owned the Warrendane Kennels at Chappaqua, N.Y. This was a famous kennel whose dogs helped to establish others, among them Canyon Crest, and are to be found in many current pedigrees.

If you are thinking in terms of a dog to show, obviously you must have learned about dog shows and must be in the habit of attending them. This is fine, but now your activity in this direction should be increased, with your attending every single dog show within a reasonable distance from your home. Much can be learned about a breed at ringside at these events. Talk with the breeders who are exhibiting. Study the dogs they are showing. Watch the judging with concentration, noting each decision made, and attempt to follow the reasoning by which the judge has reached it. Note carefully the attributes of the dogs who win and, for your later use, the manner in which each is presented. Close your ears to the ringside know-it-alls, usually novice owners of only a dog or two and very new to the Fancy, who have only derogatory remarks to make about all that is taking place unless they happen to win. This is the type of exhibitor who "comes and goes" through the Fancy and whose interest is usually of very short duration owing to lack of knowledge and dissatisfaction caused by the failure to recognize the need to learn. You, as a fancier it is hoped will last and enjoy our sport over many future years, should develop independent thinking at this stage; you should learn to draw your own conclusions about the merits, or lack of them, seen before you in the ring and, thus, sharpen your own judgement in preparation for choosing wisely and well.

Note carefully which breeders campaign winning dogs, not just an occasional isolated good one but consistent, homebred winners. It is from one of these people that you should select your own future "star."

If you are located in an area where dog shows take place only occasionally or where there are long travel distances involved, you will need to find another testing ground for your ability to select a worthy show dog. Possibly, there are some representative kennels raising this breed within a reasonable distance. If so, by all means ask permission of the owners to visit the kennels and do so when permission is granted. You may not necessarily buy then and there, as they may not have available what you are seeking that very day, but you will be able to see the type of dog being raised there and to discuss the dogs with the breeder. Every time you do this, you add to your knowledge. Should one of these kennels have dogs which especially appeal to you, perhaps you could reserve a show-prospect puppy from a coming litter. This is frequently done, and it is often worth waiting for a puppy, unless you have seen a dog with which you truly are greatly impressed and which is immediately available.

The purchase of a puppy has already been discussed. Obviously this same approach applies in a far greater degree when the purchase involved is a future show dog. The only place at which to purchase a show prospect is from a breeder who raises show-type stock; otherwise, you are almost certainly doomed to disappointment as the puppy matures. Show and breeding kennels obviously cannot keep all of their fine young stock. An active breeder-exhibitor is, therefore, happy to place promising youngsters in the hands of people also interested in showing and winning with them, doing so at a fair price according to the quality and prospects of the dog involved. Here again, if no kennel in your immediate area has what you are seeking, do not hesitate to contact top breeders in other areas and to buy at long distance. Ask for pictures, pedigrees, and a complete description. Heed the breeder's advice and recommendations, after truthfully telling exactly what your expectations are for the dog you purchase. Do you want something with which to win just a few ribbons now and then? Do you want a dog who can complete his championship? Are you thinking of the real "big time" (i.e., seriously campaigning with Best of Breed, Group wins, and possibly even Best in Show as your eventual goal)? Consider it all carefully in advance; then honestly discuss your plans with the breeder. You will be better satisfied with the results if you do this, as the breeder is then in the best position to help you choose the dog who is most likely to come through for you. A breeder selling a show dog is just as anxious as the buyer for the dog to succeed, and the breeder will represent the dog to you with truth and honesty. Also, this type of breeder does not lose interest the moment the sale has been made but when necessary will be right there ready to assist you with beneficial advice and suggestions based on years of experience.

As you make inquiries of at least several kennels, keep in mind that show-prospect puppies are less expensive than mature show dogs, the latter often costing close to four figures, and sometimes more. The reason for this is that, with a puppy, there is always an element of chance, the possibility of its developing unexpected faults as it matures or failing to develop the excellence and quality that earlier had seemed probable. There definitely is a risk factor in buying a show-prospect puppy. Sometimes all goes well, but occasionally the swan becomes an ugly duckling. Reflect on this as you consider available puppies and young adults. It just might be a good idea to go with a more mature, though more costly, dog if one you like is available.

When you buy a mature show dog, "what you see is what you get," and it is not likely to change beyond coat and condition which are dependent on your care. Also advantageous for a novice owner is the fact that a mature dog of show quality almost certainly will have received show-ring training and probably match-show experience, which will make your earliest handling ventures far easier.

Frequently it is possible to purchase a beautiful dog who has completed championship but who, owing to similarity in bloodlines, is not needed for the breeder's future program. Here you have the opportunity of owning a champion, usually in the two-to-five-year-old range, which you can enjoy campaigning as a special (for Best of Breed competition) and which will be a settled, handsome dog for you and your family to enjoy with pride.

If you are planning foundation for a future kennel, concentrate on acquiring one or two really superior bitches. These need not necessarily be top show-quality, but they should represent your breed's finest producing bloodlines from a strain noted for producing quality, generation after generation. A proven matron who is already the dam of show-type puppies is, of course, the ideal selection; but these are usually difficult to obtain, no one being anxious to part with so valuable an asset. You just might strike it lucky, though, in which case you are off to a flying start. If you cannot find such a matron available, select a young bitch of finest background from top-producing lines who is herself of decent type, free of obvious faults, and of good quality.

Great attention should be paid to the pedigree of the bitch from whom you intend to breed. If not already known to you, try to see the sire and dam. It is generally agreed that someone starting with a breed should concentrate on a fine collection of topflight bitches and raise a few litters from these before considering keeping one's own stud dog. The practice of buying a stud and then

Ch. Eagle Valley Q.E.D. belongs to the noted stage star Gretchen Wyler, for whom he is being handled to a good win by Lina Basquette.

breeding everything you own or acquire to that dog does not always work out well. It is better to take advantage of the many noted sires who are available to be used at stud, who represent all of the leading strains, and in each case to carefully select the one who in type and pedigree seems most compatible to each of your bitches, at least for your first several litters.

To summarize, if you want a "family dog" as a companion, it is best to buy it young and raise it according to the habits of your household. If you are buying a show dog, the more mature it is, the more certain you can be of its future beauty. If you are buying foundation stock for a kennel, then bitches are better, but they must be from the finest *producing* bloodlines.

When you buy a pure-bred dog that you are told is eligible for registration with the American Kennel Club, you are entitled to receive from the seller an application form which will enable you to register your dog. If the seller cannot give you the application form you should demand and receive an identification of your dog

226

consisting of the name of the breed, the registered names and numbers of the sire and dam, the name of the breeder, and your dog's date of birth. If the litter of which your dog is a part is already recorded with the American Kennel Club, then the litter number is sufficient identification.

Do not be misled by promises of papers at some later date. Demand a registration application form or proper identification as described above. If neither is supplied, do not buy the dog. So warns the American Kennel Club, and this is especially important in the purchase of show or breeding stock.

Ch. Honeygold von Overcup, one of the top Danes in the U.S. late in the 1960's, was Top Working Dog for 1969. By Ch. Sham's Sacerdotes ex Ch. Thendara Henriette Keppen, bred by Art White, owned by Jim and Edna Hatch. Photo courtesy of Elizabeth Mitchell, San Luis Rey, Calif.

Five-week-old brindle bitch puppy, typical of those raised at Rochford Kennels, Janet Quick, Kansas City, Mo.

Litter of eight puppies at 14 days. Sire, Best in Specialty Show winning Ch. Hauerdane's War Bonnet ex Ch. Kingswood Phoebe Snow. Breeders-owners, Richard E. and Kathy Varian of Rika Danes and Kathy Jacobs.

Chapter 12

The Care of Your Great Dane Puppy

PREPARING FOR YOUR PUPPY'S ARRIVAL

The moment you decide to be the new owner of a puppy is not one second too soon to start planning for the puppy's arrival in your home. Both the new family member and you will find the transition period easier if your home is geared in advance of the arrival.

The first things to be prepared are a bed for the puppy and a place where you can pen him up for rest periods. Every dog should have a crate of its own from the very beginning, so that he will come to know and love it as his special place where he is safe and happy. It is an ideal arrangement, for when you want him to be free, the crate stays open. At other times you can securely latch it and know that the pup is safely out of mischief. If you travel with him, his crate comes along in the car; and, of course, in traveling by plane there is no alternative but to have a carrier for the dog. If you show your dog, you will want him upon occasion to be in a crate a good deal of the day. So from every consideration, a crate is a very sensible and sound investment in your puppy's future safety and happiness and for your own peace of mind.

The crates most desirable are the wooden ones with removable side panels, which are ideal for cold weather (with the panels in place to keep out drafts) and in hot weather (with the panels removed to allow better air circulation). Wire crates are all right in the summer, but they give no protection from cold or drafts. Aluminum crates, due to the manner in which the metal reflects surrounding temperatures, are not recommended. If it is cold, so is the metal of the crate; if it is hot, the crate becomes burning hot.

When you choose the puppy's crate, be certain that it is roomy enough not to become outgrown. The crate should have sufficient height so the dog can stand up in it as a mature dog and sufficient area so that he can stretch out full length when relaxed. When the puppy is young, first give him shredded newspaper as a bed; the papers can be replaced with a mat or turkish towels when the dog is older. Carpet remnants are great for the bottom of the crate, as they are inexpensive and in case of accidents can be quite easily replaced. As the dog matures and is past the chewing age, a pillow or blanket in the crate is an appreciated comfort.

Sharing importance with the crate is a safe area in which the puppy can exercise and play. If you are an apartment dweller, a baby's playpen can work out well. If you have a yard, an area where he can be outside in safety should be fenced in prior to the dog's arrival at your home. This area does not need to be huge, but it does need to be made safe and secure. If you are in a suburban area where there are close neighbors, stockade fencing works out best as then the neighbors are less aware of the dog and the dog cannot see and bark at everything passing by. If you are out in the country where no problems with neighbors are likely to occur, then regular chain-link fencing is fine. For added precaution in both cases, use a row of concrete blocks or railroad ties inside against the entire bottom of the fence; this precludes or at least considerably lessens the chances of your dog digging his way out.

Be advised that if yours is a single dog, it is very unlikely that it will get sufficient exercise just sitting in the fenced area, which is what most of them do when they are there alone. Two or more dogs will play and move themselves around, but one by itself does little more than make a leisurely tour once around the area to check things over and then lie down. You must include a daily walk or two in your plans if your puppy is to be rugged and well.

230

Ch. Dinro's Taboo and Dinro Tosca, littermates from the Dinro Danes, Rosemarie Robert, Carmel, N.Y. the 1960's. Photo courtesy of Ed Lyons.

Ch. Eaglevalley Hex v Doggenhoff, Ed Lyons handling, a well-known winner from Dorothy Montgomery's Eaglevalley Kennels at New Milford, Connecticutt.

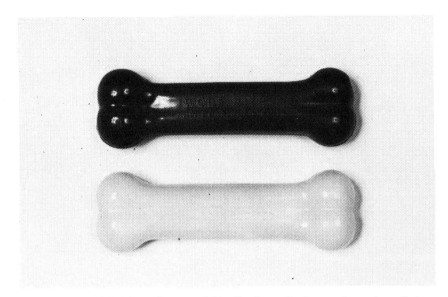

Several sizes of Nylabones® are available, like the petite for puppies and small size breeds, the regular for medium size dogs, and the giant or souper for big breeds. Your Great Dane also has the choice of either meat flavor or chocolate. Nylabone is safe, lasts long, and inexpensive. Photo by V. Serbin.

Four-week-old puppies at Keetra Kennels being taught table manners. These are from black out of Harlequin parents. Owned by the Schwartzes, Lake Forest, Illinois.

Exercise is extremely important to a puppy's muscular development and to keep a mature dog fit and trim. So make sure that those exercise periods, or walks, a game of ball, and other such activities, are part of your daily program as a dog owner.

If your fenced area has an outside gate, provide a padlock and key and a strong fastening for it, and use them, so that the gate cannot be opened by others and the dog taken or turned free. The ultimate convenience in this regard is, of course, a door (unused for other purposes) from the house around which the fenced area can be enclosed, so that all you have to do is open the door and out into his area he goes. This arrangement is safest of all, as then you need not be using a gate, and it is easier in bad weather since then you can send the dog out without taking him and becoming soaked yourself at the same time. This is not always possible to manage, but if your house is arranged so that you could do it this way, you would never regret it due to the convenience and added safety thus provided. Fencing in the entire yard, with gates to be opened and closed whenever a caller, deliveryman, postman, or some other person comes on your property, really is not safe at all because people not used to gates and their importance are frequently careless about closing and latching gates *securely*. Many heartbreaking incidents have been brought about by someone carelessly only half closing a gate which the owner had thought to be firmly latched and the dog wandering out. For greatest security a fenced *area* definitely takes precedence over a fenced *yard*.

The puppy will need a collar (one that fits now, not one to be grown into) and a lead from the moment you bring him home. Both should be an appropriate weight and type for his size. Also needed are a feeding dish and a water dish, both made preferably of unbreakable material. Your pet supply shop should have an interesting assortment of these and other accessories from which you can choose. Then you will need grooming tools of the type the breeder recommends and some toys. Equally satisfactory is Nylabone®, a nylon bone that does not chip or splinter and that "frizzles" as the puppy chews, providing healthful gum massage. Rawhide chews are safe, too, *if made in the United States*. There was a problem a few years back, owing to the chemicals with which some foreign rawhide toys had been treated. Also avoid plastics and any sort of rubber toys, *particularly those with squeakers* which the puppy may remove and swallow. If you want a ball for the puppy to use when playing with him, select one of very hard construction made for this purpose and do not leave it alone with him because he may chew off and swallow bits of the rubber. Take the ball with you when the game is over. This also applies to some of those "tug of war" type rubber toys which are fun when used with the two of you for that purpose but again should *not* be left behind for the dog to work on with his teeth. Bits of swallowed rubber, squeakers, and other such foreign articles can wreak great havoc in the intestinal tract—do all you can to guard against them.

Too many changes all at once can be difficult for a puppy. For at least the first few days he is with you, keep him on the food and feeding schedule to which he is accustomed. Find out ahead of time from the breeder what he feeds his puppies, how frequently, and at what times of the day. Also find out what, if any, food supplements the breeder has been using and recommends. Then be prepared by getting in a supply of the same food so that you will have it there when you bring the puppy home. Once the puppy is accustomed to his new surroundings, then you can switch the type of food and schedule to fit your convenience, but for the first several days do it as the puppy expects.

Your selection of a veterinarian also should be attended to before the puppy comes home, because you should stop at the vet's office for the puppy to be checked over as soon as you leave the breeder's premises. If the breeder is from your area, ask him for recommendations. Ask you dog-owning friends for their opinions of the local veterinarians, and see what their experiences with those available have been. Choose someone whom several of your friends recommend highly, then contact him about your puppy, perhaps making an appointment to stop in at his office. If the premises are clean, modern, and well equipped, and if you like the veterinarian, make an appointment to bring the puppy in on the day of purchase. Be sure to obtain the puppy's health record from the breeder, including information on such things as shots and worming that the puppy has had.

JOINING THE FAMILY

Remember that, exciting and happy an occasion as it is for you, the puppy's move from his place of birth to your home can be, for him, a traumatic experience. His mother and littermates will be

234

missed. He quite likely will be awed or frightened by the change of surroundings. the person on whom he depended will be gone. Everything should be planned to make his arrival at your home pleasant—to give him confidence and to help him realize that yours is a pretty nice place to be after all.

Never bring a puppy home on a holiday. There just is too much going on with people and gifts and excitement. If he is in honor of an "occasion," work it out so that his arrival will be a few days earlier, or perhaps even better, a few days later than the "occasion." Then your home will be back to it normal routine and the puppy can enjoy your undivided attention. Try not to bring the puppy home in the evening. Early morning is the ideal time, as then he has the opportunity of getting acquainted and the initial strangeness should wear off before bedtime. You will find it a more peaceful night that way. Allow the puppy to investigate as he likes, under your watchful eye. If you already have a pet in the household, keep a careful watch that the relationship between the two gets off to a friendly start or you may quickly find yourself with a lasting problem. Much of the future attitude of each toward the other will depend on what takes place that first day, so keep your mind on what they are doing and let your other activities slide for the moment. Be careful not to let your older pet become jealous by paying more attention to the puppy than to him, as that will start a bad situation immediately.

If you have a child, here again it is important that the relationship start out well. Before the puppy is brought home, you should have a talk with the youngster about puppies so that it will be clearly understood that puppies are fragile and can easily be injured; therefore, they should not be teased, hurt, mauled, or overly rough-housed. A puppy is not an inanimate toy; it is a living thing with a right to be loved and handled respectfully, treatment which will reflect in the dog's attitude toward your child as both mature together. Never permit your children's playmates to mishandle the puppy, tormenting the puppy until it turns on the children in self-defense. Children often do not realize how rough is too rough. You, as a responsible adult, are obligated to assure that your puppy's relationships with children is a pleasant one.

Do not start out by spoiling your puppy. A puppy is usually pretty smart and can be quite demanding. What you had considered to be "just for tonight" may be accepted by the puppy as "for keeps." Be firm with him, strike a routine, and stick to it. The puppy will learn more quickly this way, and everyone will be happier at the result. A radio playing softly or a dim night light are often comforting to a puppy as it gets accustomed to new surroundings and should be provided in preference to bring the puppy to bed with you—unless, of course, you intend him to share the bed as a permanent arrangement.

SOCIALIZING AND TRAINING

Socialization and training of your puppy should start the very day of his arrival in your home. Never address him without calling him by name. A short, simple name is the easiest to teach as it catches the dog's attention quickly, so avoid elaborate call names. Always address the dog by the same name, not a whole series of pet names; the latter will only confuse the puppy.

Use his name clearly, and call the puppy over to you when you see him awake and wandering about. When he comes, make a big fuss over him for being such a good dog. He thus will quickly associate the sound of his name with coming to you and a pleasant happening.

Several hours after the puppy's arrival is not too soon to start accustoming him to the feel of a light collar. He may hardly notice it; or he may struggle, roll over, and try to rub it off his neck with his paws. Divert his attention when this occurs by offering a tasty snack or a toy (starting a game with him) or by petting him. Before long he will have accepted the strange feeling around his neck and no longer appear aware of it. Next comes the lead. Attach it and then immediately take the puppy outside or otherwise try to divert his attention with things to see and sniff. He may struggle against the lead at first, biting at it and trying to free himself. Do not pull him with it at this point; just hold the end loosely and try to follow him if he starts off in any direction. Normally his attention will soon turn to investigating his sourroundings if he is outside or you have taken him into an unfamiliar room in your house; curiosity will take over and he will become interested in sniffing around the surroundings. Just follow him with the lead slackly held until he seems to have completely forgotten about it; then try with gentle urging to get him to follow you. Don't be rough or jerk at him; just tug gently on the lead in short quick motions

236

(steady pulling can become a battle of wills), repeating his name or trying to get him to follow your hand which is holding a bite of food or an interesting toy. If you have an older lead-trained dog, then it should be a cinch to get the puppy to follow along after *him*. In any event the average puppy learns quite quickly and will soon be trotting along nicely on the lead. Once that point has been reached, the next step is to teach him to follow on your left side, or heel. Of course this will not likely be accomplished all in one day but should be done with short training periods over the course of several days until you are satisfied with the result.

During the course of house training your puppy, you will need to take him out frequently and at regular intervals: first thing in the morning directly from the crate, immediately after meals, after the puppy has been napping, or when you notice that the puppy is looking for a spot. Choose more or less the same place to take the puppy each time so that a pattern will be established. If he does not go immediately, do not return him to the house as he will probably relieve himself the moment he is inside. Stay out with him until he has finished; then be lavish with your praise for his good behavior. If you catch the puppy having an accident indoors, grab him firmly and rush him outside, sharply saying "No!" as you pick him up. If you do not see the accident occur, there is little point in doing anything except cleaning it up, as once it has happened and been forgotten, the puppy will most likely not even realize why you are scolding him.

Especially if you live in a big city or are away many hours at a time, having a dog that is trained to go on paper has some very definite advantages. To do this, one proceeds pretty much the same way as taking the puppy outdoors, except now you place the puppy on the newspaper at the proper time. The paper should always be kept in the same spot. An easy way to paper train a puppy if you have a playpen for it or an exercise pen is to line the area with newspapers; then gradually, every day or so, remove a section of newspaper until you are down to just one or two. The puppy acquires the habit of using the paper; and as the prepared area grows smaller, in the majority of cases the dog will continue to use whatever paper is still available. It is pleasant, if the dog is alone for an excessive length of time, to be able to feel that if he needs it the paper is there and will be used.

The puppy should form the habit of spending a certain amount of time in his crate, even when you are home. Sometimes the puppy will do this voluntarily, but if not, he should be taught to do so, which is accomplished by leading the puppy over by his collar, gently pushing him inside, and saying firmly, "Down" or "Stay." Whatever expression you use to give a command, stick to the very same one each time for each act. Repetition is the big thing in training—and so is association with what the dog is expected to do. When you mean "Sit" always say exactly that. "Stay" should mean *only* that the dog should remain where he receives the command. "Down" means something else again. Do not confuse the dog by shuffling the commands, as this will create training problems for you.

As soon as he had had his immunization shots, take your puppy

Ch. Duyster's Lord Jim, 1950's, Honey Hollow's first male champion and stud dog. Owned by Lina Basquette, Honey Hollow Kennels.

Ch. Kim's Sabu of Lyndane, by Ch. Big Kim of Bella Dane ex Broadway Princess Pat, handled here by Jane Forsyth for Dr. Anthony DiNardo. Born February 1970.

with you whenever and wherever possible. There is nothing that will build a self-confident, stable dog like socialization, and it is extremely important that you plan and give the time and energy necessary for this whether your dog is to be a show dog or a pleasant, well-adjusted family member. Take your puppy in the car so that he will learn to enjoy riding and not become carsick as dogs may do if they are infrequent travelers. Take him anywhere you are going where you are certain he will be welcome: visiting friends and relative (if they do not have housepets who may resent the visit), busy shopping centers (keeping him always on lead), or just walking around the streets of your town. If someone admires him (as always seems to happen when one is out with puppies), encourage the stranger to pet and talk with him. Socialization of this type brings out the best in your puppy and helps him to grow up with a friendly outlook, liking the world and its inhabitants. The worst thing that can be done to a puppy's personality is to overly shelter him. By always keeping him at home away from things and people unfamiliar to him you may be creating a personality problem for the mature dog that will be a cross for you to bear later on.

FEEDING YOUR DOG

Time was when providing nourishing food for dogs involved a far more complicated procedure than people now feel is necessary. The old school of thought was that the daily ration must consist of fresh beef, vegetables, cereal, egg yolks, and cottage cheese as basics with such additions as brewer's yeast and vitamin tablets on a daily basis.

During recent years, however, many minds have changed regarding this procedure. Eggs, cottage cheese, and supplements to the diet are still given, but the basic method of feeding dogs has changed; and the change has been, in the opinion of many authorities, definitely for the better. The school of thought now is that you are doing your dogs a avor when you feed them some of the fine commercially prepared dog foods in preference to your own home-cooked concoctions.

The reason behind this new outlook is easily understandable. The dog food industry has grown to be a major one, participated in by some of the best known and most respected names in America. These trusted firms, it is agreed, turn out excellent products, so people are feeding their dog food preparations with confidence and the dogs are thriving, living longer, happier, and healtheir lives than ever before. What more could one want?

There are at least half a dozen absolutely top-grade dry foods to be mixed with broth or water and served to your dog according to directions. There are all sorts of canned meats, and there are several kinds of "convenience foods," those in a packet which you open and dump out into the dog's dish. It is just that simple. The convenience foods are neat and easy to use when you are away from home, but generally speaking a dry food mixed with hot water or soup and meat is preferred. It is the opinion of many that the canned meat, with its added fortifiers, is more beneficial to the dogs than the fresh meat. However, the two can be alternated or, if you prefer and your dog does well on it, by all means use fresh ground beef. A dog enjoys changes in the meat part of his diet, which is easy with the canned food since all sorts of beef are available (chunk, ground, stewed, and so on), plus lamb, chicken, and even such concoctions as liver and egg.

240

There is also prepared food geared to every age bracket of your dog's life, from puppyhood on through old age, with special additions or modifications to make it particularly nourishing and beneficial. Previous generations never had it so good where the canine dinner is concerned, because these commercially prepared foods are tasy and geared to meeting the dog's gastronomic approval.

Additionally, contents and nutrients are clearly listed on the labels, as are careful instructions for feeding just the right amount for the size, weight, and age of each dog.

With these foods the addition of extra vitamins is not necessary, but if you prefer there are several kinds of those, too, that serve as taste treats as well as being beneficial. Your pet supplier has a full array of them.

Of course there is no reason not to cook up something for your dog if you would feel happier doing so. But it seems unnecessary when such truly satisfactory rations are available with so much less trouble and expense.

How often you feed your dog is a matter of how it works out best for you. Many owners prefer to do it once a day. It is generally agreed that two meals, each of smaller quantity, are better for the digestion and more satisfying to the dog, particularly if yours is a household member who stands around and watches preparations for the family meals. Do not overfeed. This is the shortest route to all sorts of problems. Follow directions and note carefully how your dog is looking. If your dog is overweight, cut back the quantity of food a bit. If the dog looks thin, then increase the amount. Each dog is an individual and the food intake should be adjusted to his requirements to keep him feeling and looking trim and in top condition.

From the time puppies are fully weaned until they are about twelve weeks old, they should be fed four times daily. From three months to six months of age, three meals should suffice. At six months of age the puppies can be fed two meals, and the twice daily feedings can be continued until the puppies are close to one year old, at which time feeding can be changed to once daily if desired. If you do feed just once a day, do so by early afternoon at the latest and give the dog a snack, a biscuit or two, at bedtime.

Remember that plenty of fresh water should always be available to your puppy or dog for drinking. This is of utmost importance to his health.

CROPPING OF YOUR GREAT DANE PUPPY'S EARS

If you live in one of the countries where ear cropping is legal and widely accepted, and you are planning to show your Great Dane in conformation competition, you almost certainly will want to have his ears cropped as it does add enormously to a show dog's appearance, especially when he will be in competition with other dogs, the majority of whom will have cropped ears. There are people who truly like, and even prefer, the uncropped look; but it is an uphill climb endeavoring to win with an uncropped Great Dane in the high quality competition of our dog show rings against many other splendid representatives of the breed whose ears are cropped in the conventional (wherever customary) manner.

Ear cropping is usually best done between the ages of six and eight weeks, the closer to six weeks the better as then the ear is thinner, thus easier to cut, causing less trauma for the puppy and increasing your chances of a really good job. Do not, however, permit cropping unless the puppy is in top physical condition. It is better to wait a week or two longer than to work on the ears of a weak or sickly puppy.

The most important part of getting a good ear cropping job is the careful selection of the person who will be doing it. Many people go to their veterinarian for this, which is fine IF the veterinarian understands the importance of what he is doing for the show dog, the Great Dane standard, and if he has had experience cropping *successfully*. A poor job, with ears off balance, of unequal size, made too short, or done in such a manner as to leave them lacking the correct upstanding carriage, can completely ruin the future of a promising show puppy. So choose carefully and choose well. The best way to find someone expert at really excellent ear cropping is by word of mouth. Discuss the matter ahead of time with the breeder from whom you acquired your bitch, the owner of the stud dog who will sire the puppies, and any friends you have made in your area who raise and show Danes. From them you should be able to locate an expert, but before making any commitments, try to have a look at some ears he has done in order to judge for yourself.

Never, ever, under any circumstances decide to undertake this operation yourself. It *must* be done by a qualified, experienced person or you may find yourself with a large problem on your

A Honey Hollow black puppy at nine weeks, just after ear cropping. Lina Basquette, owner, Honey Hollow Great Danes.

Stone Valley puppies, their ears taped following cropping, owned by Chuck and Darcy Quinlan, Kennesaw, Ga.

Ch. Rika's Rendition of Kingswood being gaited for the judge by handler Doug Toomey, as another exhibitor "stacks" (sets up) her dog in the background. Rendition is owned by Richard and Kathy Varian, Rika Kennels, Reseda, Calif.

hands and suffering for the puppy.

Sharing the importance with the actual cropping is the after-care period, which rests squarely in your hands. This can make or break the entire matter, so be careful and conscientious about following instructions *exactly*. You want the ears to heal quickly, cleanly, and with no infection. Your part of bringing this about is the care and attention you exercise during the healing process.

Chapter 13

The Making of a Show Dog

If you have decided to become a show dog exhibitor, you have accepted a very real and very exciting challenge. The groundwork has been accomplished with the selection of your future show prospect. If you have purchased a puppy, it is assumed that you have gone through all the proper preliminaries concerning good care, which should be the same if the puppy is a pet or future show dog with a few added precautions for the latter.

GENERAL CONSIDERATIONS

Remember the importance of keeping your future winner in trim, top condition. Since you want him neither too fat nor too thin, his appetite for his proper diet should be guarded, and children and guests should not be permitted to constantly feed him "goodies." The best treat of all is a small wad of raw ground beef or a packaged dog treat. To be avoided are ice cream, cake, cookies, potato chips, and other fattening items which will cause the dog to put on weight and may additionally spoil his appetite for the proper, nourishing, well-balanced diet so essential to good health and condition.

The importance of temperament and showmanship cannot possibly be overestimated. They have put many a mediocre dog across while lack of them can ruin the career of an otherwise outstanding specimen. From the day your dog joins your family, socialize him. Keep him accustomed to being with people and to being handled by people. Encourage your friends and relatives to "go over" him as the judges will in the ring so this will not seem a strange and upsetting experience. Practice showing his "bite" (the manner in which his teeth meet) quickly and deftly. It is quite simple to slip the lips apart with your fingers, and the puppy should be willing to accept this from you or the judge without struggle.

Some judges prefer that the exhibitors display the dog's bite and other mouth features themselves. These are the considerate ones, who do not wish to chance the spreading of possible infection from dog to dog with their hands on each one's mouth—a courtesy particularly appreciated in these days of virus epidemics. But the old-fashioned judges still insist in doing it themselves, so the dog should be ready for either possibility.

Take your future show dog with you in the car, thus accustoming him to riding so that he will not become carsick on the day of a dog show. He should associate pleasure and attention with going in the car, van, or motor home. Take him where it is crowded: downtown, to the shops, everywhere you go that dogs are permitted. Make the expeditions fun for him by frequent petting and words of praise; do not just ignore him as you go about your errands.

Do not overly shelter your future show dog. Instinctively you may want to keep him at home where he is safe from germs or danger. This can be foolish on two counts. The first reason is that a puppy kept away from other dogs builds up no natural immunity against all the things with which he will come in contact at dog shows, so it is wiser actually to keep him well up to date on all protective shots and then let him become accustomed to being among dogs and dog owners. Also, a dog who never is among strange people, in strange places, or among strange dogs, may grow up with a shyness or timidity of spirit that will cause you real problems as his show career draws near.

Keep your show prospect's coat in immaculate condition with frequent grooming and daily brushing. When bathing is necessary, use a mild dog shampoo or whatever the breeder of your

246

Another "great" from
Dinro's past. Int'l. Ch.
Dinro Beau Geste of
Airways. Photo
courtesy of Ed Lyons.

Ch. Von Raseac's
Great Caesar's Quote,
by Great Caesar's
Ghost V Raseac ex
Cameo's Lilabet of
Jason. A nationally
ranked showman in
1973, Quote sired nine
champions.

The final few moments of a dog show, as the judge selects Best in Show. Ann Stevenson points her finger at the lovely Dane bitch, Ch. Brierdane's Indian Amber, as handler Sylvia Rodwell raises her arm in victory.

The late and very famous Great Dane breeder, Mrs. Rosemarie Robert, at Westchester in 1970 handling her Ch. Dinro Strictly Taboo to a good win under another noted Dane authority, William (Pop) Gilbert, whose own Danes are among the most famous, judging the breed at Westchester K.C. in 1970. Photo courtesy of Ed Lyons.

puppy may suggest. Several of the brand-name products do an excellent job. Be sure to rinse thoroughly so as not to risk skin irritation by traces of soap left behind and protect against soap entering the eyes by a drop of castor oil in each before you lather up. Use warm water (be sure it is not uncomfortably hot or chillingly cold) and a good spray. Make certain you allow your dog to dry thoroughly in a warm, draft-free area (or outdoors, if it is warm and sunny) so that he doesn't catch cold. Then proceed to groom him to perfection.

Toenails should be watched and trimmed every few weeks. It is important not to permit nails to grow excessively long, as they will ruin the appearance of both the feet and pasterns.

A show dog's teeth must be kept clean and free of tartar. Hard dog biscuits can help toward this, but if tartar accumulates, see that it is removed promptly by your veterinarian. Bones for chewing are not suitable for show dogs as they tend to damage and wear down the tooth enamel.

Assuming that you will be handling the dog yourself, or even if he will be professionally handled, a few moments each day of dog show routine is important. Practice setting him up as you have seen the exhibitors do at the shows you've attended, and teach him to hold this position once you have him stacked to your satisfaction. Make the learning period pleasant by being firm but lavish in your praise when he responds correctly. Teach him to gait at your side at a moderate rate on a loose lead. When you have mastered the basic essentials at home, then hunt out and join a training class for future work. Training classes are sponsored by show-giving clubs in many areas, and their popularity is steadily increasing. If you have no other way of locating one, perhaps your veterinarian would know of one through some of his other clients; but if you are sufficiently aware of the dog show world to want a show dog, you will probably be personally acquainted with other people who will share information of this type with you.

Accustom your show dog to being in a crate (which you should be doing with a pet dog as well). He should relax in his crate at the shows "between times" for his own well being and safety.

MATCH SHOWS

Your show dog's initial experience in the ring should be in match show competition for several reasons. First, this type of event is intended as a learning experience for both the dog and the exhibitor. You will not feel embarrassed or out of place no matter how poorly your puppy may behave or how inept your attempts at handling may be, as you will find others there with the same type of problems. The important thing is that you get the puppy out and into a show ring where the two of you can practice together and learn the ropes.

Only on rare occasions is it necessary to make match show entries in advance, and even those with a pre-entry policy will usually accept entries at the door as well. Thus you need not plan several weeks ahead, as is the case with point shows, but can go when the mood strikes you. Also there is a vast difference in the cost, as match show entries only cost a few dollars while entry fees for the point shows may be over ten dollars, an amount none of us needs to waste until we have some idea of how the puppy will behave or how much more pre-show training is needed.

Match shows very frequently are judged by professional handlers who, in addition to making the awards, are happy to help new exhibitors with comments and advice on their puppies and their presentation of them. Avail yourself of all these opportunities before heading out to the sophisticated world of the point shows.

POINT SHOWS

As previously mentioned, entries for American Kennel Club point shows must be made in advance. This must be done on an official entry blank of the show-giving club. The entry must then be filed either personally or by mail with the show superintendent or the show secretary (if the event is being run by the club members alone and a superintendent has not been hired, this information will appear on the premium list) in time to reach its destination prior to the published closing date or filling of the quota. These entries must be made carefully, must be signed by the owner of the dog or the owner's agent (your professional handler), and must be accompanied by the entry fee; otherwise they will not be accepted. Remember that it is not when the entry leaves your hands that counts but the date of arrival at its destination. If you are relying on the mails, which are not always dependable, get the entry off well before the deadline to avoid disappointment.

A dog must be entered at a dog show in the name of the actual owner at the time of the entry closing date of that specific show.

Ch. Bit O'Tallbrook's Brenda, by Tallbrook's Darby Dan ex Ch. Tallbrook's Bit O'Honey, dam of two champions, here taking Winners Bitch for her second major en route to her title at the Great Dane Club of San Diego Specialty. Dick Schaefer handling for owners, Tallbrook Farms, Kathleen Twaits and Jacqueline White, Los Angeles, Calif.

From the 1950's, Ch. Hycrest Prince, owned by Lester T. and Alice C. Sawyer, Hy Crest Great Danes, Leominster, Mass., is becoming the first male Great Dane to win Best of Breed at Westminster K.C. two years successively. As of May 1956, Prince had won two Bests in Show, seven Group 1sts, and Best of Breed on 49 occasions. The judge is noted Dane fancier Mrs. Nelli T. Williams.

Ch. Highfields Buchanan, by Ch. Paethan of Mountdania ex Sabrina of Mountdania, going Best in Show at Pasadena Kennel Club in 1963. Bred by Marilyn L. Schick, owned by Keith and Ann Kelsey. This is a grandsire to Caesar, the sire of Annie Oakley, and is of pure Mountdania pedigree.

If a registered dog has been acquired by a new owner, it must be entered in the name of the new owner in any show for which entries close after the date of acquirement, regardless of whether the new owner has or has not actually received the registration certificate indicating that the dog is recorded in his name. State on the entry form whether or not transfer application has been mailed to the American Kennel Club, and it goes without saying that the latter should be attended to promptly when you purchase a registered dog.

In filling out your entry blank, type, print, or write clearly, paying particular attention to the spelling of names, correct registration numbers, and so on. Also, if there is more than one variety in your breed, be sure to indicate into which category your dog is being entered.

The Puppy Class is for dogs or bitches who are six months of age and under twelve months, were whelped in the United States, and are not champions. The age of a dog shall be calculated up to and inclusive of the first day of a show. For example, the first day a dog whelped on January 1st is eligible to compete in a Puppy Class at a show is July 1st of the same year; and he may continue to compete in Puppy Classes up to and including a show on December 31st of the same year, but he is *not* eligible to compete in a Puppy Class at a show held on or after January 1st of the following year.

The Puppy Class is the first one in which you should enter your puppy. In it a certain allowance will be made for the fact that they *are* puppies, thus an immature dog or one displaying less than perfect showmanship will be less severely penalized than, for instance, would be the case in Open. It is also quite likely that others in the class will be suffering from these problems, too. When you enter a puppy, be sure to check the classification with care, as some shows divide their Puppy Class into a 6-9 months old section and a 9-12 months old section.

The Novice Class is for dogs six months of age and over, whelped in the United States or Canada, who *prior to the official closing date for entries* have *not* won three first prizes in the Novice Class, any first prize at all in the Bred-by-Exhibitor, American-bred, or Open Classes, or one or more points toward championship. The provisions for this class are confusing to many people, which is probably the reason exhibitors do not enter in it more frequently. A dog may win any number of first prizes in the Puppy Class and still retain his eligibility for Novice. He may place second, third, or fourth not only in Novice on an unlimited number of occasions but also in Bred-by-Exhibitor, American-bred and Open and still remain eligible for Novice. But he may no longer be shown in Novice when he has won three blue ribbons in that class, when he has won even one blue ribbon in either Bred-by-Exhibitor, American-bred, or Open, or when he has won a single championship point.

In determining whether or not a dog is eligible for the Novice Class, keep in mind the fact that previous wins are calculated according to the official published date for closing of entries, not by the date on which you may actually have made the entry. So if in the interim, between the time you made the entry and the official closing date, your dog makes a win causing him to become ineligible for Novice, change your class *immediately* to another for which he will be eligible, preferably either Bred-by-Exhibitor or American-bred. To do this, you must contact the show's superintendent or secretary, at first by telephone to save time and at the same time confirm it in writing. The Novice Class always seems to have the fewest entries of any class, and therefore it is a splendid "practice ground" for you and your young dog while you are getting the "feel" of being in the ring.

Bred-by-Exhibitor Class is for dogs whelped in the United States or, if individually registered in the American Kennel Club Stud Book, for dogs whelped in Canada who are six months of age or older, are not champions, and are owned wholly or in part by the person or by the spouse of the person who was the breeder or one of the breeders of record. Dogs entered in this class must be handled in the class by an owner or by a member of the immediate family of the owner. Members of an immediate family for this purpose are husband, wife, father, mother, son, daughter, brother, or sister. This is the class which is really the "breeders' showcase," and the one which breeders should enter with particular pride to show off their achievements.

The American-bred Class is for all dogs excepting champions, six months of age or older, who were whelped in the United States by reason of a mating which took place in the United States.

The Open Class is for any dog six months of age or older (this is the only restriction for this class). Dogs with championship points compete in it, dogs who are already champions are eligible to do so, dogs who are imported can be entered, and, of course, American-bred dogs compete in it. This class is, for some strange reason, the favorite of exhibitors who are "out to win." They rush to enter their pointed dogs in it, under the false impression that by doing so they assure themselves of greater attention from the judges. This really is not so, and some people feel that to enter in one of the less competitive classes, with a better chance of winning it and thus earning a second opportunity of gaining the judge's approval by returning to the ring in the Winners Class, can often be a more effective strategy.

One does not enter the Winners Class. One earns the right to compete in it by winning first prize in Puppy, Novice, Bred-by-Exhibitor, American-bred, or Open. No dog who has been defeated on the same day in one of these classes is eligible to compete for Winners, and every dog who has been a blue-ribbon winner in one of them and not defeated in another, should he have been entered in more than one class (as occasionally happens), *must* do so. Following the selection of the Winners Dog or the Winners Bitch, the dog or bitch receiving that award leaves the ring. Then the dog or bitch who placed second in that class, unless previously beaten by another dog or bitch in another class at the same show, re-enters the ring to compete against the remaining first-prize winners for Reserve. The latter award indicates that the dog or bitch selected for it is standing "in reserve" should the one who received Winners be disqualified or declared ineligible through any technicality when the awards are checked at the American Kennel Club. In that case, the one who placed Reserve is moved up to Winners, at the same time receiving the appropriate championship points.

Winners Dog and Winners Bitch are the awards which carry points toward championship with them. The points are based on the number of dogs or bitches actually in competition, and the points are scaled one through five, the latter being the greatest number available to any one dog or bitch at any one show. Three-, four-, or five-point wins are considered majors. In order to become a champion, a dog or bitch must have won two majors under two different judges, plus at least one point from a third judge, and the additional points necessary to bring the total to fifteen. When your dog has gained fifteen points as described above, a championship certificate will be issued to you, and your dog's name will be published in the champions of record list in the *Pure-Bred Dogs/American Kennel Gazette*, the official publication of the American Kennel Club.

The scale of championship points for each breed is worked out by the American Kennel Club and reviewed annually, at which time the number required in competition may be either changed (raised or lowered) or remain the same. The scale of championship points for all breeds is published annually in the May issue of the *Gazette*, and the current ratings for each breed within that area are published in every show catalog.

When a dog or bitch is adjudged Best of Winners, its championship points are, for that show, compiled on the basis of which sex had the greater number of points. If there are two points in dogs and four in bitches and the dog goes Best of Winners, then *both* the dog and the bitch are awarded an equal number of points, in this case four. Should the Winners Dog or the Winners Bitch go on to win Best of Breed or Best of Variety, additional points are accorded for the additional dogs and bitches defeated by so doing, provided, of course, that there were entries specifically for Best of Breed competition or Specials, as these specific entries are generally called.

If your dog or bitch takes Best of Opposite Sex after going Winners, points are credited according to the number of the same sex defeated in both the regular classes and Specials competition. If Best of Winners is also won, then whatever additional points for each of these awards are available will be credited. Many a one- or two-point win has grown into a major in this manner.

Moving further along, should your dog win its Variety Group from the classes (in other words, if it has taken either Winners Dog or Winners Bitch), you then receive points based on the greatest number of points awarded to any member of any breed included within that Group during that show's competition. Should the day's winning also include Best in Show, the same rule of thumb applies, and your dog or bitch receives the highest number of points awarded to any other dog of any breed at that event.

256

Ch. Dinro San Maramutch, by Ch. Dinro Taboo ex Psass v Maramutch, owner-handled by Rosemarie Robert, Dinro Danes, Carmel, N.Y., finished with two Specialties to his credit during the mid-1960's. Here he is handled by his owner to Best of Winners at Lancaster K.C. in 1965 taking Best of Winners in an entry of 110. Photo courtesy of Ed Lyons.

Am. and Can. Ch. Tallbrook's Dapper Dan, by Ch. Hizoner Gilbert's Judge ex Laurel of Tallbrook Farms, a Group and Specialty winner. Top Sire in America for 1979, has a total of 17 champions. Bred and owned by Jacqueline F. White and Kathleen Twaits, Los Angeles, Calif.

Ch. Dinro Bo Jangles owned by Dinro Danes, the late Mrs Rosemarie Robert, Carmel, N.Y. Photo courtesy of Ed Lyons.

Best of Breed competition consists of the Winners Dog and the Winners Bitch, who automatically compete on the strength of those awards, in addition to whatever dogs and bitches have been entered specifically for this class for which champions of record are eligible. Since July 1980, dogs who, according to their owner's records, have completed the requirements for a championship after the closing of entries for the show, but whose championships are unconfirmed, may be transferred from one of the regular classes to the Best of Breed competition, provided this transfer is made by the show superintendent or show secretary *prior to the start of any judging at the show.*

This has proved an extremely popular new rule, as under it a dog can finish on Saturday and then be transferred and compete as a Special on Sunday. It must be emphasized that *the change must be made prior to the start of any part of the day's judging, not for just your individual breed.*

In the United States, Best of Breed winners are entitled to compete in the Variety Group which includes them. This is not mandatory; it is a privilege which exhibitors value. (In Canada, Best of Breed winners *must* compete in the Variety Group, or they lose any points already won.) The dogs winning *first* in each of the seven Variety Groups *must* compete for Best in Show. Missing the opportunity of taking your dog in for competition in its Group is foolish as it is there where the general public is most likely to notice your breed and become interested in learning about it.

Non-regular classes are sometimes included at the all-breed shows, and they are almost invariably included at Specialty shows. These include Stud Dog Class and Brood Bitch Class, which are judged on the basis of the quality of the two offspring accompanying the sire or dam. The quality of the latter two is beside the point and should not be considered by the judge; it is the youngsters who count, and the quality of *both* are to be averaged to decide which sire or dam is the best and most consistent producer. Then there is the Brace Class (which, at all-breed shows, moves up to Best Brace in each Variety Group and then Best Brace in Show), which is judged on the similarity and evenness of appearance of the two members of the brace. In other words, the two dogs should look like identical twins in size, color, and conformation and should move together almost as a single dog, one person

259

Ch. Honey Hollow Rameses, "the perfect Great Dane head in profile." Representative of the quality Danes from Lina Basquette's famed kennel. Owned by J. Council Parker.

Ch. Jecamo's Lucy Ann, C.D. at nine years of age. Dam of Ch. Abner Lowell Davis, Ch. Archibald Davis, and Jecamo's Alexander Davis (pointed). Lucy was a Great Dane Club of California Specialty winner, made her show debut by going Winners Bitch at their 1965 event. Owners, Mr. and Mrs. Lowell K. Davis, Covina, Calif.

handling with precision and ease. The same applies to the Team Class competition, except that four dogs are involved and, if necessary, two handlers.

The Veterans Class is for the older dogs, the minimum age of whom is seven years. This class is judged on the quality of the dogs, as the winner competes in Best of Breed competition and has, on a respectable number of occasions, been known to take that top award. So the point is *not* to pick out the oldest dog, as some judges seem to believe, but the best specimen of the breed, exactly as in the regular classes.

Then there are Sweepstakes and Futurity Stakes sponsored by many Specialty clubs, sometimes as part of their regular Specialty shows and sometimes as separate events on an entirely different occasion. The difference between the two stakes is that Sweepstakes entries usually include dogs from six to eighteen months age with entries made at the same time as the others for the show, while for a Futurity the entries are bitches nominated when bred and the individual puppies entered at or shortly following their birth.

If you already show your dog, if you plan on being an exhibitor in the future, or if you simply enjoy attending dog shows, there is a book which you will find to be an invaluable source of detailed information about all aspects of show dog competition. This book is *Successful Dog Show Exhibiting* (T.F.H. Publications, Inc.) and is available wherever the one you are reading was purchased.

JUNIOR SHOWMANSHIP COMPETITION

If there is a youngster in your family between the ages of ten and sixteen there is no better or more rewarding hobby than becoming an active participant in Junior Showmanship. This is a marvelous activity for young people. It teaches responsibility, good sportsmanship, the fun of competition where one's own skills are the deciding factor of success, proper care of a pet, and how to socialize with other young folks. Any youngster may experience the thrill of emerging from the ring a winner and the satisfaction of a good job well done.

Entry in Junior Showmanshiop Classes is open to any boy or girl who is at least ten years old and under seventeen years old on the day of the show. The Novice Junior Showmanship Class is open to youngsters who have not already won, at the time the entries close, three firsts in this class. Youngsters who have won three firsts in Novice may compete in the Open Junior Showmanship Class. Any junior handler who wins his third first-place award in Novice may participate in the Open Class at the same show, provided that the Open Class has at least one other junior handler entered and competing in it that day. The Novice and Open Classes may be divided into Junior and Senior Classes. Youngsters between the ages of ten and twelve, inclusively, are eligible for the Junior division; and youngsters between thirteen and seventeen, inclusively, are eligible for the Senior division.

Any of the foregoing classes may be separated into individual classes for boys and for girls. If such a division is made, it must be so indicated on the premium list. The premium list also indicates the prize for Best Junior Handler, if such a prize is being offered at the show. Any youngster who wins a first in any of the regular classes may enter the competition for this prize, provided the youngster has been undefeated in any other Junior Showmanship Class at that show.

Junior Showmanship Classes, unlike regular conformation classes in which the quality of the dog is judged, are judged solely on the skill and ability of the junior handling the dog. Which dog is best is not the point—it is which youngster does the best job with the dog that is under consideration. Eligibility requirements for the dog being shown in Junior Showmanship, and other detailed information, can be found in *Regulations for Junior Showmanship*, available from the American Kennel Club.

A junior who has a dog that he or she can enter in both Junior Showmanship and conformation classes has twice the opportunity for success and twice the opportunity to get into the ring and work with the dog, a combination which can lead to not only awards for expert handling, but also, if the dog is of sufficient quality, for making a conformation champion.

In less than two years of handling her Great Dane in Junior Showmanship, Jodi Sherman, daughter of the Mike Shermans of Sheridane fame, has obtained a very impressive list of exciting wins.

As her father is a successful breeder and professional handler, Jodi has grown up with dogs and has had many advantages in this regard.

Ch. Dinro Za-Rina winning the 9-12 months Puppy Bitch Class at the Great Dane Club of Pennsylvania Specialty Show, October 1967. Owned by the late Rosemarie Robert, Carmel, N.Y. Photo courtesy of Ed Lyons.

Rochford Devon, a 10-month-old puppy bitch, visiting an orphanage. Janet Quick, Rochford Great Danes, Kansas City, Mo.

Like her parents, Jodi chose the Great Dane as her breed because she considers it to be unique. As she says, "It is the only breed that has the characteristics of being "awestriking" because of its great size, and at the same time elegant. These qualities make the Great Dane a most special and beautiful breed. I could never call any other my own."

Jodi considers Junior Showmanship to be the most influential growing and learning experience thus far in her life. From it she has learned not only to become a better handler, but a better person as well. It has taught her to be more sociable, making it possible to form some very special friendships which otherwise would not have come about.

In the future, Jodi plans to continue with the Sheridane name and goal, which is always to strive for a better animal through carefully thought out breeding plans. She intends, also, to become a professional handler, and perhaps someday a judge.

To other youngsters, Jodi makes this statement: "Junior Showmanship is a wonderful part of dog shows. More people should be made aware of its existence. Unfortunately, I did not discover my love for it until I was 15 years of age; but these past two years have been the most fulfilled ones so far in my life."

In addition to her wins with the Great Danes, Jodi has also achieved lots of additional placements, including wins with other breeds such as Boxers, English Cockers, American Cockers, Whippets, and a Miniature Pinscher—all of which widens her experience and teaches the skill of working with many breeds.

We predict that Jodi will grow up to become a very successful breeder and professional handler, judging by her ability and enthusiasm. We know that her parents must take pride in her talent!

Junior Showmanship competition has been heightened considerably by the success of Stacy Ann Dewey, daughter of Larry and Penny Dewey of Stafford, Texas, with her family's Great Dane, Champion Rojon's The Striker of Ruffian. As a team, Stacy Ann and Striker were #1 in Working Group Junior Showmanship competition during 1984, and #6 All Breeds that same year. The accompanying picture shows them winning the Junior Showmanship Award at the Astro Hall Series of Dog Shows in 1985, at which events the entries run between 60 and 70 Juniors. Striker is four years old in this picture on the latter occasion; Stacy Ann, 16.

We congratulate them on their success, and hope that it will encourage other Juniors to compete with their Great Danes in this very exciting type of competition.

Ch. Rojon's The Striker of Ruffian is owned by Larry and Penny Dewey of Stafford, Texas, helping the Deweys' 16-year-old daughter, Stacy Ann, win first in Junior Showmanship at San Jacinto K. C. in 1985, which was part of the Astro Hall Dog Show series each August in Houston, Texas.

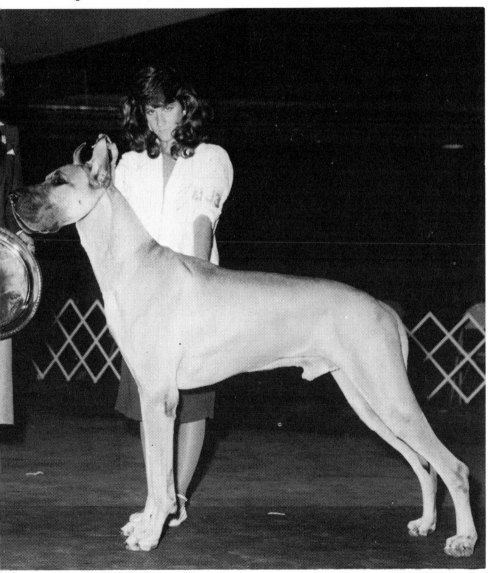

Ch. Jeffrey McDavis, handled here by Lowell Davis, is one of four titled littermates by Ch. Sunridge's Chief Justice ex Ch. Abigail Davis of Tallbrook. This dog made his debut by taking Best Puppy in Show at the Great Dane Club of California Independent Specialty, then two years later won the Stud Dog Class at the Great Dane Club of California under famed Dane expert Mrs. Rose Sabetti. At this same show, his son, Nova Lanqueteau McDavis repeated his sire's accomplishment by taking Best Puppy in Show. Jeffrey was bred by Arlene and Lowell K. Davis, later co-owned by them with Peggy McQuillan, also from Covina, Calif.

PRE-SHOW PREPARATIONS

Preparations of the items you will need as a dog show exhibitor should not be left until the last moment. They should be planned and arranged for at least several days in advance of the show in order for you to remain calm and relaxed as the countdown starts.

266

The importance of the crate has already been mentioned, and should already be part of your equipment. Of equal importance is the grooming table, which very likely you have also already acquired for use at home. You should take it along with you to the shows, as your dog will need last minute touches before entering the ring. Should you have not yet made this purchase, folding tables with rubber tops are made specifically for this purpose and can be purchased at most dog shows, where concession booths with marvelous assortments of "doggy" necessities are to be found, or at your pet supplier. You will also need a sturdy tack box (also available at the dog show concessions) in which to carry your grooming tools and equipment. The latter should include brushes, comb, scissors, nail clippers, whatever you use for last minute clean-up jobs, cotton swabs, first-aid equipment, and anything you are in the habit of using on the dog, including a leash or two of the type you prefer, some well-cooked and dried-out liver or any of the small packaged "dog treats" for use as bait in the ring, an atomizer in case you wish to dampen your dog's coat when you are preparing him for the ring, and so on. A large turkish towel to spread under the dog on the grooming table is also useful.

Take a large thermos or cooler of ice, the biggest one you can accommodate in your vehicle, for use by "man and beast." Take a jug of water (there are lightweight, inexpensive ones available at all sporting goods shops) and a water dish. If you plan to feed the dog at the show, or if you and the dog will be away from home more than one day, bring food for him from home so that he will have the type to which he is accustomed.

You may or may not have an exercise pen. While the shows do provide areas for exercise of the dogs, these are among the most likely places to have your dog come in contact with any illnesses which may be going around, and having a pen of your own for your dog's use is excellent protection. Such a pen can be used in other ways, too, such as a place other than the crate in which to put the dog to relax (that is roomier than the crate) and a place in which the dog can exercise at motels and rest stops. These pens are available at the show concession stands and come in a variety of heights and sizes. A set of "pooper scoopers" should also be

267

part of your equipment, along with a package of plastic bags for cleaning up after your dog.

Bring along folding chairs for the members of your party, unless all of you are fond of standing, as these are almost never provided anymore by the clubs. Have your name stamped on the chairs so that there will be no doubt as to whom the chairs belong. Bring whatever you and your family enjoy for drinks or snacks in a picnic basket or cooler, as show food, in general, is expensive and usually not great. You should always have a pair of boots, a raincoat, and a rain hat with you (they should remain permanently in your vehicle if you plan to attend shows regularly), as well as a sweater, a warm coat, and a change of shoes. A smock or big cover-up apron will assure that you remain tidy as you prepare the dog for the ring. Your overnight case should include a small sewing kit for emergency repairs, bandaids, headache and indigestion remedies, and any personal products or medications you normally use.

In your car you should always carry maps of the area where you are headed and an assortment of motel directories. Generally speaking, Holiday Inns have been found to be the nicest about taking dogs. Ramadas and Howard Johnsons generally do so cheerfully (with a few exceptions). Best Western generally frowns on pets (not always, but often enough to make it necessary to find out which do). Some of the smaller chains welcome pets; the majority of privately owned motels do not.

Have everything prepared the night before the show to expedite your departure. Be sure that the dog's identification and your judging program and other show information are in your purse or briefcase. If you are taking sandwiches, have them ready. Anything that goes into the car the night before the show will be one thing less to remember in the morning. Decide upon what you will wear and have it out and ready. If there is any question in your mind about what to wear, try on the possibilities before the day of the show; don't risk feeling you may want to change when you see yourself dressed a few moments prior to departure time!

In planning your outfit, make it something simple that will not detract from your dog. Remember that a dark dog silhouettes attractively against a light background and vice-versa. Sport clothes always seem to look best at dog shows, preferably conservative in

Ch. Von Raseac's Quintessence, by Great Caesar's Ghost V Raseac ex Cameo's Lilabet of Jason, the dam of four champions, all of whom went on to become Group winners. Bred by R. Harris and Brucie Mitchell; owners, Kenyon and Harriet Larkin and Brucie Mitchell. Pictured with Gene Mitchell.

This is the very handsome Constant Comment who has been so tremendous an asset to the Lyons' Pride Great Danes owned by Lucy and Ed Lyons at Somers, Conn. Pictured winning under Maxwell Riddle.

type and not overly "loud" as you do not want to detract from your dog, who should be the focus of interest at this point. What you wear on your feet is important. Many types of flooring can be hazardously slippery, as can wet grass. Make it a habit to wear rubber soles and low or flat heels in the ring for your own safety, especially if you are showing a dog that likes to move out smartly.

Your final step in pre-show preparation is to leave yourself plenty of time to reach the show that morning. Traffic can get amazingly heavy as one nears the immediate area of the show, finding a parking place can be difficult, and other delays may occur. You'll be in better humor to enjoy the day if your trip to the show is not fraught with panic over fear of not arriving in time!

ENJOYING THE DOG SHOW

From the moment of your arrival at the show until after your dog has been judged, keep foremost in your mind the fact that he is your reason for being there and that he should therefore be the center of your attention. Arrive early enough to have time for those last-minute touches that can make a great difference when he enters the ring. Be sure that he has ample time to exercise and that he attends to personal matters. A dog arriving in the ring and immediately using it as an exercise pen hardly makes a favorable impression on the judge.

When you reach ringside, ask the steward for your arm-card and anchor it firmly into place on your arm. Make sure that you are where you should be when your class is called. The fact that you have picked up your arm-card does not guarantee, as some seem to think, that the judge will wait for you. The judge has a full schedule which he wishes to complete on time. Even though you may be nervous, assume an air of calm self-confidence. Remember that this is a hobby to be enjoyed, so approach it in that state of mind. The dog will do better, too, as he will be quick to reflect your attitude.

Always show your dog with an air of pride. If you make mistakes in presenting him, don't worry about it. Next time you will do better. Do not permit the presence of more experienced exhibitors to intimidate you. After all, they, too, once were newcomers.

The judging routine usually starts when the judge asks that the dogs be gaited in a circle around the ring. During this period the judge is watching each dog as it moves, noting style, topline, reach and drive, head and tail carriage, and general balance. Keep your mind and your eye on your dog, moving him at his most becoming gait and keeping your place in line without coming too close to the exhibitor ahead of you. Always keep your dog on the inside of the circle, between yourself and the judge, so that the judge's view of the dog is unobstructed.

Calmly pose the dog when requested to set up for examination. If you are at the head of the line and many dogs are in the class, go all the way to the end of the ring before starting to stack the dog, leaving sufficient space for those behind you to line theirs up as well, as requested by the judge. If you are not at the head of the line but between other exhibitors, leave sufficient space ahead of your dog for the judge to examine him. The dogs should be spaced so that the judge is able to move among them so see them from all angles. In practicing to "set up" or "stack" your dog for the judge's examination, bear in mind the importance of doing so quickly and with dexterity. The judge has a schedule to meet and only a few moments in which to evaulate each dog. You will immeasurably help yours to make a favorable impression if you are able to "get it all together" in a minimum amount of time. Practice at home before a mirror can be a great help toward bringing this about, facing the dog so that you see him from the same side that the judge will and working to make him look right in the shortest length of time.

Listen carefully as the judge describes the manner in which the dog is to be gaited, whether it is straight down and straight back; down the ring, across, and back; or in a triangle. The latter has become the most popular pattern with the majority of judges. "In a triangle" means the dog should move down the outer side of the ring to the first corner, across that end of the ring to the second corner, and then back to the judge from the second corner, using the center of the ring in a diagonal line. Please learn to do this pattern without breaking at each corner to twirl the dog around you, a senseless maneuver that has been noticed on occasion. Judges like to see the dog in an uninterrupted triangle, as they are thus able to get a better idea of the dog's gait.

It is impossible to overemphasize that the gait at which you move your dog is tremendously important and considerable study

272

and thought should be given to the matter. At home, have someone move the dog for you at different speeds so that you can tell which shows him off to best advantage. The most becoming action almost invariably is seen at a moderate gait, head up and topline holding. Do not gallop your dog around the ring or hurry him into a speed atypical of his breed. Nothing being rushed appears at its best; give your dog a chance to move along at his (and the breed's) natural gait. For a dog's action to be judged accurately, that dog should move with strength and power, but not excessive speed, holding a straight line as he goes to and from the judge.

As you bring the dog back to the judge, stop him a few feet away and be sure that he is standing in a becoming position. Bait him to show the judge an alert expression, using whatever tasty morsel he has been trained to expect for this purpose or, if that works better for you, use a small squeak-toy in your hand. A reminder, please, to those using liver or treats. Take them with you when you leave the ring. Do not just drop them on the ground where they will be found by another dog.

When the awards have been made, accept yours graciously, no matter how you actually may feel about it. What's done is done, and arguing with a judge or stomping out of the ring is useless and a reflection on your sportsmanship. Be courteous, congratulate the winner if your dog was defeated, and try not to show your disappointment. By the same token, please be a gracious winner; this, surprisingly, sometimes seems to be still more difficult.

Ch. Abner Lowell Davis, #1 Great Dane, #4 Working Dog, #5 All Breeds in 1971, all systems. Handled by Jack Dexter for breeders-owners Arlene and Lowell K. Davis, Covina, California.

Chapter 14

Your Great Dane and Obedience

For its own protection and safety, every dog should be taught, at the very least, to recognize and obey the commands "Come," "Heel," "Down," "Sit," and "Stay." Doing so at some time might save the dog's life and in less extreme circumstances will certainly make him a better behaved, more pleasant member of society. If you are patient and enjoy working with your dog, study some of the excellent books available on the subject of obedience and then teach your canine friend these basic manners. If you need the stimulus of working with a group, find out where obedience training classes are held (usually your veterinarian, your dog's breeder, or a dog-owning friend can tell you) and you and your dog can join up. Alternatively, you could let someone else do the training by sending the dog to class, but this is not very rewarding because you lose the opportunity of working with your dog and the pleasure of the rapport thus established.

If you are going to do it yourself, there are some basic rules which you should follow. You must remain calm and confident in attitude. Never lose your temper and frighten or punish your dog unjustly. Be quick and lavish with praise each time a command is correctly followed. Make it fun for the dog and he will be eager to please you by responding correctly. Repetition is the keynote, but it should not be continued without recess to the point of tedium. Limit the training sessions to ten- or fifteen-minute periods at a time.

Formal obedience training can be followed, and very frequently is, by entering the dog in obedience competition to work toward an obedience degree, or several of them, depending on the dog's aptitude and your own enjoyment. Obedience trials are held in conjunction with the majority of all-breed conformation dog shows, with Specialty shows, and frequently as separate Specialty events. If you are working alone with your dog, a list of trial dates might be obtained from your dog's veterinarian, your dog breeder, or a dog-owning friend; the AKC *Gazette* lists shows and trials to be scheduled in the coming months; and if you are a member of a training class, you will find the information readily available.

The goals for which one works in the formal AKC Member or Licensed Trials are the following titles: Companion Dog (C.D.), Companion Dog Excellent (C.D.X.), and Utility Dog (U.D.). These degrees are earned by receiving three "legs," or qualifying scores, at each level of competition. The degrees must be earned in order, with one completed prior to starting work on the next. For example, a dog must have earned C.D. prior to starting work on C.D.X.; then C.D.X. must be completed before U.D. work begins. The ultimate title attainable in obedience work is Obedience Trial Champion (O.T.Ch.)

When you see the letters C.D. following a dog's name, you will know that this dog has satisfactorily completed the following exercises: heel on leash and figure eight, heel free, stand for examination, recall, long sit, and long down. C.D.X. means that tests have been passed on all of those just mentioned plus heel free and figure eight, drop on recall, retrieve on flat, retrieve over high jump, broad jump, long sit, and long down. U.D. indicates that the dog has additionally passed tests in scent discrimination (leather article), scent discrimination (metal article), signal exercise, directed retrieve, directed jumping, and group stand for examination. The letters O.T.Ch. are the abbreviation for the only obedience title which precedes rather than follows a dog's name. To gain an obedience trial championship, a dog who already holds a Utility Dog degree must win a total of one hundred points and must win three firsts, under three different judges, in Utility and Open B Classes.

There is also a Tracking Dog title (T.D.) which can be earned at tracking trials. In order to pass the tracking tests the dog must follow the trail of a stranger along a path on which the trail was laid between thirty minutes and two hours previously. Along this track there must be more than two right-angle turns, at least two of which are well out in the open where no fences or other boundaries exist for the guidance of the dog or the handler. The dog wears a harness and is connected to the handler by a lead twenty to forty feet in length. Inconspicuously dropped at the end of the track is an article to be retrieved, usually a glove or wallet, which the dog is expected to locate and the handler to pick up. The letters T.D.X. is the abbreviation for Tracking Dog Excellent, a more difficult version of the Tracking Dog test with a longer track and more turns to be worked through.

ZOLLY IN THE OBEDIENCE RING

Beth and Dale Meyer live at Auburn, Washington, and have two Great Danes at the present time. These were not the first Danes Beth had owned; she had black ones in the past; but when she saw a Boston puppy in a litter it was more than she could resist as a pet, so home with her the youngster came to be named RNR's Sweet Sadie. She was also the first Dane whose ears Beth had had cropped, and of that she says "probably also my last."

Beth bought Sadie on a breeder's contract arrangement, so in due time she was bred. The sire used was American and Canadian Champion Kimo's Rock of Cashel, who was a Harlequin. Out of the seven puppies, Beth got three show marked Harlequins and kept the male whom they named Zoltan, King of the Hill.

Zolly started his obedience training when he was four months old. He is mostly an outdoor dog, Beth explains, therefore the toughest part of the class the first few weeks was getting him to walk on the slick floors and to stop imitating a pancake. Zolly was three years old on November 8, 1985, and has been in obedience classes since his first puppy class at four months.

Beth tells us,"He enjoyed the work, and so did I. So when he was around 14 months old we thought that we would try towards competitive obedience. So what if I do have a Dane, and everyone knows Danes do not move fast enough to look anything but funny! I was wrong about this, however! Our instructor asked us to be part of a demonstration for a local kennel club so that they could see that a Dane, too, can be quick and precise."

The Meyers next decided that they would like to try showing in conformation competition while training for the obedience ring. Beth wanted to help the Harlequin color become more accepted. Also she wanted, hopefully, to show that uncropped Danes can win, too. Showing an uncropped Harlequin Dane was certainly more than a slight challenge, and so Beth was delighted when, at his second show, Zolly was awarded reserve in a major entry. After that he gained blues, a couple of reds. This was Beth's first attempt at conformation handling, so she felt that her owner-handled uncropped Harlequin Dane was really doing rather well, and while so far they have limited their showing to Washington and Oregon, the Meyers are looking towards Canada for their next step.

But returning to Zolly the obedience dog! He and Beth train at Canine College in Bellevue, Washington where Zolly is the biggest dog in the class. Some of the exercises had to be modified a little due to his size, since he is over 36 inches tall and weighs in at about 200 pounds, mostly muscle. He surprises everyone by how fast he does everything, and how straight he can sit. Again quoting Beth, "It hasn't been easy, but it's been a LOT of fun."

Zolly has always been a "people attracter." He and Beth can walk into a building full of people and dogs and have everyone turn and look. Then Beth has Dale hold Zolly's lead so that she can get away and watch the pattern for the breed or obedience ring. People are constantly (non-stop) coming up to whoever is with Zolly seeking permission to pet him, and obviously admiring. The applause following Zolly's obedience routine is amazing.

The Meyers—and Zolly—are very proud of their three scores so far in Novice A: 196, 196, and 197. Next they will start working towards his C.D.X.

Says Beth Meyer, "I'd like to encourage all Dane owners to join us in the obedience ring. Attitude is important for both you and your Dane, the trick being to make it fun for both yourself and your dog. A Great Dane wants to please, and as long as you keep

This is the mother of Zolly, Beth Meyer's Boston-marked Dane whom she was unable to resist. We have heard the thought expressed in some circles that this attractive pattern *should* be admitted as an acceptable show color for a Harlequin. Perhaps one day in the future that may come to pass.

Winning his second C.D. leg, Zolly doing recall at the Washington State Obedience Training Club.

"Well, what'd you stop for? Let's go," says Zolly to owner-trainer-handler Beth Meyer, who replies, "I was nervous — he was not."

Ch. Shadam's Chessa, along with being an outstanding show bitch, has had some training as a gun dog and works well in the field. She also works in tracking and has successfully executed some medium length tracks so far. Owned by Nancy L. Gilbert, Everett, Wash., and June Herbst, Albany, Ore.

giving positive reinforcement he will do anything for you. A Dane can move as fast as you ask of him. You make it slow and they will move slow."

Zolly is truly a *companion dog*. He swims, retrieves, is good with horses, loves children and other dogs. And he now has earned his C.D.

There you have it, the story of how One Dane's Family enjoys their Dane. You can do likewise with time and patience. The rewards are generous.

A FIELD AND RETRIEVING GREAT DANE

Champion Shadam's Chessa is an excellent example of the diverse talents of a Great Dane. For who would think of one of this breed for work as a retriever, in the field, and for tracking? Yet Chessa excels in all three of these areas, as well as in the show ring.

Chessa belongs to Nancy L. Gilbert of Everett, Washington, who has been working with her in the field and on the tracking course; and by Mrs. June Herbst of Albany, Oregon, at whose home Chessa's first litter has recently been whelped, and who has primarily handled this lovely bitch.

Chessa is a granddaughter of Champion Rojon's The Hustler on her sire's and dam's sides. She is predominantly von Reisenhof and Marydane breeding. Her championship was completed at age two years with a 4-point major under Great Dane Club of America President, Donald Booxbaum.

Chessa is trained to retrieve, and will be used as a gun dog during hunting season. She has good bird instincts. Also she is being trained for a tracking degree, and will be entered in obedience classes following the weaning of her puppies.

During about nine months as a special in 1985, Chessa has won three Bests of Breed over specials, two under California breeder-judges, and a dozen Bests of Opposite Sex. During 1986 she will be shown in Canada as well as entered in obedience trials.

Headstudy, by Missy Yuhl, of the great sire and Best in Show winner. Am., Can., and Mex. Ch. Jecamo's Caesar of AAA. Owned by Gene Mitchell, bred by Jerry and Carolyn Mobley, sired by Trailblazer of Los Vientos ex Ch. Kelsey's Annie Laurie.

Chapter 15

Breeding Your Great Dane

An earlier chapter discussed selection of a bitch you plan to use for breeding. In making this important purchase, you will be choosing a bitch who you hope will become the foundation of your kennel. Thus she must be of the finest producing bloodlines, excellent in temperament, of good type, and free of major faults or unsoundness. If you are offered a "bargain" brood bitch, be wary, as for this purchase you should not settle for less than the best and the price will be in accordance with the quality.

Conscientious breeders feel quite strongly that the only possible reason for producing puppies is the ambition to improve and uphold quality and temperament within the breed—definitely *not* because one hopes to make a quick cash profit on a mediocre litter, which never seems to work out that way in the long run and which accomplishes little beyond perhaps adding to the nation's heartbreaking number of unwanted canines. The only reason ever for breeding a litter is, with conscientious people, a desire to improve the quality of dogs in their own kennel or, as pet owners, to add to the number of dogs they themselves own with a puppy or two from their present favorites. In either case breeding should not take place unless one definitely has prospective owners for as many puppies as the litter may contain, lest you find yourself with several fast-growing young dogs and no homes in which to place them.

THE GREAT DANE BROOD BITCH

Bitches should not be mated earlier than their second season, by which time they should be from fifteen to eighteen months old. Many breeders prefer to wait and first finish the championships of their show bitches before breeding them, as pregnancy can be a disaster to a show coat and getting the bitch back in shape again takes time. When you have decided what will be the proper time, start watching at least several months ahead for what you feel would be the perfect mate to best complement your bitch's quality and bloodlines. Subscribe to the magazines which feature your breed exclusively and to some which cover all breeds in order to familiarize yourself with outstanding stud dogs in areas other than your own for there is no necessity nowadays to limit your choice to a local dog unless you truly like him and feel that he is the most suitable. It is quite usual to ship a bitch to a stud dog a distance away, and this generally works out with no ill effects. The important thing is that you need a stud dog strong in those features where your bitch is weak or lacking, a dog whose bloodlines are compatible with hers. Compare the background of both your bitch and the stud dog under consideration, paying particular attention to the quality of the puppies from bitches with backgrounds similar to your bitch's. If the puppies have been of the type and quality you admire, then this dog would seem a sensible choice for yours, too.

Stud fees may be a few hundred dollars, sometimes even more under special situations for a particularly successful sire. It is money well spent, however. *Do not* ever breed to a dog because he is less expensive than the others unless you honestly believe that he can sire the kind of puppies who will be a credit to your kennel and your breed.

Contacting the owners of the stud dogs you find interesting will bring you pedigrees and pictures which you can then study in relation to your bitch's pedigree and conformation. Discuss your plans with other breeders who are knowledgeable (including the one who bred your own bitch). You may not always receive an entirely unbiased opinion (particularly if the person giving it also has an available stud dog), but one learns by discussion so listen to what they say, consider their opinions, and then you may be better qualified to form your own opinion.

This is the famed Ch. Mountdania's Timber, bred and owned by Leon E. Reimert, Coatesville, Pa. Although used sparingly at stud, Timber, prior to his untimely death, produced nine champions of which two were Best in Show winners, among them the lovely bitch Ch. Sunridge's Lil Liza Jane, who was Best in Show at Westchester in September 1974, owned by M.A. and J.A. Lawrence. Timber, by Danel's Caius of Mountdania ex Danel's Angee of Mountdania, here taking Best of Breed at the Great Dane Club of Central Pennsylvania Specialty in 1970 under Joe Gregory.

Ch. C. and B.'s Special-K, after retirement, "at home" in Wheeling with her devoted Lina!

Ch. Dinro Taboo, sire of Ch. Dinro Taboo Again and numerous other winners. Handled by his breeder-owner, the late Rosemarie Robert, Carmel, N.Y.

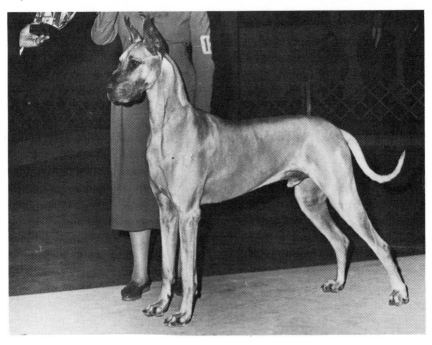

As soon as you have made a choice, phone the owner of the stud dog you wish to use to find out if this will be agreeable. You will be asked about the bitch's health, soundness, temperament, and freedom from serious faults. A copy of her pedigree may be requested, as might a picture of her. A discussion of her background over the telephone may be sufficient to assure the stud's owner that she is suitable for the stud dog and of type, breeding, and quality herself to produce puppies of the quality for which the dog is noted. The owner of a top-quality stud is often extremely selective in the bitches permitted to be bred to his dog, in an effort to keep the standard of his puppies high. The owner of a stud dog may require that the bitch be tested for brucellosis, which should be attended to not more than a month previous to the breeding.

Check out which airport will be most convenient for the person meeting and returning the bitch if she is to be shipped and also what airlines use that airport. You will find that the airlines are also apt to have special requirements concerning acceptance of animals for shipping. These include weather limitations and types of crates which are acceptable. The weather limits have to do with extreme heat and extreme cold at the point of destination, as some airlines will not fly dogs into temperatures above or below certain levels, fearing for their safety. The crate problem is a simple one, since, if your own crate is not suitable, most of the airlines have specially designed crates available for purchase at a fair and moderate price. It is a good plan to purchase one of these if you intend to be shipping dogs with any sort of frequency. They are made of fiberglass and are the safest type to use for shipping.

Normally you must notify the airline several days in advance to make a reservation, as they are able to accommodate only a certain number of dogs on each flight. Plan on shipping the bitch on about her eighth or ninth day of season, but be careful to avoid shipping her on a weekend when schedules often vary and freight offices are apt to be closed. Whenever you can, ship your bitch on a direct flight. Changing planes always carries a certain amount of risk of a dog being overlooked or wrongly routed at the middle stop, so avoid this danger if at all possible. The bitch must be accompanied by a health certificate which you must obtain from your veterinarian before taking her to the airport. Usually it will be necessary to have the bitch at the airport about two hours prior

287

Int'l. Ch. Zeila von Loheland, a very important bitch and famous importation to Ernest E. Ferguson's Estid Kennels circa 1940.

to flight time. Before finalizing arrangements, find out from the stud's owner at what time of day it will be most convenient to have the bitch picked up promptly upon arrival.

It is simpler if you can plan to bring the bitch to the stud dog yourself. Some people feel that the trauma of the flight may cause the bitch to not conceive; and, of course, undeniably there is a slight risk in shipping which can be avoided if you are able to drive the bitch to her destination. Be sure to leave yourself sufficient time to assure your arrival at the right time for her for breeding (normally the tenth to fourteenth day following the first signs of color); and remember that if you want the bitch bred twice, you should allow a day to elapse between the two matings. Do not expect the stud's owner to house you while you are there. Locate a nearby motel that takes dogs and make that your headquarters.

Just prior to the time your bitch is due in season, you should take her to visit your veterinarian. She should be checked for worms and should receive all the booster shots for which she is due plus one for parvovirus, unless she has had the latter shot fairly recently. The brucellosis test can also be done then, and the health certificate can be obtained for shipping if she is to travel by air. Should the bitch be at all overweight, now is the time to get the surplus off. She should be in good condition, neither underweight nor overweight, at the time of breeding.

The moment you notice the swelling of the vulva, for which you should be checking daily as the time for her season approaches, and the appearance of color, immediately contact the stud's owner and settle on the day for shipping or make the appointment for your arrival with the bitch for breeding. If you are shipping the bitch, the stud fee check should be mailed immediately, leaving ample time for it to have been received when the bitch arrives and the mating takes place. Be sure to call the airline, making her reservation at that time, too.

Do not feed the bitch within a few hours before shipping her. Be certain that she has had a drink of water and been well exercised before closing her in the crate. Several layers of newspapers, topped with some shredded newspaper, make a good bed and can be discarded when she arrives at her destination; these can be replaced with fresh newspapers for her return home. Remember that the bitch should be brought to the airport about two hours before flight time as sometimes the airlines refuse to accept late arrivals.

If you are taking your bitch by car, be certain that you will arrive at a reasonable time of day. Do not appear late in the evening. If your arrival in town is not until late, get a good night's sleep at your motel and contact the stud's owner first thing in the morning. If possible, leave children and relatives at home, as they will only be in the way and perhaps unwelcome by the stud's owner. Most stud dog owners prefer not to have any unnecessary people on hand during the actual mating.

After the breeding has taken place, if you wish to sit and visit for awhile and the stud's owner has the time, return the bitch to her crate in your car (first ascertaining, of course, that the temperature is comfortable for her and that there is proper ventilation). She should not be permitted to urinate for at least one hour following the breeding. This is the time when you get the business part of the transaction attended to. Pay the stud fee, upon which you should receive your breeding certificate and, if you do not already have it, a copy of the stud dog's pedigree. The owner of the stud dog does not sign or furnish a litter registration application until the puppies have been born.

Upon your return home, you can settle down and plan in happy anticipation a wonderful litter of puppies. A word of caution! Remember that although she has been bred, your bitch is still an interesting target for all male dogs, so guard her carefully for the next week or until you are absolutely certain that her season has entirely ended. This would be no time to have any unfortunate incident with another dog.

THE GREAT DANE STUD DOG

Choosing the best stud dog to complement your bitch is often very difficult. The two principal factors to be considered should be the stud's conformation and his pedigree. Conformation is fairly obvious; you want a dog that is typical of the breed in the words of the Standard of perfection. Understanding pedigrees is a bit more subtle since the pedigree lists the ancestry of the dog and involves individuals and bloodlines with which you may not be entirely familiar.

290

Am., Can., and Mex Ch. Jecamo's Caesar of AAA, foundation stud for Von Raseac Kennels, bred by Jerry and Carolyn Mobley. Owned by Gene Mitchell, San Luis Rey, Calif. Son of Trailblazer of Los Vientos ex Ch. Kelsey's Annie Laurie. A Best in Show and Group winner; the sire of 10 champions.

Am. and Can. Ch. Von Raseac's Quite A Gal, by Great Caesar's Ghost v Raseac ex Cameo's Lilabet of Jacon, owned by Gene and Brucie Mitchell. A Best in Show winner and a "winner" in the whelping box — dam of seven champions. Portrait by Michael.

A special salute goes to the dog who is not only the #1 Great Dane Sire in history but who is the sire, as well, of the dog who will succeed him for this honor. This is Champion Ashbun Acres Avant-Garde who was born on September 22, 1971, bred by John W. and Constance Bungart, owned by Hugo and Sally Gamboa, Champaign, Illinois, and died on April 10, 1979. Avant-Garde sired a total of 37 champions, among them the "heir apparent" to his throne, Champion Mountdania's Ashley, who is pressing close in number of champions sired as we write. Ashley is from Mountdania's Katie O'Kauffman.

The champions sired by Avant-Garde in addition to Ashley, and their dams, are listed below:

Ch. Sheenwater Joker's Wild (D), ex Sheenwater Grassfire.

Ch. Psyche's Aurora V Ravenna (B), ex Glorilane Psyche of Bella-D.

Ch. Yoredane's Ms D.D. Marston (B) ex Ch. Cranedane's Javelin.

Ch. Hayron's Pretty Penny (B), ex D.D.'s Lady Lorelei of Carl-Mar.

Ch. Marstondane's Javelin (B), ex Ch. Crandane's Javelin.

Ch. Sheenwater Knock Out (D), ex Sheenwater Grassfire.

Ch. Sheenwater Joie De Vivre (B), ex Sheenwater Grassfire.

Ch. Brandelyn's Rhiannon (B), ex Ch. Brandelyn's Encore.

Ch. Sheenwater Kiss and Tell (B), ex Sheenwater Grassfire.

Ch. Gabet Brandelyn Avant Viking (D), ex Ch. Brandelyn's Encore.

Ch. Brandelyn's Tantamount (D), ex Ch. Brandelyn's Encore.

Ch. Honey Lane's Once Upon A Dream (B), ex Honeylane's Keeley.

Ch. Mountdania's Ms. Avant Garde (B), ex Ch. Mountdania's Heather.

Ch. Daichi's Drumbshanbo (D), ex Ch. Rockhill's Fancy Britches.

Ch. Jerita's The Midas Touch (D), ex Arndale's Miss Sydney of Betts.

Ch. Devroks Zartanian V Sheboane, ex Devrok's Quite A Doll.

Ch. Jonlyn's Miss Elizabeth Z (B), ex Arndale's Miss Sydney of Betts.

Ch. Honey Lane's One More Time (B), ex Honeylane's Keeley.

Ch. Sheenwater Jackpot (D), ex Sheenwater Grassfire.

Ch. Brandelyn's Keridwen (B), ex Ch. Brandelyn's Encore.

Ch. Perridane's Reno (D), ex Arndale's Phaedra V Perridane.

Ch. Brandelyn Derek of Woodcliff (D), ex Ch. Brandelyn's Encore.

Ch. Sheenwater Jubilee (B), ex Sheenwater Grassfire.

Ch. Yoredane's Mr. President (D), ex Von Riesenhof's Lady Godiva.

Ch. Sheenwater Koenig V Ashbun A (D), ex Sheenwater Grassfire.

Ch. Rodane Tourister (D), ex Rodane Sophisticated Lady.

Ch. Mountdania's Serendipity (B), ex Mountdania's Katie O'Kauffman.

Ch. Reann's French Aristocrat (D), ex Ch. Reann's Barefoot Contessa.

Ch. Jonlyn's Ms Helen Coates (B), ex Murlo Razz Ma Tazz.

Ch. Allegra's Avant-Arpeggio (B), ex Ch. Mountdania's Heather.

Ch. Fowler's Forget Me Not (B), ex Ch. Rojan's Please Me.

Ch. Reann Granada's Fiesta (B), ex Ch. Reann's Barefoot Contessa.

Ch. Waldenthree's Tecumseh (D), ex Hearth Hill Curie Waldenthree.

Ch. Reann's Forever Amber (D), ex Ch. Reann's Barefoot Contessa.

Ch. Waldenthree's Tecumseh (D), ex Hearth Hill Curie Waldenthree.

Ch. Lazycroft Zoe Sandale (B), ex Lazycroft Topaz.

Ch. Reann's French Connection (D), ex Ch. Reann's Barefoot Contessa.

As a show dog, "Alfie" was a multiple Best in Show and Specialty winner, including the Great Dane Club Of America National.

To a novice in the breed, then, the correct interpretation of a pedigree may at first be difficult to grasp. Study the pictures and text of this book and you will find many names of important bloodlines and members of the breed. Also make an effort to discuss the various dogs behind the proposed stud with some of the more experienced breeders, starting with the breeder of your own bitch. Frequently these folks will be personally familiar with many of the dogs in question, can offer opinions of them, and may have access to additional pictures which you would benefit by seeing. It is very important that the stud's pedigree be harmonious with that of the bitch you plan on breeding to him. Do not rush out and breed to the latest winner with no thought of whether or not he can produce true quality. By no means are all great show dogs great producers. It is the producing record of the dog in question and the dogs and bitches from which he has come that should be the basis on which you make your choice.

Breeding dogs is never a money-making operation. By the time you pay a stud fee, care for the bitch during pregnancy, whelp the litter, and rear the puppies through their early shots, worming, and so on, you will be fortunate to break even financially once the puppies have been sold. Your chances of doing this are greater if you are breeding for a show-quality litter which will bring you higher prices, as the pups are sold as show prospects. Therefore, your wisest investment is to use the best dog available for your bitch regardless of the cost; then you should wind up with more valuable puppies. Remember that it is equally costly to raise mediocre puppies as it is top ones, and your chances of financial return are better on the latter. To breed to the most excellent, most suitable stud dog you can find is the only sensible thing to do, and it is poor economy to quibble over the amount you are paying in a stud fee.

It will be your decision which course you decide to follow when you breed your bitch, as there are three options: linebreeding, inbreeding, and outcrossing. Each of these methods has its supporters and its detractors! Linebreeding is breeding a bitch to a dog belonging originally to the same canine family, being descended from the same ancestors, such as half brother to half sister, grandsire to granddaughter, niece to uncle (and vice-versa) or cousin to cousin. Inbreeding is breeding father to daughter, mother to son, or full brother to sister. Outcross breeding is breeding a dog and a bitch with no or only a few mutual ancestors.

Linebreeding is probably the safest course, and the one most likely to bring results, for the novice breeder. The more sophisticated inbreeding should be left to the experienced, longtime breeders who throroughly know and understand the risks and the possibilities involved with a particular line. It is usually done in an effort to intensify some ideal feature in that strain. Outcrossing is the reverse of inbreeding, an effort to introduce improvement in a specific feature needing correction, such as a shorter back, better movement, more correct head or coat, and so on.

It is the serious breeder's ambition to develop a strain or bloodline of their own, one strong in qualities for which their dogs will become distinguished. However, it must be realized that this will involve time, patience, and at least several generations before the achievement can be claimed. The safest way to embark on this plan, as we have mentioned, is by the selection and breeding of one or two bitches, the best you can buy and from top-producing kennels. In the beginning you do *not* really have to own a stud dog. In the long run it is less expensive and sounder judgement to pay a stud fee when you are ready to breed a bitch than to purchase a stud dog and feed him all year; a stud dog does not win any popularity contests with owners of bitches to be bred until he becomes a champion, has been successfully Specialed for a while, and has been at least moderately advertised, all of which adds up to quite a healthy expenditure.

The wisest course for the inexperienced breeder just starting out in dogs is as outlined above. Keep the best bitch puppy from the first several litters. After that you may wish to consider keeping your own stud dog if there has been a particularly handsome male in one of your litters that you feel has great potential or if you know where there is one available that you are interested in, with the feeling that he would work in nicely with the breeding program on which you have embarked. By this time, with several litters already born, your eye should have developed to a point enabling you to make a wise choice, either from one of your own litters or from among dogs you have seen that appear suitable.

The greatest care should be taken in the selection of your own stud dog. He must be of true type and highest quality as he may be responsible for siring many puppies each year, and he should come from a line of excellent dogs on both sides of his pedigree which themselves are, and which are descended from, successful producers. This dog should have no glaring faults in conformation; he should be of such a quality that he can hold his own in keenest competition within his breed. He should be in good health, be virile and be a keen stud dog, a proven sire able to transmit his correct qualities to his puppies. Need I say that such a dog will be enormously expensive unless you have the good fortune to produce him in one of your own litters? To buy and use a lesser stud dog, however, is downgrading your breeding program unnecessarily since there are so many dogs fitting the description of a fine stud whose services can be used on payment of a stud fee.

You should *never* breed to an unsound dog or one with any serious disqualifying faults according to the breed's standard. Not all champions by any means pass along their best features; and by the same token, occasionally you will find a great one who can pass along his best features but never gained his championship title due to some unusual circumstances. The information you need about a stud dog is what type of puppies he has produced and with what bloodlines and whether or not he possesses the bloodlines and attributes considered characteristic of the best in your breed.

If you go out to buy a stud dog, obviously he will not be a puppy but rather a fully mature and proven male with as many of the best attributes as possible. True, he will be an expensive investment, but if you choose and make his selection with care and forethought, he may well prove to be one of the best investments you have ever made.

Of course, the most exciting of all is when a young male you have decided to keep from one of your litters due to his tremendous show potential turns out to be a stud dog such as we have described. In this case he should be managed with care, for he is a valuable property that can contribute inestimably to this breed as a whole and to your own kennel specifically.

Do not permit your stud dog to be used until he is about a year old, and even then he should be bred to mature, proven matron accustomed to breeding who will make his first experience pleasant and easy. A young dog can be put off forever by a maiden bitch who fights and resists his advances. Never allow this to happen. Always start a stud dog out with a bitch who is mature, has been bred previously, and is of even temperament. The first breeding should be performed in quiet surroundings with only you and one other person to hold the bitch. Do not make it a circus, as the experience will determine the dog's outlook about future stud work. If he does not enjoy the first experience or associates it with any unpleasantness, you may well have a problem in the future.

Your young stud must permit help with the breeding, as later there will be bitches who will not be cooperative. If right from the beginning you are there helping him and praising him, whether or not your assistance is actually needed, he will expect and accept this as a matter of course when a difficult bitch comes along.

Things to have handy before introducing your dog and the bitch are K-Y jelly (the only lubricant which should be used) and a length of gauze with which to muzzle the bitch should it be necessary to keep her from biting you or the dog. Some bitches put up a fight; others are calm. It is best to be prepared.

At the time of the breeding, the stud fee comes due, and it is expected that it will be paid promptly. Normally a return service is offered in case the bitch misses or fails to produce one live puppy. Conditions of the service are what the stud dog's owner makes them, and there are no standard rules covering this. The stud fee is paid for the act, not the result. If the bitch fails to conceive, it is customary for the owner to offer a free return service; but this is a courtesy and not to be considered a right, particularly in the case of a proven stud who is siring consistently and whose fault the failure obviously is *not*. Stud dog owners are always anxious to see their clients get good value and to have in the ring winning young stock by their dog; therefore, very few refuse to mate the second time. It is wise, however, for both parties to have the terms of the transaction clearly understood at the time of the breeding.

If the return service has been provided and the bitch has missed a second time, that is considered to be the end of the matter and the owner would be expected to pay a further fee if it is felt that the bitch should be given a third chance with the stud dog. The management of a stud dog and his visiting bitches is quite a task, and a stud fee has usually been well earned when one service has been achieved, let alone by repeated visits from the same bitch.

The accepted litter is one live puppy. It is wise to have printed a breeding certificate which the owner of the stud dog and the owner of the bitch both sign. This should list in detail the conditions of the breeding as well as the dates of the mating.

Upon occasion, arrangements other than a stud fee in cash are made for a breeding, such as the owner of the stud taking a pick-of-the-litter puppy in lieu of money. This should be clearly specified on the breeding certificate along with the terms of the age at which the stud's owner will select the puppy, whether it is to be a specific sex, or whether it is to be the pick of the entire litter.

The price of a stud fee varies according to circumstances. Usually, to prove a young stud dog, his owner will allow the first breeding to be quite inexpensive. Then, once a bitch has become pregnant by him, he becomes a "proven stud" and the fee rises accordingly for bitches that follow. The sire of championship quality puppies will bring a stud fee of at least the purchase price of one show puppy as the accepted "rule-of-thumb." Until at least one champion by your stud dog has finished, the fee will remain equal to the price of one pet puppy. When his list of champions starts to grow, so does the amount of the stud fee. For a top-producing sire of champions, the stud fee will rise accordingly.

Almost invariably it is the bitch who comes to the stud dog for the breeding. Immediately upon having selected the stud dog you wish to use, discuss the possibility with the owner of that dog. It is the stud dog owner's prerogative to refuse to breed any bitch deemed unsuitable for this dog. Stud fee and method of payment should be stated at this time and a decision reached on whether it is to be a full cash transaction at the time of the mating or a pick-of-the-litter puppy, usually at eight weeks of age.

If the owner of the stud dog must travel to an airport to meet the bitch and ship her for the flight home, an additional charge will be made for time, tolls, and gasoline based on the stud owner's proximity to the airport. The stud fee includes board for the day on the bitch's arrival through two days for breeding, with a day in between. If it is necessary that the bitch remain longer, it is very likely that additional board will be charged at the normal per-day rate for the breed.

Be sure to advise the stud's owner as soon as you know that your bitch is in season so that the stud dog will be available. This is especially important because if he is a dog being shown, he and his owner may be unavailable, owing to the dog's absence from home.

As the owner of a stud dog being offered to the public, it is essential that you have proper facilities for the care of visiting bitches. Nothing can be worse than a bitch being insecurely housed and slipping out to become lost or bred by the wrong dog. If you are taking people's valued bitches into your kennel or home, it is imperative that you provide them with comfortable, secure housing and good care while they are your responsibility.

There is no dog more valuable than the proven sire of champions, Group winners, and Best in Show dogs. Once you have such an animal, guard his reputation well and do *not* permit him to be bred to just any bitch that comes along. It takes two to make the puppies; even the most dominant stud cannot do it all himself, so never permit him to breed a bitch you consider unworthy. Remember that when the puppies arrive, it will be your stud dog who will be blamed for any lack of quality, while the bitch's shortcomings will be quickly and conveniently overlooked.

Going into the actual management of the mating is a bit superfluous here. If you have had previous experience in breeding a dog and bitch you will know how the mating is done. If you do not have such experience, you should not attempt to follow direction given in a book but should have a veterinarian, breeder friend, or handler there to help you with the first few times. You do not just turn the dog and bitch loose together and await developments, as too many things can go wrong and you may altogether miss getting the bitch bred. Someone should hold the dog and the bitch (one person each) until the "tie" is made and these two people should stay with them during the entire act.

If you get a complete tie, probably only the one mating is absolutely necessary. However, especially with a maiden bitch or one that has come a long distance for this breeding, we prefer following up with a second breeding, leaving one day in between the two matings. In this way there will be little or no chance of the bitch missing.

Once the tie has been completed and the dogs release, be certain that the male's penis goes completely back within its sheath. He should be allowed a drink of water and a short walk, and then he should be put into his crate or somewhere alone where he can settle down. Do not allow him to be with other dogs for a while as they will notice the odor of the bitch on him, and, particularly with other males present, he may become involved in a fight.

PREGNANCY, WHELPING, AND THE LITTER

Once the bitch has been bred and is back at home, remember to keep an ever watchful eye that no other males get to her until at least the twenty-second day of her season has passed. Until then, it will still be possible for an unwanted breeding to take place, which at this point would be catastrophic. Remember that she actually can have two separate litters by two different dogs, so take care.

In other ways, she should be treated normally. Controlled exercise is good, and necessary for the bitch throughout her pregnancy, tapering it off to just several short walks daily, preferably on lead, as she reaches about her seventh week. As her time grows close, be careful about her jumping or playing too roughly.

The theory that a bitch should be overstuffed with food when pregnant is a poor one. A fat bitch is never an easy whelper, so the overfeeding you consider good for her may well turn out to be a hindrance later on. During the first few weeks of pregnancy, your bitch should be fed her normal diet. At four to five weeks along, calcium should be added to her food. At seven weeks her food may be increased if she seems to crave more than she is getting, and a meal of canned milk (mixed with an equal amount of water) should be introduced. If she is fed just once a day, add another meal rather than overload her with too much at one time. If twice a day is her schedule, then a bit more food can be added to each feeding.

A week before the pups are due, your bitch should be introduced to her whelping box so that she will be accustomed to it and feel at home there when the puppies arrive. She should be encouraged to sleep there but permitted to come and go as she wishes. The box should be roomy enough for her to lie down and stretch out in but not too large, lest the pups have more room than is

300

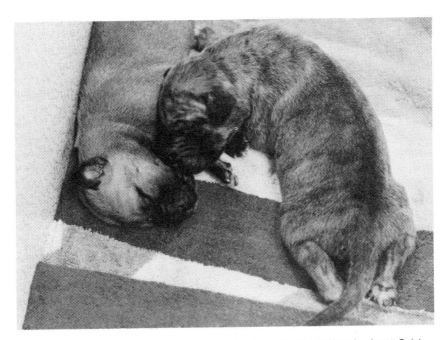

Fawn and brindle newborn Great Dane puppies from Rochford Kennels, Janet Quick, Kansas City, Mo.

The dam of these black puppies was fawn from brindle and fawn parents. This litter whelped in 1957 sired by Ch. Honey Hollow Rameses consisted of seven black puppies. Lina Basquette, owner, Honey Hollow Great Danes, Chalfont, Pa.

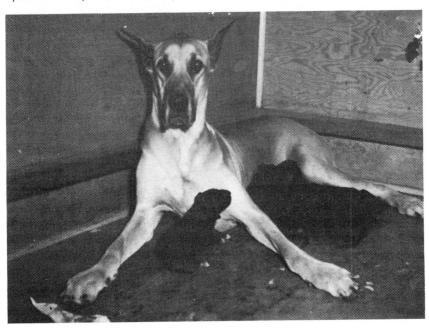

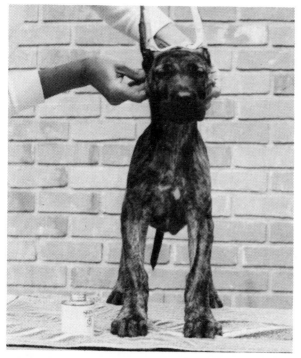

Front view of a show-prospect puppy, age nine weeks. Thor Dane's Stroh Du Lite was bred by Ed and Linda Springthorpe and is owned by Paul and Sally Harris.

Two fawn male Great Dane puppies at age eight weeks. By Ch. Rika's Rendition of Kingswood ex Laurado's Shana. Breeder-owners Larry Burgess and Katie Wood.

needed in which to roam and possibly get chilled by going too far away from their mother. Be sure that the box has a "pig rail"; this will prevent the puppies from being crushed against the sides. The room in which the box is placed, either in your home or in the kennel, should be kept at about 70 degrees Fahrenheit. In winter it may be necessary to have an infrared lamp over the whelping box, in which case be careful not to place it too low or close to the puppies.

Newspapers will become a very important commodity, so start collecting them well in advance to have a big pile handy for the whelping box. With a litter of puppies, one never seems to have papers enough, so the higher pile to start with, the better off you will be. Other necessities for whelping time are clean, soft turkish towels, scissors, and a bottle of alcohol.

You will know that her time is very near when your bitch becomes restless, wandering in and out of her box and of the room. She may refuse food, and at that point her temperature will start to drop. She will dig at and tear up the newspapers in her box, shiver, and generally look uncomfortable. Only you should be with your bitch at this time. She does not need spectators; and several people, even though they may be family members whom she knows, hanging over her may upset her to the point where she may harm the puppies. You should remain nearby, quietly watching, not fussing or hovering; speak calmly and frequently to her to instill confidence. Eventually she will settle down in her box and begin panting; contractions will follow. Soon thereafter a puppy will start to emerge, sliding out with the contractions. The mother immediately should open the sac, sever the cord with her teeth, and then clean up the puppy. She will also eat the placenta, which you should permit. Once the puppy is cleaned, it should be placed next to the bitch unless she is showing signs of having the next one immediately. Almost at once the puppy will start looking for a nipple on which to nurse, and you should ascertain that it is able to latch on successfully.

If the puppy is a breech (*i.e.*, born feet first), you must watch carefully for it to be completely delivered as quickly as possible and for the sac to be removed quickly so that the puppy does not drown. Sometimes even a normally positioned birth will seem extremely slow in coming. Should this occur, you might take a clean towel, and as the bitch contracts, pull the puppy out, doing so gently and with utmost care. If, once the puppy is delivered, it shows little signs of life, take a rough turkish towel and massage the puppy's chest by rubbing quite briskly back and forth. Continue this for about fifteen minutes, and be sure that the mouth is free of liquid. It may be necessary to try mouth-to-mouth breathing, which is done by pressing the puppy's jaws open and, using a finger, depressing the tongue which may be stuck to the roof of the mouth. Then place your mouth against the puppy's and blow hard down the puppy's throat. Rub the puppy's chest with the towel again and try artificial respiration, pressing the sides of the chest together slowly and rhythmically—in and out, in and out. Keep trying one method or the other for at least twenty minutes before giving up. You may be rewarded with a live puppy who otherwise would not have made it.

If you are successful in bringing the puppy around, do not immediately put it back with the mother as it should be kept extra warm. Put it in a cardboard box on an electric heating pad or, if it is the time of year when your heat is running, near a radiator or near the fireplace or stove. As soon as the rest of the litter has been born, it then can join the others.

An hour or more may elapse between puppies, which is fine so long as the bitch seems comfortable and is neither straining nor contracting. She should not be permitted to remain unassisted for more than an hour if she does continue to contract. This is when you should get her to your veterinarian, whom you should already have alerted to the possibility of a problem existing. He should examine her and perhaps give her a shot of Pituitrin. In some cases the veterinarian may find that a Caesarean section is necessary due to a puppy being lodged in a manner making normal delivery impossible. Sometimes this is caused by an abnormally large puppy, or it may just be that the puppy is simply turned in the wrong position. If the bitch does require a Caesarean section, the puppies already born must be kept warm in their cardboard box with a heating pad under the box.

Once the section is done, get the bitch and the puppies home. Do not attempt to put the puppies in with the bitch until she has regained consciousness as she may unknowingly hurt them. But do get them back to her as soon as possible for them to start nursing.

Should the mother lack milk at this time, the puppies must be fed by hand, kept very warm, and held onto the mother's teats several times a day in order to stimulate and encourage the secretion of milk, which should start shortly.

Assuming that there has been no problem and that the bitch has whelped naturally, you should insist that she go out to exercise, staying just long enough to make herself comfortable. She can be offered a bowl of milk and a biscuit, but then she should settle down with her family. Freshen the whelping box for her with fresh newspapers while she is taking this respite so that she and the puppies will have a clean bed.

Unless some problem arises, there is little you must do about the puppies until they become three to four weeks old. Keep the box clean and supplied with fresh newspapers the first few days, but then turkish towels should be tacked down to the bottom of the box so that the puppies will have traction as they move about.

If the bitch has difficulties with her milk supply, or if you should be so unfortunate as to lose her, then you must be prepared to either hand-feed or tube-feed the puppies if they are to survive. Tube-feeding is so much faster and easier. If the bitch is available, it is best that she continues to clean and care for the puppies in the normal manner excepting for the food supplements you will provide. If it is impossible for her to do this, then after every feeding you must gently rub each puppy's abdomen with wet cotton to make it urinate, and the rectum should be gently rubbed to open the bowels.

Newborn puppies must be fed every three to four hours around the clock. The puppies must be kept warm during this time. Have your veterinarian teach you how to tube-feed. You will find that it is really quite simple.

After a normal whelping, the bitch will require additional food to enable her to produce sufficient milk. In addition to being fed twice daily, she should be given some canned milk several times each day.

When the puppies are two weeks old, their nails should be clipped, as they are needle sharp at this age and can hurt or damage the mother's teats and stomach as the pups hold on to nurse.

Future Ch. Rochford's Cumbria, five-month-old fawn bitch who at that point had not quite grown into her ears. A definite show prospect from Rochford Great Danes, Janet Quick, Kansas City, Mo.

Rochford's Cumbria at age ten months and in the show ring. By Ch. Temple Dell's Odin v Branstock ex Ch. Edeldane's Celebration. Bred and owned by Gary and Janet Quick, Rochford Great Danes, Kansas City, Mo.

Between three and four weeks of age, the puppies should begin to be weaned. Scraped beef (prepared by scraping it off slices of beef with a spoon so that none of the gristle is included) may be offered in very small quantities a couple of times daily for the first few days. Then by the third day you can mix puppy chow with warm water as directed on the package, offering it four times daily. By now the mother should be kept away from the puppies and out of the box for several hours at a time so that when they have reached five weeks of age she is left in with them only over-night. By the time the puppies are six weeks old, they should be entirely weaned and receiving only occasional visits from their mother.

Most veterinarians recommend a temporary DHL (distemper, hepatitis, leptospirosis) shot when the puppies are six weeks of age. This remains effective for about two weeks. Then at eight weeks of age, the puppies should receive the series of permanent shots for DHL protection. It is also a good idea to discuss with your vet the advisability of having your puppies inoculated against the dreaded parvovirus at the same time. Each time the pups go to the vet for shots, you should bring stool samples so that they can be examined for worms. Worms go through various stages of development and may be present in a stool sample even though the sample does not test positive in every checkup. So do not neglect to keep careful watch on this.

The puppies should be fed four times daily until they are three months old. Then you can cut back to three feedings daily. By the time the puppies are six months of age, two meals daily are sufficient. Some people feed their dogs twice daily throughout their lifetime; others go to one meal daily when the puppy becomes one year of age.

The ideal age for puppies to go to their new homes is between eight and twelve weeks, although some puppies successfully adjust to a new home when they are six weeks old. Be sure that they go to their new owners accompanied by a description of the diet you've been feeding them and a schedule of the shots they have already received and those they still need. These should be included with the registration application and a copy of the pedigree.

Ch. Eaglevalley Fireaway by Ch. Dinro Taboo ex Eaglevalley Extravagant was one of the outstanding Great Danes from the 1960's owned by Mrs. Sewall Montgomery, Eaglevalley Kennels, New Milford, Conn. Photo courtesy of Ed Lyons.

Chapter 16

Traveling with Your Great Dane

When you travel with your dog, to shows or on vacation or wherever, remember that everyone does not share your enthusiasm or love for dogs and that those who do not, strange creatures though they seem to us, have their rights, too. These rights, on which your should not encroach, include not being disturbed, annoyed, or made uncomfortable by the presence and behavior of other people's pets. Your dog should be kept on lead in public places and should recognize and promptly obey the commands "Down," "Come," "Sit," and "Stay."

Take along his crate if you are going any distance with your dog. And keep him in it when riding in the car. A crated dog has a far better chance of escaping injury than one riding loose in the car, should an accident occur or an emergency arise. If you do permit your dog to ride loose, never allow him to hang out a window, ears blowing in the breeze. An injury to his eyes could occur in this manner. He could also become overly excited by something he sees and jump out, or he could lose his balance and fall out.

If you are staying at a hotel or motel with your dog, exercise him somewhere other than in the flower beds and parking lot of the property. People walking to and from their cars really are not thrilled at "stepping in something" left by your dog. Should an accident occur, pick it up with a tissue or paper towel and deposit it in a proper receptacle; do not just walk off leaving it to remain there. Usually there are grassy areas on the sides of and behind motels where dogs can be exercised. Use them rather than the more conspicuous, usually carefully tended, front areas or those close to the rooms. If you are becoming a dog show enthusiast, you will eventually need an exercise pen to take with you to the show. Exercise pens are ideal to use when staying at motels, too, as they permit you to limit the dog's roaming space and to pick up after him more easily.

Never leave your dog unattended in the room of a motel unless you are absolutely, positively certain that he will stay there quietly and not damage or destroy anything. You do not want a long list of complaints from irate guests, caused by the annoying barking or whining of a lonesome dog in strange surroundings or an over-zealous watch dog barking furiously each time a footstep passes the door or he hears a sound from an adjoining room. And you certainly do not want to return to torn curtains or bedspreads, soiled rugs, or other embarrassing evidence of the fact that your dog is not really house-reliable after all.

If yours is a dog accustomed to traveling with you and you are positive that his behavior will be acceptable when left alone, that is fine. But if the slightest uncertainty exists, the wise course is to leave him in the car while you go to dinner or elsewhere; then bring him into the room when you are ready to retire for the night.

When you travel with a dog, it is often simpler to take along from home the food and water he will need rather than to buy food and look for water while you travel. In this way he will have the rations to which he is accustomed and which you know agree with him, and there will be no fear of problems due to different drinking water. Feeding on the road is quite easy now, at least for short trips, with all the splendid dry prepared foods and high-quality canned meats available. A variety of lightweight, refillable water containers can be bought at many types of stores.

Be careful always to leave sufficient openings to ventilate your car when the dog will be alone in it. Remember that during the summer, the rays of the sun can make an inferno of a closed car within only a few minutes, so leave enough window space open to provide air circulation. Again, if your dog is in a crate, this can be done quite safely. The fact that you have left the car in a shady spot is not always a guarantee that you will find conditions the same when you return. Don't forget that the position of the sun changes in a matter of minutes, and the car you left nicely shaded half an hour ago can be getting full sunlight far more quickly than you may realize. So, if you leave a dog in the car, make sure there is sufficient ventilation and check back frequently to ascertain that all is well.

If you are going to another country, you will need a health certificate from your veterinarian for each dog you are taking with you, certifying that each has had rabies shots within the required time preceding your visit.

Ch. Archibald Davis, 1966–1971, by Ch. Greenwood's Zip of Mountdania ex Ch. Jecamo's Lucy Ann, C.D., litter brother to Ch. Abner Lowell Davis. Archie was Best of Winenrs at the Great Dane Club of Northern California and the Great Dane Club of Southern California Specialties. Although he never competed against Abner in the show ring, he too was an immensely popular stud, and used by many breeders who recognized his quality. Breeders and owners, Arlene and Lowell K. Davis, Covina, Calif.

Brandt's Barrister of Dane Oaks winning the Great Dane Club of America National Specialty in conjunction with Westchester K.C. in September 1979. The judge is William P. Gilbert. Jane Forsyth is handling for the owners.

Chapter 17

Responsibilities of Breeders and Owners

The first responsibility of any person breeding dogs is to do so with care, forethought, and deliberation. It is inexcusable to breed more litters than you need to carry on your show program or to perpetuate your bloodlines. A responsible breeder should not cause a litter to be born without definite plans for the safe and happy disposition of the puppies.

A responsible dog breeder makes absolutely certain, so far as is humanly possible, that the home to which one of his puppies will go is a good home, one that offers proper care and an enthusiastic owner. To be admired are those breeders who insist on visiting (although doing so is not always feasible) the prospective owners of their puppies to see if they have suitable facilities for keeping a dog and to find out if they understand the responsibility involved, and if all members of the household are in accord regarding the desirability of owning one. All breeders should carefully check out the credentials of prospective purchasers to be sure that the puppy is being placed in responsible hands.

No breeder ever wants a puppy or grown dog he has raised to wind up in an animal shelter, in an experimental laboratory, or as

313

a victim of a speeding car. While complete control of such a situation may be impossible, it is at important to make every effort to turn over dogs to responsible people. When selling a puppy, it is a good idea to do so with the understanding that should it become necessary to place the dog in other hands, the purchaser will first contact you, the breeder. You may want to help in some way, possibly by buying back or taking back the dog or placing it elsewhere. It is not fair to just sell puppies and then never again give a thought to their welfare. Family problems arise, people may be forced to move where dogs are prohibited, or people just plain grow bored with a dog and its care. Thus the dog becomes a victim. You, as the dog's breeder, should concern yourself with the welfare of each of your dogs and see to it that the dog remains in good hands.

The final obligation every dog owner shares, be there just one dog or an entire kennel involved, is that of making detailed, explicit plans for the future of these dearly loved animals in the event of the owner's death. Far too many of people are apt to procrastinate and leave this very important matter unattended to, feeling that everything will work out or that "someone will see to them." The latter is not too likely, at least not to the benefit of the dogs, unless you have done some advance planning which will assure their future well-being.

Life is filled with the unexpected, and even the youngest, healthiest, most robust of us may be the victim of a fatal accident or sudden illness. The fate of your dogs, so entirely in our hands, should never be left to chance. If you have not already done so, please get together with your lawyer and set up a clause in your will specifying what you want done with each of your dogs, to whom they will be entrusted (after first making absolutely certain that the person selected is willing and able to assume the responsibility), and telling the locations of all registration papers, pedigrees, and kennel records. Just think of the possibilities which might happen otherwise! If there is another family member who shares your love of the dogs, that is good and you have less to worry about. But if your heirs are not dog-oriented, they will hardly know how to proceed or how to cope with the dogs themselves, and they may wind up disposing of or caring for your dogs

Two of the handsome Danes from Honey Hollow Kennels, from the 1950's era. Lina Basquette, Honey Hollow, Chalfont, Pa.

in a manner that would break your heart were you around to know about it.

It is advisable to have in your will specific instructions concerning each of your dogs. A friend, also a dog person who regards her own dogs with the same concern and esteem as we do, may agree to take over their care until they can be placed accordingly and will make certain that all will work out as you have planned. This person's name and phone number can be prominently displayed in your van or car and in your wallet. Your lawyer can be made aware of this fact. This can be spelled out in your will. The friend can have a signed check of yours to be used in case of an emergency or accident when you are traveling with the dogs; this check can be used to cover her expense to come and take over the care of your dogs should anything happen to make it impossible for us to do so. This is the least any dog owner should do in preparation for the time their dogs suddenly find themselves alone. There have been so many sad cases of dogs unprovided for by their loving owners, left to heirs who couldn't care less and who disposed of them in any way at all to get rid of them, or left to heirs who kept and neglected them under the misguided idea that they were providing them "a fine home with lots of freedom." These misfortunes must be prevented from befalling your own dogs who have meant so much you!

Index

318